Interactive Read–Alouds

Linking Standards, Fluency, and Comprehension

K–1

Linda Hoyt

firsthand
HEINEMANN

Heinemann, Portsmouth, NH

*first*hand
An imprint of Heinemann
A division of Reed Elsevier Inc.
361 Hanover Street
Portsmouth, NH 03801-3912
www.firsthand.heinemann.com

Offices and agents throughout the world

Library of Congress Cataloguing-in-Publications Data
CIP data is on file with the Library of Congress

ISBN 0-325-00735-7 (Lesson Book)
　　0-325-01055-2 (Teachers Guide)
　　0-325-01056-0 (set)

Printed in the United States of America on acid-free paper

10　09　08　07　06　　ML　　1　2　3　4　5　6

The Author and Publisher would like to thank those who have generously given permission to reprint borrowed material.

From MAKE WAY FOR DUCKLINGS by Robert McCloskey, copyright 1941, renewed © 1969 by Robert McCloskey. Used by permission of Viking Penguin, A Division of Penguin Young Readers Group, A Member of Penguin Group (USA) Inc., 345 Hudson Street, New York, NY 10014. All rights reserved.

From THE BREMEN-TOWN MUSICIANS by Ilse Plume, copyright © 1980 by Ilse Plume. Used by permission of Random House Children's Books, a division of Random House, Inc.

From THE ART LESSON by Tomie de Paola, copyright © 1989 by Tomie de Paola. Used by permission of G.P. Putnam's Sons, A Division of Penguin Young Readers Group, A Member of Penguin Group (USA) Inc., 345 Hudson Street, New York, NY 10014. All rights reserved.

Reprinted with the permission of Simon & Schuster Books for Young Readers, an imprint of Simon & Schuster Children's Publishing Division from STREGA NONA by Tomie de Paola. Text copyright © 1975 Tomie de Paola.

From FROG AND TOAD ARE FRIENDS by Arnold Lobel. Used by permission of HarperCollins Publishers.

From INCH BY INCH copyright 1960 by Leo Lionni renewed 1988 by Leo Lionni, published by Astor-Honor, New York. Reprinted by permission of Ann Lionni and Astor-Honor, Inc.

Reprinted with the permission of Simon & Schuster Books for Young Readers, an imprint of Simon & Schuster Children's Publishing Division from HATTIE AND THE FOX by Mem Fox. Text copyright © 1986 Mem Fox.

To Lois Bridges

Teacher

Mentor

Friend

Visionary

Thank you

TABLE OF CONTENTS

ACKNOWLEDGMENTS

A project such as this is always the work of many. I feel especially honored to have had input from teachers whose shared thinking, willingness to pilot lessons, and advocacy for children have helped to shape and mold this resource. Special thanks go to Sally Wells, Marie Govro, Leah Shook, Katy Taylor, Kathryn McInnis, Ellen Arnold, Nick Gelbard, Kathryn Welch, Linda Watson, Jan Woodbury, Mary Hurliman, Teresa Therriault, Kendra Evans, and Gretchen Nelson.

Jan McCall has been a key player in the development of this concept over the last four years. Her knowledge of children's books, commitment to developmentally appropriate practice, and love of literacy have been a guiding light as this project has evolved. We spent many hours joyfully reading and thinking together while selecting books for the lessons and the Booklinks.

Pat Dragon, Heinemann author and wonderful primary teacher, shared her thinking and suggested books guaranteed to delight young children.

Lynnette Brent has become my pen pal and trusted writing colleague. She has deep knowledge of literacy instruction, is one of those rare individuals who understands how to shepherd reading development from emergent to fluent readers, and has an uncanny ability to craft language that will entice and extend the thinking of children. Her humorous poetry and several smartly crafted Readers Theater scripts grace this resource.

Many thanks go to the Heinemann *first*hand team, especially Lesa Scott, Tina Miller, Charles McQuillen, and Michael Cirone, and to Karen Billip of Eliot House Productions for their expertise and careful shepherding of the manuscript as it moved through production.

Lesson Matrix

This chart identifies the mentor text used in the model lesson for each standard. (Standards for Writing Traits have two mentor texts and model lessons.) Booklinks are other wonderful books that help children expand and practice the standard. Use the lesson planner provided in this guide and on the *Resources for Interactive Read-Alouds* CD-ROM to create your own lessons using the Booklinks.

LESSON MATRIX							
Standards for COMPREHENSION							
Page Ref	Standard	K/1 Mentor Text	Booklink 1	Booklink 2	Booklink 3	Booklink 4	Booklink 5
1	Use prior knowledge	*Goodnight Moon*	Frog and Toad Are Friends	Stellaluna	The Hello, Goodbye Window	Olivia	Snowflake Bentley
5	Ask/answer questions	*Where's Spot?*	Owl Moon	The Relatives Came	No, David!	Click, Clack, Moo: Cows That Type	Officer Buckle and Gloria
9	Make connections	*Frog and Toad Are Friends, "A Lost Button"*	Blueberries for Sal	Goodnight Moon	Little Bear's Visit	"More More More," Said the Baby	The Relatives Came
13	Connect to experience of others	*Wilfred Gordon McDonald Partridge*	Galimoto	Crow Boy	No, David!	The Relatives Came	Grandfather's Journey
17	Analyze and evaluate	*Miss Nelson Is Missing!*	When Sophie Gets Angry	Strega Nona	A Chair for My Mother	Sam, Bangs & Moonshine	It Could Always Be Worse
23	Interpret through explanation	*Kitten's First Full Moon*	Don't Let the Pigeon Drive the Bus!	Stellaluna	Swimmy	Where the Wild Things Are	What Do You Do With a Tail Like This?
29	Interpret through performance (drama, music, art)	*Don't Let the Pigeon Drive the Bus!*	Tops & Bottoms	Chicka Chicka Boom Boom	Goldilocks and the Three Bears	Joseph Had a Little Overcoat	Snow
33	Infer	*No, David!*	Have You Seen My Duckling?	The Polar Express	Good Dog, Carl	Officer Buckle and Gloria	Where the Wild Things Are
37	Predict	*Blueberries for Sal*	Farmer Duck	Hattie and the Fox	Puss In Boots	Have You Seen My Duckling?	Tuesday
41	Draw conclusions	*Olivia*	Chicken Sunday	Frederick	Swimmy	Sam, Bangs & Moonshine	Crow Boy
45	Compare and contrast (text structure and plot)	*Goldilocks and the Three Bears*	Julius, the Baby of the World and Lilly's Purple Plastic Purse	Q is for Duck and Alphabet City	Martin's Big Words and My Brother Martin	The Three Pigs and The True Story of the Three Little Pigs	Lon Po Po and Little Red Riding Hood
49	Compare and contrast (characters and settings)	*Frederick*	Frog and Toad	"More More More," Said the Baby	Officer Buckle and Gloria	In the Small, Small Pond and Have You Seen My Duckling?	Snowy Day and Owl Moon
53	Identify cause and effect	*If You Give a Mouse a Cookie*	The Little House	Julius, the Baby of the World	It Could Always Be Worse	Joseph Had a Little Overcoat	The Stray Dog

continued

LESSON MATRIX

Standards for COMPREHENSION, continued

Page Ref	Standard	K/1 Mentor Text	Booklink 1	Booklink 2	Booklink 3	Booklink 4	Booklink 5
57	Identify main ideas and supporting details	*The Grouchy Ladybug*	The Important Book	Lilly's Purple Plastic Purse	My Friend Rabbit	When Sophie Gets Angry	The Art Lesson
61	Rank important vs. unimportant information	*The Wednesday Surprise*	Make Way for Ducklings	Mike Mulligan and His Steam Shovel	Tops & Bottoms	Rosie's Walk	The Biggest Bear
65	Represent text graphically	*A Pocket for Corduroy*	The Mitten	Blueberries for Sal	What Do You Do With a Tail Like This?	Tomorrow's Alphabet	The Dinosaurs of Waterhouse Hawkins
71	Read classic and contemporary works	*Mike Mulligan and His Steam Shovel*	One Morning in Maine	The Biggest Bear	Chrysanthemum	The Polar Express	Make Way for Ducklings
75	Read for a purpose	*King Bidgood's in the Bathtub*	The Ghost Eye Tree	Martin's Big Words	Q is for Duck	Knots on a Counting Rope	What Do You Do With a Tail Like This?
79	Use pictures to support comprehension	*Farmer Duck*	The Snowy Day	Dr. DeSoto	Stellaluna	King Bidgood's in the Bathtub	The Ghost-Eye Tree
85	Summarize	*Hattie and the Fox*	The Dinosaurs of Waterhouse Hawkins	What Do You Do With a Tail Like This?	Inch by Inch	Officer Buckle and Gloria	Hansel and Gretel
89	Distinguish real from make-believe	*The Very Hungry Caterpillar*	The Popcorn Book	Sam Bangs & Moonshine	When Sophie Gets Angry	The Snowy Day	Stellaluna

Standards for STORY ELEMENTS

Page Ref	Standard	K/1 Mentor Text	Booklink 1	Booklink 2	Booklink 3	Booklink 4	Booklink 5
95	Distinguish fiction/ nonfiction	*The Bremen-Town Musicians*	How Many Days to America?	The Popcorn Book	Snowflake Bentley	The Polar Express	Martin's Big Words
99	Sequence of Events/Plot	*Tops & Bottoms*	Alexander and the Wind Up Mouse	Make Way for Ducklings	Goldilocks and the Three Bears	Julius, the Baby of the World	Goggles!
103	Beginning/middle/end	*The Wednesday Surprise*	Swimmy	Blueberries for Sal	The Art Lesson	Miss Rumphius	Owen
107	Climax	*The Ghost-Eye Tree*	Little Red Riding Hood	Inch By Inch	Officer Buckle and Gloria	Kitten's First Full Moon	Casey at the Bat
111	Main idea	*Joseph Had A Little Overcoat*	A House is a House for Me	A Chair for My Mother	No, David!	Have You Seen My Duckling?	The Stray Dog
115	Setting	*The Art Lesson*	The Hello, Goodbye Window	Miss Rumphius	How Many Days to America?	Sylvester and the Magic Pebble	Owl Moon
119	Character development	*Strega Nona*	Swimmy	Tops & Bottoms	Song and Dance Man	No, David!	Mufaro's Beautiful Daughters
125	Personification	*Click, Clack, Moo: Cows That Type*	The Little House	The Snowman	Rotten Ralph	Dr. DeSoto	Little Bear's Visit

continued

LESSON MATRIX

Standards for STORY ELEMENTS, continued

Page Ref	Standard	K/1 Mentor Text 1	Booklink 1	Booklink 2	Booklink 3	Booklink 4	Booklink 5
129	Narration	*Frog and Toad are Friends,* "The Swim"	*Don't Let the Pigeon Drive the Bus!*	*The Three Little Wolves and the Big Bad Pig*	*The Polar Express*	*Sleeping Ugly*	*When Sophie Gets Angry—Really, Really Angry...*
135	Theme/author's purpose	*When Sophie Gets Angry—Really, Really Angry...*	*The True Story of the Three Little Pigs*	*The Art Lesson*	*The Hello Goodbye Window*	*Julius, the Baby of the World*	*The Ugly Duckling*
139	Connect to cultures	*Galimoto*	*Grandfather's Journey*	*Lon Po Po*	*Going Home*	*Mufaro's Beautiful*	*Crow Boy*
143	Problem/solution structure	*Inch by Inch*	*Lon Po Po*	*Miss Nelson is Missing!*	*King Bidgood's in the Bathtub*	*Little Red Riding Hood*	*My Friend Rabbit*
147	Circular/cumulative structure	*If You Give A Mouse a Cookie*	*We're Going On a Bear Hunt*	*There Was an Old Lady Who Swollowed a Fly*	*It Could Always Be Worse*	*A House is a House for Me*	*The House That Jack Built*

Standards for VOCABULARY/LITERARY LANGUAGE

Page Ref	Standard	K/1 Mentor Text 1	Booklink 1	Booklink 2	Booklink 3	Booklink 4	Booklink 5
151	Vocabulary	*Owen*	*When I Was Young In the Mountains*	*Dr. DeSoto*	*In the Small, Small Pond*	*Lilly's Purple Plastic Purse*	*Sylvester and the Magic Pebble*
155	Context clues	*Where the Wild Things Are*	*Chrysanthemum*	*Owen*	*Stellaluna*	*Lon Po Po*	*Officer Buckle and Gloria*
161	Literary/figurative language leads	Leads: *Owl Moon; Blueberries for Sal, Goldilocks and the Three Bears, Farmer Duck, Stellaluna*	Endings: *Cinderella, Rumplestiltskin, Make Way for Ducklings*	Endings: *Goodnight Moon; Brown Bear, Brown Bear, What Do You See?*	*Officer Buckle and Gloria*	*The Snowy Day Where the Wild Things Are*	*Hansel and Gretel*
165	Alliteration	*Chicken Little*	*How the Grinch Stole Christmas*	*Shrek!*	*Dr. Seuss's ABC*	*There's an Ant in Anthony*	*Some Smug Slug*
169	Rhyme (recognize and appreciate)	*Noisy Nora*	*King Bidgood's in the Bathtub*	*In the Small Small Pond*	*A House is a House for Me*	*Ten, Nine, Eight*	*Dr. Seuss's ABC*
173	Rhyme (interpret)	*Brown Bear, Brown Bear What Do You See?*	*Chicka Chicka Boom Boom*	*There Was an Old Lady Who Swollowed A Fly*	*Goodnight Moon*	*In the Small, Small Pond*	*A House Is a House for Me*
179	Onomatopoeia	*We're Going on a Bear Hunt*	*Farmer Duck*	*Click, Clack, Moo: Cows That Type*	*The Wheels on the Bus*	*The Little Engine That Could*	*Kitten's First Full Moon*
183	Transitional words	*The Snowy Day*	*Stone Soup*	*The Mitten*	*Bremen-Town Musicians*	*Make Way for Ducklings*	*Goldilocks and the Three Bears*

continued

LESSON MATRIX

Standards for LITERARY ELEMENTS AND DEVICES

Page Ref	Standard	K/1 Mentor Text	Booklink 1	Booklink 2	Booklink 3	Booklink 4	Booklink 5
187	Point of view	Click, Clack, Moo: Cows That Type	A Chair For My Mother	Where the Wild Things Are	Tuesday	Don't Let the Pigeon Drive the Bus!	The True Story of the Three Little Pigs
193	Foreshadowing	Rosie's Walk	The Little House	Strega Nona	Hattie and the Fox	Miss Rumphius	Mike Mulligan and His Steam Shovel5
197	Flashback	A Chair for My Mother	The Dinosaurs of Waterhouse Hawkins	The Keeping Quilt	The Day Jimmy's Boa Ate the Wash	Roxaboxen	The True Story of the Three Little Pigs
203	Simile/metaphor	Quick as a Cricket	Owl Moon	Snowflake Bentley	The Polar Express	The Night Before Christmas	Wilfrid Gordon McDonald Partridge
207	Allusion	Goodnight Moon	Goldilocks Returns	Each Peach Pear Plum	The Frog Prince Continued	Goodnight Goodnight	Sleeping Ugly
211	Repetition	Have You Seen My Duckling?	Rain Makes Applesauce	"More More More," Said the Baby	The Happy Day	King Bidgood's in the Bathtub	When I Was Young In the Mountains
215	Exaggeration	Rotten Ralph	My Friend Rabbit	May I Bring A Friend?	Millions of Cats	Cloudy with a Chance of Meatballs	There Was An Old Lady Who Swallowed a Fly

Standards for GENRE

Page Ref	Standard	K/1 Mentor Text	Booklink 1	Booklink 2	Booklink 3	Booklink 4	Booklink 5
219	Distinguishing features of genres	Fiction and nonfiction selections	The Wheels on the Bus	The Dinosaurs of Waterhouse Hawkins	Ten, Nine, Eight	A House Is a House for Me	Little Red Riding Hood
223	Nonfiction	Q is for Duck	What Do You Do With a Tail Like This?	Snowflake Bentley	The Popcorn Book	Mailing May	Tomorrow's Alphabet
227	Fairy Tale/folktale	Rumplestiltskin	Little Red Riding Hood	Cinderella	The Three Little Pigs	The Ugly Duckling	The Bremen-Town Musicians
231	Drama/play	Hattie and the Fox	Ira Sleeps Over	Stone Soup	The Hello, Goodbye Window	Don't Let the Pigeon Drive the Bus!	The Snowy Day
235	Alphabet book	Tomorrow's Alphabet	Q is for Duck	Dr. Seuss's ABC	Chicka Chicka Boom Boom	Alphabatics	Alphabet City
239	Counting book	The Very Hungry Caterpillar	1 is One	Moja Means One	Ten Little Monkeys	The Icky Bug Counting Book	Ten, Nine, Eight

continued

LESSON MATRIX

Standards for WRITING TRAITS

Page Ref	Standard	K/1 Mentor Text 1	K/1 Mentor Text 2	Booklink 1	Booklink 2	Booklink 3	Booklink 4
243	Ideas	*Good Dog, Carl*	*Goodnight Moon*	*Alphabet City*	*The Important Book*	*A Tree Is Nice*	*When Sophie Gets Angry— Very, Very Angry...*
251	Organization	*Brown Bear, Brown Bear, What Do You See?*	*Ten, Nine, Eight*	*The Snowy Day*	*Tomorrow's Alphabet*	*The Art Lesson*	*The Important Book*
259	Voice	*Have You Seen My Duckling?*	*Farmer Duck*	*The Grouchy Ladybug*	*If I Were In Charge of the World*	*No, David!*	*Officer Buckle and Gloria*
267	Word choice	*Rosie's Walk*	*Diary of a Worm*	*Chrysanthemum*	*Snowflake Bentley*	*The Snowman*	*Owl Moon*
275	Sentence fluency	*Where the Wild Things Are*	*The Snowy Day*	*If You Give a Mouse a Cookie*	*The Very Hungry Caterpillar*	*Olivia*	*How the Grinch Stole Christmas*
283	Conventions	*No, David!*	*Don't Let the Pigeon Drive the Bus!*	*Yo! Yes?*	*Brown Bear, Brown Bear, What Do You See?*	*Click, Clack Moo: Cows That Type*	*Where's Spot?*

Comprehension

This strand—from utilizing prior knowledge and asking questions to summarizing and distinguishing real from make-believe—focuses on strategies that help learners negotiate the meaning of texts. Within this strand, you will find familiar terms such as main idea, cause and effect, analyze, and evaluate that commonly appear in lists of standards for comprehension.

Goodnight Moon
By Margaret Wise Brown

FOCUS THE LEARNING

Introduction: Prior knowledge helps us all of the time. When we do something for the first time, it can feel kind of hard because we don't have much prior knowledge. After we do something several times, we have a lot of prior knowledge and it feels easier. I am thinking of riding a bike. I remember trying to learn and it wasn't very easy. But now I have a lot of prior knowledge so it is fun instead of hard.

 Think together. What are some things you have a lot of prior knowledge about? Soccer, cartoons, best pizza toppings?

Let's use our prior knowledge to remember some of our favorite nursery rhymes and stories. I am going to start, and when you remember, join in! "Hey, diddle diddle, the cat and the fiddle. The cow jumped over the _____." You remembered. Your prior knowledge really helped. Let's try another one.

"Once upon a time, there was a little girl named Goldilocks who went into the house of the three _____." You have it. Your prior knowledge is ready for *Goodnight Moon* by Margaret Wise Brown.

INTERACTIVE READ-ALOUD
Model and Guide Practice

Look at the cover. This is a book about bedtime and saying goodnight to things in your room.

READ TO THE PAGE WITH THE COW JUMPING OVER THE MOON.
Okay. Get your prior knowledge ready. "Hey, diddle diddle..." Isn't this great. Our prior knowledge is helping us think about the picture on the wall. That isn't just any cow. That is the cow jumping over the moon!

READ THE NEXT PAGE.

 Put your heads together. Use your prior knowledge to remember the story about the Three Bears.

READ TO THE PAGE THAT SHOWS THE ENTIRE ROOM. "Goodnight room" is such a nice way to think about going to sleep, isn't it? If I were going to use my prior knowledge here, I would think about my own bedroom and the things I could say goodnight to...Are you thinking about your room? Do you have a special stuffed animal? Or a favorite chair...maybe a pillow?

 Think together.

CONTINUE TO THE END OF THE STORY TO ENJOY THE LANGUAGE.

END OF STORY REFLECTION

Our prior knowledge helps us in life and in books. Now, this story has added to your prior knowledge. Everything we learn and everything we do help our prior knowledge to get bigger and bigger. What is important is that we use what we already know. Someone who didn't know about the Three Bears might not have noticed the picture on the wall. Aren't you glad you were using your prior knowledge and could think about the story that made that picture special?

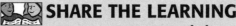

SHARE THE LEARNING
Focus on Prior Knowledge

Tip for Share the Reading

Read the "Goodnight" poem to the children several times while you track under the line of print. As they are ready, encourage them to join in and read or chant with you. You could dramatize by having students stand and point to or hold up the individual items as they are mentioned. You might also have the children use prior knowledge to write a new version of the poem: they could think of favorite storybook characters they remember from read-alouds and write a poem saying goodnight to their favorite characters.

Goodnight

Goodnight chairs
Goodnight clock
Goodnight windows
Goodnight books
Goodnight pencils
Goodnight pens
Goodnight crayons
Goodnight friends

Tip for Readers Theater Script

For emergent readers, enjoy "Good Morning" as an echo poem: teacher reads and children echo. As they gain confidence, encourage them to read with partners or independently. For developing readers, after enjoying a fluent, expressive reading of the script, have them write their own versions and perform them.

"Good Morning!"
Readers Theater Adaptation by Linda Hoyt

Good Morning Cow

Good Morning Frog

Good Morning Spider

Good Morning Rooster

Good Morning Animals!

EXTEND THE LEARNING

☆ Make a point to pause before reading and say: "This is a book about _____." Let's activate our prior knowledge and think about what we already know.

☆ In small group instruction, encourage children to make connections to prior knowledge as they preview their books.

☆ Introduce a topic and ask children to draw and write what they already know on the topic before you begin reading.

☆ Pair fiction and nonfiction titles on the same topic and explain to the children that the nonfiction titles will help them build prior knowledge for the fiction selection.

ASSESS THE LEARNING

➤ Listen in as partners share prior knowledge with one another to see if they are focusing on the topic.

➤ Confer with readers during independent reading, and ask them to share prior knowledge on the topic. Assess their ability to share the information orally.

INFUSION OF FORMAL LANGUAGE
Test-style language

Goodnight Moon is told by:
  A. the bears
  B. the cow
  C. the kitten
  D. the rabbit in the bed

This story was *mostly* about:
  A. Pictures on the wall
  B. Kittens with yarn
  C. The moon
  D. Saying goodnight to things you enjoy

Goodnight

Goodnight chairs

Goodnight clock

Goodnight windows

Goodnight books

Goodnight pencils

Goodnight pens

Goodnight crayons

Goodnight friends

"Good Morning!"

Readers Theater adaptation by Linda Hoyt

 Good Morning Cow

 Good Morning Frog

 Good Morning Spider

 Good Morning Rooster

Good Morning Animals!

Where's Spot?
By Eric Hill

INTERACTIVE READ-ALOUD
Model and Guide Practice

SHOW THE BACK COVER OF THE BOOK FIRST. THEN READ THE COVER. I have a lot of questions. I wonder how old the puppy might be. I wonder what kind of dog he is to have spots like that on his body. What are you wondering? Do you have any questions?

 Thinking partners, share your questions.

LOOKING AT THE COVER. Did you notice the title? It says "Where's Spot?" See this question mark? This tells us that the title is a question. *Where's Spot?* I am not going to talk to a partner. I am going to think by myself: Where is he? Where could he be? I am wondering if that means the little dog is named Spot? I wonder if he is lost? Think by yourself for a moment. What are your questions?

OPEN TO THE TITLE PAGE. I see a question mark so I know this first page will be a question. I wonder why the mom is looking for Spot? I wonder why he didn't eat his dinner? Why wouldn't a puppy want to eat? Read up to the page with the door, but do not open the door.

 What are your questions? What are you wondering?

OPEN THE BLUE DOOR. I have a question! What is a bear doing in the closet? Why isn't the dog afraid of the bear?

CONTINUE TO THE END OF THE STORY. Point out question marks, inviting the children to ask and answer questions.

END OF STORY REFLECTION

Let's work together to think of questions about the story. Let's choose questions that we can answer so we can write them here in our chart. I am going to write my first question, "What is the puppy's name?" Notice my question mark. That shows everyone that this is a question.

 Think together: What is the answer? That's right. The puppy's name is Spot. I will write that under "Answers." Notice that I am putting a period because this is not a question. It is an answer. Continue adding questions and answers on the chart.

Our Questions	Answers
What is the puppy's name?	*The puppy's name is Spot.*

SHARE THE LEARNING
Focus on Asking and Answering Questions

Tip for Share the Thinking

Engage the children in a conversation about the photograph. List their questions, making sure you emphasize the addition of a question mark at the end of each. When possible, also write their answers. Unanswered questions could generate interest in finding some books on spiders.

Questions	Answers
What is this?	A spider.

Tip for Readers Theater Script

For emergent readers, enjoy "Where's Frog?" as an echo poem: teacher reads and children echo. Then have the children read the poem chorally tracking under each line of print. Encourage them in trying to navigate the text independently. For developing readers, you might want to enjoy the script as a two-team experience: team one reads the question and Team two gives an answer. For a focus on fluency, have partners read the script in unison.

EXTEND THE LEARNING

☆ Create class question books called Where's _____? The focus of the books could be searching around the school for the principal, looking for a classroom pet, finding the children in the classroom, and so on.

☆ Have parents get involved in helping their children ask and answer questions at home.

☆ Give children numerous opportunities to question texts they listen to or read, sharing their questions orally, in the form of a sketch, or a few words on a sticky note.

☆ Post a list of words and phrases that are helpful in questioning: Who, what, when, where, why, how, what if, I wonder, Do you think?

☆ After reading, have partners write questions they can also answer and then share them with the class.

ASSESS THE LEARNING

> Assess questioning during small group instruction to identify learners who can separate a question from a statement.

> Confer with readers during independent reading to see if they can generate a question about the books they are reading.

> Gather written questions to assess ability to generate a question and use a question mark.

INFUSION OF FORMAL LANGUAGE
Test-style language

At the end of a question, we use a ____.
  A. "
  B. *
  C. -
  D. ?

Spot's mother found him in:
  A. The kitchen
  B. The closet
  C. The basket
  D. The clock

Questions	Answers
What is this?	A spider.

"Where's Frog?"

By Linda Hoyt

Is he in the wagon?

Is he in the boat?

Is he in the flowers?

No! He is in a tree!

MAKE CONNECTIONS

Frog and Toad Are Friends
"A Lost Button"
By Arnold Lobel

FOCUS THE LEARNING

Introduction: If we started talking about going swimming, could you make a connection and tell about a time you went swimming? What about eating a hamburger? Could you make a connection and think of a time you ate a hamburger or went to a McDonald's?

 Share a hamburger connection with your thinking partner.

Connections can help us while we are reading. If you are reading about a frog and you make a connection to a time when you saw or heard a frog…or perhaps make a connection to another book about frogs, you learn more and understand better.

INTERACTIVE READ-ALOUD
Model and Guide Practice

I am going to read one of the stories in *Frog and Toad Are Friends* by Arnold Lobel. This story is called "A Lost Button." The title tells me that this is going to be about losing a button. I am already making a connection! This makes me think of when I lost the keys to my car. It was terrible. I looked everywhere. I thought about each place I had been and then went back to look for my keys. The more I looked, the more upset I got. Have you ever lost something and had to go looking for it? Let's make some connections with Frog and Toad.

READ PAGES 28–29. Poor Toad. He has sore feet and he lost a button. If you have ever lost something or had sore feet, you can make a connection to how he is feeling.

 Thinking partners, tell each other. How do you think he is feeling? What do you think he will do now? If you connect to losing something yourself, what would you do?

READ TO PAGE 33. I am really connecting with Toad right now. I am wondering if he is feeling like I did when I lost my keys. I felt sad and frustrated, and I got really tired of looking.

 Think together. Can you connect to the way Toad is probably feeling? Can you remember a time when you felt like that?

READ TO PAGE 36. Can you connect with Toad's feelings now? Have you ever been so angry you screamed?

 Think together. Share your connections.

READ PAGE 37. I am going to read the last three lines again. I am having a connection and I want to think about it. Toad is feeling bad because Frog was so nice and used so much time to help him…and Toad hadn't been very nice. Remember when he was yelling?

 Have you been mad about something and then felt badly that you didn't act very nice? Share your connections.

CONTINUE TO THE END OF THE STORY. Pause occasionally to give partners time to connect.

END OF STORY REFLECTION

We made a lot of connections with that story, didn't we? We connected to losing things and we connected to the feelings that Toad was having. Connections are really good as long as they help us understand the story better.

 Think together. Which connections do you think helped you understand the story better?

 **SHARE THE LEARNING**
Focus on Connections

Tip for Share the Reading

As the story progressed, Toad continued to get more and more upset. Our connections to Toad's emotions were invited by the verbs Arnold Lobel selected. Careful word choice by an author stimulates connections in the reader. Have the children practice reading the statements dramatically, connecting to the correct behavior with each successive line.

"That is not my button," said Toad.

"That is not my button," cried Toad.

"That is not my button," wailed Toad.

"That is not my button," shouted Toad.

"That is not my button," screamed Toad.

Tip for Readers Theater Script

Sing the song "A Lost Button" to the children several times so they have a strong sense of the language of the song and understand how to sing it. Next, read the song without singing and encourage the students to track under the lines of print as they move through the lyrics. Have partners read and sing the song together, tracking the print as they sing. Some children might enjoy creating additional verses for the song.

Frog and Toad, "A Lost Button"
Reader's Theater adaptation by Linda Hoyt
Sing to the tune of Mary Had a Little Lamb)

Toad lost a button from his coat.
From his coat,
From his coat.
Toad lost a button from his coat.
He felt very sad.

The more he looked, the worse he felt,
Worse he felt,
Worse he felt.
The more he looked, the worse he felt.
Toad got really mad!

EXTEND THE LEARNING

☆ Have children make a paper chain adding links when they make connections in stories. They can then share their connections with partners.

☆ Guide text-to-text connections by reading additional Frog and Toad selections and comparing the various stories.

☆ Have children illustrate connections by sketching the scene in a story on one side of a page and sketching a connection to their life or another story on the opposite side of the page.

☆ During independent time with books, have children place strips of sticky note material in their books when they think of connections. Provide time for partners to share their favorite connections after reading.

ASSESS THE LEARNING

➤ Analyze the sketches showing connections. Confer with the illustrator/connector to see if explanations reflect understanding.

➤ Confer with readers during independent reading to see if they are able to make connections.

➤ Have emergent readers make connections focusing on photographs and illustrations.

INFUSION OF FORMAL LANGUAGE
Test-style language

Which statement is *not true*?
  A. Frog lost a button.
  B. Toad lost a button.
  C. Frog and Toad looked for the missing button.
  D. The sparrow and the raccoon helped look for the button.

You could tell Frog was a good friend because
  A. he talked to Toad.
  B. he helped look for the button.
  C. he went for a walk with Toad.
  D. all of the above.

"That is not my button," said Toad.

"That is not my button," cried Toad.

"That is not my button," wailed Toad.

"That is not my button," shouted Toad.

"That is not my button," screamed Toad.

Frog and Toad, "A Lost Button"

Reader's Theater adaptation by Linda Hoyt

(Sing to the tune of Mary Had a Little Lamb)

Toad lost a button from his coat

From his coat,

From his coat.

Toad lost a button from his coat.

He felt very sad.

The more he looked, the worse he felt,

Worse he felt,

Worse he felt.

The more he looked, the worse he felt.

Toad got really mad!

CONNECT TO EXPERIENCE OF OTHERS

Wilfrid Gordon McDonald Partridge
By Mem Fox

FOCUS THE LEARNING

Introduction: Memories are something special that we all treasure. I remember our first day of school this year. I remember seeing all of you walk in the door and the way we began to form a family.

Can you remember something from your first day in our class? Do you have a memory of a special holiday? A birthday? Moving into your home? going on a trip? Share your thinking.

As people get old, sometimes their memories fade a bit. They forget things. In this story, *Wilfrid Gordon McDonald Partridge* by Mem Fox, a little boy helps an old lady find her memories, and he tries to understand what is special to her.

INTERACTIVE READ-ALOUD
Model and Guide Practice

READ TO THE PAGE WHERE WILFRID TELLS MISS NANCY ALL OF HIS SECRETS. I am thinking that secrets are kind of like memories and how nice it is that Wilfrid and Miss Nancy were friends. If he told her his secrets or his memories, I would guess that she was a good listener and made connections to what he was telling her.

READ THE NEXT PAGE WHERE WILFRID'S PARENTS ARE TALKING ABOUT MISS NANCY. Miss Nancy lost her memory. We know that happens to some people when they get old. She must have liked listening to Wilfrid's secrets and memories since she couldn't remember her own. Memories are like special treasures we all carry with us...

Think together. Have you ever been around someone who is old and is losing their memory? What would it be like to be getting old and not be able to remember things?

READ TO WHERE MR. DRYSDALE TALKS ABOUT MEMORIES.

Talk to your thinking partner. The old people described memories as precious as gold, something that makes you laugh, something that makes you cry, and something from long ago. What can you say about memories?

CONTINUE TO THE END OF THE STORY. Pause occasionally to give partners time to talk about Miss Nancy's memories and the things that helped her to remember. What connections can they make to Miss Nancy's memories? Have they ever found a bird nest? Gone to the beach? Had a brother or a sister? Played with a puppet or a doll? Played with a football, basketball, or soccer ball? What connections can they make to Miss Nancy?

END OF STORY REFLECTION

Memories are precious and so are the connections we make to each other's experiences. You were able to make connections to Miss Nancy's experiences and so was Wilfrid Gordon. Let's practice a bit more. Tell a story about something the children are likely to connect to, such as going out for pizza, eating a big juicy hamburger, riding a bike, and so on. Invite them to make connections, and try to understand the memory you are sharing.

Think together about being a good listener and making connections to the experiences of another person. Share your memories, and try to make connections to each other's experiences.

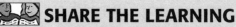 **SHARE THE LEARNING**

Focus on Connecting to Other People's Experiences

Tip for Share the Reading

Reflect on another memory you have experienced. Then write it on the overhead while the children watch you write. Read the passage aloud when you are finished, inviting the children to read along with you. Then have the children orally share the connections they are making.

I have a special memory.

Tip for Readers Theater Script

For emergent readers, read "A Special Memory" to the children, pausing to give them time to make connections with each stanza. As you provide repeated readings, invite learners to chorally read the repeating lines labeled "children" while you read the other lines of

text. For developing readers, after choral reading, try reading as partners with one student reading the children section and one reading the teacher section. For all readers, extend the last stanza into writing and illustrating, encouraging the children to write and draw about special memories.

EXTEND THE LEARNING

☆ Have children draw and write about favorite memories. Then share with partners. Challenge the partners to try to connect to the experiences they are hearing about by asking questions, sharing common experiences, and so on.

☆ During Read-Alouds, take time for children to make connections to personal experiences that they think are helping them to understand.

☆ Invite a guest speaker to tell the children about an experience. Encourage the children to make connections to the speaker and the experience that is being shared.

☆ Have children create illustrations to show the connections they are making to a book.

ASSESS THE LEARNING

> Listen in as partners make connections with each other's experiences to determine understanding.

> During small group instruction, read and discuss connections that help us to understand the experience of the narrator or the speaker in the selection.

> Have children draw connections they are able to make to another person's experience.

INFUSION OF FORMAL LANGUAGE

Test-style language

Wilfrid Gordon helped Miss Nancy *connect* to her memories when he

  A. played in the old people's home.

  B. asked questions.

  C. took her the basket with the egg, the medal, the seashell, and the ball.

  D. danced with the puppet.

There is enough information to suggest that

  A. Miss Nancy liked Wilfrid Gordon.

  B. Wilfrid Gordon's parents wished he would stay home.

  C. Mr. Tippet was crazy.

  D. Wilfrid Gordon went to the beach.

I have a special memory.

"A Special Memory"

By Linda Hoyt

Children

I have a special memory…

I picture it now in my head.

Children

I have a special memory…

I picture it now in my head.

Children

I have a special memory…

I picture it now in my head.

Children

I have a special memory…

I picture it now in my head.

Children

I have a special memory…

I picture it now in my head.

Teacher

I remember rolling in the grass

And playing with one of my friends.

Teacher

I remember running barefoot

And feeling rocks poke into my feet.

Teacher

I remember running ever so fast

And feeling the wind in my face.

Teacher

I remember holding a special book

And turning from page to page.

Teacher

I remember…

Miss Nelson Is Missing
By Harry Allard and James Marshall

FOCUS THE LEARNING

Introduction: When we analyze or evaluate, our job is to think critically and offer opinions. For example, if we were going to analyze or evaluate our classroom library, we would want to give our opinions about it. Do we have enough books that you enjoy? Is there a good balance between fiction and nonfiction in our class library? How did we do in decorating it and posting signs to remind us of how to select good books?

 How might you analyze our library? What opinions do you have?

Today as we read *Miss Nelson Is Missing!* by Harry Allard and James Marshall, you are going to analyze and evaluate. I am going to ask you to share opinions and make suggestions. When we evaluate, we don't retell a story. We give opinions about it.

INTERACTIVE READ-ALOUD
Model and Guide Practice

READ PAGES 3–7. I have an opinion here. I don't think those kids should get away with acting like this in school at all. If these were my students, we would certainly have to evaluate the way we were doing things and make some changes.

 Think together. What opinions do you have? How would you analyze this situation? What should the teacher do?

READ TO PAGE 14. Interesting. I am thinking about how to evaluate the situation now. It seems that these kids are mean to a nice teacher and cooperate with a mean teacher.

 What opinions can you offer? How would you analyze this? Is it OK for kids to act like that?

READ TO PAGE 17. I am wondering about going to the police. Was that a good idea?

What do you think of their decision to go to the police? What is your opinion?

READ TO PAGE 24. As I evaluate the story so far, I realize the authors have done a really good job at making me feel involved. These kids need to learn to act better, but I want to know what happened to Miss Nelson.

 Work together to evaluate the situation. Is there anything else the children could be doing? What is your opinion about the story so far?

CONTINUE TO THE END OF THE STORY. Pause occasionally to give partners time to analyze, evaluate, and offer opinions.

END OF STORY REFLECTION

Remember, when we analyze and evaluate, we are not just retelling. We are giving opinions. If we were to evaluate this book, what kind of rating might you give it?

 Think together. If you could rate the book on a scale of 1–5, what rating would you give it and why?

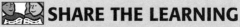 **SHARE THE LEARNING**
Focus on Analyze and Evaluate

Tip for Share the Thinking

Guide the children in a conversation comparing Miss Swamp and Miss Nelson. What might each of them sound like when they talk to children? Analyze the way they would stand and the way their faces would look. Act out the behaviors of the two teachers. Read the

lines as though you are Miss Swamp. Chorally read the selection. Read it again as though they were Miss Nelson. What are the differences? Explain that it is important to analyze and think about what the character is like so we can change our reading to sound like the character would really sound.

Tip for Readers Theater Script

Read the script "Miss Nelson Is Missing!" to the children with fluency and expression. Engage them in a conversation about the script. What is their opinion of it? Read it again and have students dramatize as you read. Have emergent readers create illustrations to

go with the poem. For developing readers, practice and then present the poem as a readers theater.

EXTEND THE LEARNING

☆ Evaluate and give opinions about settings, characters, poems, or playground rules.

☆ Have students evaluate and analyze books used in small group and independent reading experiences.

☆ Do Sticky Note Reviews: Have students rate books they read in independent reading on a 1–5 scale. Then place their rating and explanation on a sticky inside the front cover as a gift to the next reader.

☆ Encourage students to identify whether they are evaluating or doing a retell of a selection.

☆ Solicit opinions about books, characters, artwork, word choice, and so on.

ASSESS THE LEARNING

> Have students fold a sheet of paper in half. On the left, they draw and write a retell. On the right, they draw and write to evaluate and offer opinions about the selection.

> Confer with readers during independent reading to assess their ability to offer opinions and analyze a story.

> During small group time, engage students in evaluating while you listen to the quality of their responses.

INFUSION OF FORMAL LANGUAGE
Test-style language

If we were to evaluate the character of Viola Swamp, we could say she
  A. had black hair.
  B. had long fingernails.
  C. was mean.
  D. made the kids work hard.

When you analyze or evaluate, you need to:
  A. Talk
  B. Write
  C. Go to the principal
  D. Give opinions and think critically

"Children, sit down."

"You have work to do."

"We'll have no story hour today."

"Sit still. Be quiet."

"Get your work done."

Miss Nelson Is Missing!

Readers Theater adaptation by Linda Hoyt

Team

1 Once there was a classroom of very naughty kids.

2 They whispered and they giggled

1 and didn't do their work.

2 Miss Nelson was their teacher.

1 She was sweet and kind and nice.

2   But all that changed on the day

Viola Swamp arrived.

1   She made them do their lessons,

2   She had them work and work.

1   No stories and no talking . . .

2   It really was the worst.

1   In the end the kids were learning.

2   They smiled and did their work.

All   They got Miss Nelson back again

before they went beserk!

INTERPRET THROUGH EXPLANATION

Kitten's First Full Moon

By Kevin Henkes

INTERACTIVE READ-ALOUD
Model and Guide Practice

READ PAGE 1. There's our answer. Kitten thinks the moon is a bowl of milk in the sky. If the kitten was hungry, what would she think she should do to get that milk?

Thinking partners, what would the kitten be thinking?

READ TO WHERE KITTEN GETS A BUG ON HER TONGUE. We have been trying to *interpret* what is happening. I am thinking that she stretched her neck, opened her mouth, and licked, because she didn't know the moon was so far away. She thought the moon . . . that bowl of milk . . . was right there where she could reach it with her tongue. She got a bug on her tongue instead.

Think together. Let's interpret what the kitten thought when she got the bug on her tongue!

READ TO THE PLACE WHERE THE KITTEN TUMBLES OFF THE PORCH. I am going to try to interpret what kitten just did. She figured out that she couldn't reach the bowl of milk by sticking out her tongue, so I interpret that she jumped because she thought the bowl of milk was just a little bit further than her tongue could reach.

How I am doing? Would you interpret her jump in the same way?

READ TO THE PLACE WHERE KITTEN IS IN THE TREE.

Think together. How would you interpret this? Why would the kitten climb up a tree? Let's try to explain what is happening.

Continue to the end of the story, pausing occasionally to give partners time to talk.

END OF STORY REFLECTION

I am going to ask you and your thinking partner to think together for a moment. If you were to interpret this story and explain it to someone who hadn't heard it, what would you tell that person? How would you explain the way the kitten behaved, and what details would you add?

Your job is to interpret this story and prepare to explain it to someone else. Be sure to add details that help you to interpret the story. Give me a thumbs-up when you and your partner are ready.

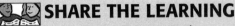

SHARE THE LEARNING
Focus on Interpretation

Tip for Share the Reading

Read the poem slowly with expression and ask the children to join you in interpreting the poem. What is happening? How would you explain this? What details are important? How might the children act it out? How could they explain this to someone who hadn't read the poem? There aren't a lot of words. Ask the children to add details based on what they visualize as they read.

I am Cat

Creeping slowly

Paws lifting one at a time

Ready, ready

Dinner is near

Pounce.

Hmm.

Tip for Readers Theater Script

Read "Dogs" to emergent learners so they catch on to the pattern. Then invite them to join you in chorally reading the selection. Children will have fun taking responsibility for a single line, enjoying the selection with a partner, or adding new lines.

"Dogs"
By Linda Hoyt

B is for dog.
Why? Because a dog barks.

F is for dog.
Why? Because a dog has fur.

R is for dog.
Why? Because a dog runs.

T is for dog.
Why? Because a dog has a long tongue.

W is for dog.
Why? Because a dog has a wet nose.

Read "Kitten's First Full Moon" to developing readers. Ask them to think about the story as they listen. Pause frequently to engage them in conversing about interpretation. Should you read it faster? slower? with more expression? Would a quiet voice be good for some parts of the script? Should you sound excited at any particular points? As they gain confidence, engage learners as readers of the script, reading in unison, in teams, or in small groups. As the children are ready, play soft instrumental music in the background to help them celebrate fluent and expressive interpretation of the script.

EXTEND THE LEARNING

☆ Use the word *interpret* in daily classroom events. For example: I notice that Miguel and Jaylynn are sitting together on the rug. I could interpret that they are ready to be thinking partners today.

☆ Give classroom artists an opportunity to "interpret" their creations for partners.

☆ Watch classroom pets closely. Can we interpret anything from what they are doing?

☆ Use hand motions and charades to communicate a message and ask the children to interpret your meaning.

☆ Interpret stories and poems by explaining their meaning and adding details that the author has left the reader to infer.

ASSESS THE LEARNING

> Listen in as partners share their interpretations of stories to assess understanding.

> Have children interpret a story by creating a picture about it and planning how to explain it to their parents.

INFUSION OF FORMAL LANGUAGE
Test-style language

To *interpret* this story, it is important to notice that:

A. the kitten thought she could reach the moon.

B. the kitten thought the moon was a bowl of milk.

C. the kitten was hungry.

D. All of the above.

You could *explain* the kitten's behavior by saying

A. the kitten was silly.

B. the kitten licked her paw.

C. the kitten thought she could reach the moon.

D. the pictures were in black and white.

I am Cat

Creeping slowly

Paws lifting one at a time

Ready, ready

Dinner is near

Pounce.

Hmm.

"Dogs"

By Linda Hoyt

B is for dog.

Why? Because a dog **b**arks.

F is for dog.

Why? Because a dog has **f**ur.

R is for dog.

Why? Because a dog **r**uns.

T is for dog.

Why? Because a dog has a long **t**ongue.

W is for dog.

Why? Because a dog has a **w**et nose.

Kitten's First Full Moon

Readers Theater adaptation by Linda Hoyt

Narrator 1:   On a night with a full moon

Narrator 2:   a hungry kitten looked at the moon

Narrator 3:   and thought it was a bowl of milk.

Narrator 4:   The kitten didn't know that the moon was far away.

Narrator 2:   All she knew is that she wanted some milk.

Narrator 3:   She tried to reach it with her tongue

Narrator 1:   and only caught a bug.

Narrator 4: She tried to jump to it from the stairs

Narrator 2: and ended up bumping her nose.

Narrator 3: She tried climbing a tree

Narrator 4: but got really scared.

Narrator 1: Kitten was tired and very hungry.

Narrator 2: She went back home

Narrator 3: and there was a great big bowl of milk on the porch.

Everyone: Right where she could reach it.

Everyone: Goodnight little kitten.

INTERPRET THROUGH DRAMA/PERFORMANCE

Don't Let the Pigeon Drive the Bus!
By Mo Willems

FOCUS THE LEARNING

Introduction: We know that tantrums and begging for things are not nice behaviors. But we do see people who do those things. I know you are so grown up that you wouldn't do this, but I watched a three-year-old ask over and over and over again for a piece of candy. When his mom kept saying no, he had a tantrum. He yelled and cried and kept begging for the candy. He didn't understand that no meant NO!

 Think together. Have you ever seen someone act like that?

In *Don't Let the Pigeon Drive the Bus!* by Mo Willems, you are going to meet a very determined pigeon.

INTERACTIVE READ-ALOUD
Model and Guide Practice

READ THE TITLE PAGE. Show the illustration of the driver leaving…and the pigeon peering in on the opposite page. This is interesting. The driver is talking to us! He is asking us to watch the bus and make sure the pigeon doesn't try to drive it. I wonder if that means he has had trouble with the pigeon before?

 Put your heads together. Would the pigeon make a good bus driver? Why?

READ UP TO THE PAGE WHERE THE PIGEON SAYS HE WILL BE CAREFUL. Now the pigeon is talking to us! He knows the driver asked us to watch the bus for him and the pigeon is trying to talk us into letting him drive. Notice how polite he is. He said, "please" and he even said he will be careful.

 Think together. Should pigeon get on the bus? Why?

READ UP TO THE PAGE WHERE THE PIGEON SAYS, "PIGEON AT THE WHEEL!" This pigeon is trying all kinds of things to get on the bus.

 What should we tell him? If the pigeon was standing right here, what would you say to him? Tell your partner what you would say to the pigeon.

READ UP TO THE PAGE WHERE HE SAYS, "I NEVER GET TO DO ANYTHING." Have you ever felt like that when you are told you can't do something?

 Show your partner what you think the pigeon looks like right now. Use your body to show how he is feeling.

READ UP TO THE PAGES WITH EIGHT PICTURES AND STATEMENTS. The pigeon just doesn't give up! Let's read these pages again. Listen to all of the ways he tried to talk us into letting him drive!

 Pretend you are the pigeon and convince your partner to let you drive.

CONTINUE TO THE END OF THE STORY. Have partners talk about the pigeon's tantrum and then his dream of driving…a truck!

END OF STORY REFLECTION

Partners, you are going to use drama to interpret this story. If you are the partner guarding the bus, it is your job to protect the bus. Don't let the pigeon drive the bus! Pigeons: try to convince the driver to let you drive. Those of you who are the pigeon need to think hard and try to convince your partner that you should be able to drive the bus. Think. How would your character sound? What actions would your character use? How would your character stand or move? Find a place in the room where you and your partner can dramatize. Ready, set, action!

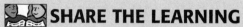 **SHARE THE LEARNING**
Focus on Interpreting Through Drama

Tip for Share the Reading

Read the passage to the students, stopping occasionally to help them visualize what an astronaut would have to do to walk on the moon. Read the passage again and have the students help you identify words that are important to consider in interpreting the passage. You might

Walking on the Moon

Walking on the moon is challenging. There is no gravity so each time you lift a foot, your leg wants to float up in the air. Astronauts wear big, heavy weights in their boots so they don't float away. Imagine having big bricks attached to each foot and you will begin to get the idea of what it is like to walk on the moon.

want to use a marker to underline or circle these key words. Have students interpret the passage by dramatizing what it would be like. Challenge them to represent the key words in their dramatization.

Tip for Readers Theater Script

For emergent readers, enjoy "Feelings" as an echo poem: teacher reads and children echo. The children then could create dramatic actions or illustrations to support each line. For developing readers, you might want to enjoy the script chorally, in partners or as a team

"Feelings"
By Linda Hoyt

Happy
Sad
Angry
Weeping
Wishing
Thinking
Laughing
Sleeping
So many feelings
All part of life
How are you going to feel tonight?

experience before shifting to independent reading of the script. Be sure to engage learners in dramatizing to interpret meaning.

EXTEND THE LEARNING

☆ Have students interpret stories by illustrating character emotions and actions.

☆ During a fiction experience in which characters change, have students use their faces to interpret how the character is feeling and acting.

☆ Provide time for readers to dramatize selections from small group reading experiences.

☆ Rewrite a favorite story as a play or readers theater during interactive writing.

☆ Dramatize mathematical equations and relationships.

☆ Write songs about stories…interpret through music.

ASSESS THE LEARNING

> Observe partner dramatization to assess ability to interpret.

> During independent reading conferences, ask individuals to interpret a portion of a story by dramatizing it.

> Have students illustrate key points they would include if they were to dramatize.

INFUSION OF FORMAL LANGUAGE
Test-style language

We could *interpret* the pigeon's behavior by saying:
  A. He was very determined
  B. He didn't give up
  C. He really wanted to drive the bus
  D. All of the above.

If you were going to *dramatize* the behavior of the pigeon, you would need to:
  A. Beg
  B. Have a tantrum
  C. Think of lots of reasons you should drive a bus
  D. All of the above.

Walking on the Moon

Walking on the moon is challenging. There is no gravity so each time you lift a foot, your leg wants to float up in the air. Astronauts wear big, heavy weights in their boots so they don't float away. Imagine having big bricks attached to each foot and you will begin to get the idea of what it is like to walk on the moon.

"Feelings"

By Linda Hoyt

Happy

Sad

Angry

Weeping

Wishing

Thinking

Laughing

Sleeping

So many feelings

All part of life

How are you going to feel tonight?

No, David!
By David Shannon

INTERACTIVE READ-ALOUD
Model and Guide Practice

SHOW THE COVER AND READ THE TITLE. Then pause to think aloud. I am going to stop reading for a minute and think about clues that might help me to infer. It looks like this boy is trying to pull the fishbowl off of the table and everything is about to crash. The title says, "No, David!" so I am going to *infer* that a mom or dad is yelling at him to stop pulling on the fishbowl.

TURN TO THE TITLE PAGE. As I look at the title page, I can see that it is a woman's body. So now I can *infer* that the person who wants David to stop is a woman...maybe a mom, a grandma, or a babysitter.

READ TO THE PAGE WHERE DAVID IS REACHING FOR THE COOKIE JAR.

 Turn to your thinking partner. What can you infer? What is David trying to do? The words are "No, David!" What does the person saying those words really want?

READ TO THE PAGE WHERE DAVID IS IN THE BATHTUB.

 Think with your partner. What can we infer here? Use the stem, "I can infer that _____.

CONTINUE READING. Pause after each two-page spread to have partners infer what David is doing and what the speaker wants to have happen. Have the partners use the stem "I can infer _____" as they share their thinking.

END OF STORY REFLECTION

We have been able to make so many inferences with this book. The author didn't use a lot of words, but he sure gave us a lot of clues about what was happening so we could infer.

 Turn and talk to your partner. What was your favorite inference in this book?

SHARE THE THINKING
Focus on Inferring

Tip for Share the Thinking

Place the text on the overhead projector. Using a sheet of paper, expose only the first line of text. Explain to the students that our inferences affect the way we read. Model reading line 1 in a mono-tone, lifeless voice. What could we infer about the person who talked like that? Then model it again with gusto, really showing emotion. What could we infer about a person who said it now? Model reading that sounds sleepy, angry, in a hurry. Repeat for each line.

Tip for Readers Theater Script

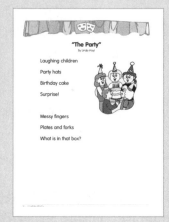

Guide the children in making inferences from only the illustration. What can they infer is happening? What are the clues? Encourage them to look closely at individual portions of the illustration, as images in various sections offer different invitations to infer. Read "The Party" to the children and ask them to consider additional inferences. What kind of party is it? What can we infer? Finally, engage the children in chorally reading the entire poem for fluency.

EXTEND THE LEARNING

☆ During small group reading instruction, help the students find places where they can infer.

☆ Focus students on inferences they can make in school. Thomas put his coat on. We can infer that he is cold.

☆ Look for inferences in additional Read-Alouds and ask students to use the stem, "I can infer…" to share their observations.

☆ Show students how we can make inferences from drawings. Example: I am looking at Daisia's drawing of going out for pizza. I can infer that she had pepperoni pizza because of the little round circles on the pizza.

ASSESS THE LEARNING

➤ Listen in as partners converse about inferences they were able to make while listening to *No, David!*

➤ Confer with readers to see if they can make inferences within the classroom about a drawing or about a reading selection.

INFUSION OF FORMAL LANGUAGE
Test-style language

In *No, David!* we could infer that

   A. David is a very busy boy.

   B. David made a lot of messes.

   C. David had to sit in the corner for being naughty.

   D. All of the above.

Another name for this story might be:

   A. *David Causes Trouble*

   B. *David's Mom Loves Him*

   C. *David Finds a Fishbowl*

   D. *David Plays Baseball*

David, be quiet

Don't play with your food

Go to your room

Will you PLEASE sit still

It is time for a bath

"The Party"
By Linda Hoyt

Laughing children

Party hats

Birthday cake

Surprise!

Messy fingers

Plates and forks

What is in that box?

Blueberries for Sal
By Robert McCloskey

FOCUS THE LEARNING

Introduction: We predict in a lot of ways in our lives. If we see big black clouds, we can sometimes predict it will rain. If we smell something really wonderful coming from the cafeteria, we can predict we are going to have a great lunch. As readers, we predict too. We look at pictures, at the title, and think about what is likely to happen. We also think about the story and use what is happening in a story to help us predict what is coming next. Today as we read *Blueberries for Sal* by Robert McCloskey, we will be predicting and thinking about what is likely to happen next.

INTERACTIVE READ-ALOUD
Model and Guide Practice

READ PAGES 6–7. I predict that they are going to start looking for blueberry bushes so they can begin to put blueberries in their pails. Let's read on and see if I was correct.

READ PAGES 8–13. I can see that my prediction was right. They found blueberry bushes and Little Sal is already eating them. I am thinking about what Little Sal is doing, and I remember that her mother said she wanted to can blueberries so they would have some in the winter.

What might we predict that Sal's mother is going to say to her?

READ PAGES 14–16. That is interesting. I predicted that Sal's mother would tell her to stop eating. She didn't do that. She just told her to pick her own berries. This is a good reminder that our predictions aren't always correct. I am not sure what is going to happen next so I am going to take a peek at the picture on the next page. [Show the illustration on page 19.] Oh, my. A mother bear and her cub.

Think together. What might we predict is going to happen?

READ PAGES 18–23. Isn't this interesting? Little Bear and his mother are a lot like Little Sal and her mother, aren't they? I wonder what will happen next.

READ PAGES 24–26.

Predict together. What do you think is making that noise?

CONTINUE TO PAGE 38. Pause occasionally to give partners time to predict. We have to really think now. Little Bear and Little Sal are with the wrong mothers. What do you predict will happen now?

Predict together.

CONTINUE TO THE END OF THE STORY. Pause for predictions between partners.

END OF STORY REFLECTION

We made a lot of predictions. Think for a minute...What helped you make predictions? Did you look at the pictures? Did you think about the story? Did you think about what you know about bears or people picking berries? How were you able to do it?

Talk together. What helped you make good predictions?

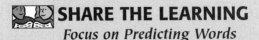

SHARE THE LEARNING
Focus on Predicting Words

Tip for Share the Reading

Explain to the children that we can predict ideas in a story and we can also predict words that are likely to appear. Place the cloze passage on the overhead and read it straight through once. Then read it again more slowly, and when you come to each blank, ask them to talk to a

> Little Frog heard a big noise and turned his head to _____. He wasn't really afraid, he just wanted to know what was making that big _____. Suddenly the ground started to shake. The bushes shook and the tree that Little Frog was sitting on began to _____. A huge _____ came running out of the bushes straight at the tree where Little Frog was hiding. Quick as a wink, Little Frog hopped down from his tree and disappeared into a _____. Safe!

partner about words they predict would fit well and make sense. After they have inserted the words they like, read the passage with expression and act it out. Try reading it with different words in the blanks for fun and variety.

Tip for Readers Theater Script

For emergent readers, read "Little Sal and Little Bear" to the children as though it was written for one person. As the children gain confidence, encourage them to read along with their own copies of the script. The children then could create illustrations. For develop-

ing readers, you might want to enjoy the script as a two-team experience. Team 1 reads the left column, and Team 2 reads the right column. With increased proficiency, partners can read the poem together for fluency and expression.

EXTEND THE LEARNING

☆ Provide opportunities to predict in a wide range of selections including nonfiction texts such as directions.

☆ During small group instruction, use prediction as a prereading tool. Focus on predicting words they think will appear as well as ideas that they think will be part of a story.

☆ During Read-Alouds, pause to have children quickly sketch their predictions. Then use their sketches to develop postreading retells.

ASSESS THE LEARNING

➤ Listen in as partners share their predictions to assess understanding.

➤ Confer with readers during independent reading to assess ability to make predictions independently.

➤ After a picture preview, ask students to make two predictions about a book and jot them down (drawing and writing). After reading, have them record what actually happened and compare.

INFUSION OF FORMAL LANGUAGE
Test-style language

If this story were to continue, we could *predict* that next winter

   A. Little Sal and her family would have canned blueberries to eat.

   B. Little Bear and his mother would be sleeping.

   C. There wouldn't be any blueberries on Blueberry Hill.

   D. All of the above.

When Little Sal's mother saw that Little Bear was behind her, she probably felt:

   A. Happy

   B. Mad

   C. Worried about Little Sal

   D. Like singing

Little Frog heard a big noise and turned his head to _____. He wasn't really afraid, he just wanted to know what was making that big _____. Suddenly the ground started to shake. The bushes shook and the tree that Little Frog was sitting on began to _____. A huge _____ came running out of the bushes straight at the tree where Little Frog was hiding. Quick as a wink, Little Frog hopped down from his tree and disappeared into a _____. Safe!

"Little Sal and Little Bear"
—A Poem for Two Voices

By Linda Hoyt

Team 1	Team 2	
We like	books!	
We like	writing!	
We like	our friends!	
We like	school!	

Olivia

By Ian Falconer

FOCUS THE LEARNING

Introduction: As we read *Olivia* by Ian Falconer today, we are going to be using clues in the story to draw conclusions about the characters. The idea is to think about the clues in the book and use those clues to think more deeply. To get started, let's look at the cover. I can see that Olivia is a little girl pig and that she is wearing a dress. The book doesn't tell us, but I can conclude that this is fiction because real pigs don't wear dresses. Ask a child to stand and make a sad face. How is _____ feeling when he looks like this? He isn't telling us but we can *conclude* that he is feeling _____.

Partners, one of you needs to make a face, and the other one needs to say, "I can conclude that you are feeling _____."

INTERACTIVE READ-ALOUD
Model and Guide Practice

READ PAGES 1–3. Then pause to think aloud. The book says that Olivia is very good at wearing people out...and even wearing herself out. The book doesn't say this *but I can conclude* that if she wears everyone out, she must be really busy.

READ PAGES 4–5. It says Olivia has to be firm to get Ian to leave her alone, but she is wearing a scary mask. I could conclude that Ian is running away because he is afraid. I can conclude that Olivia put the mask on because she *wanted* to scare her little brother.

READ PAGES 6–7. It shows Olivia moving the cat, twice! The book doesn't say it, but I could conclude that the cat is a pest and gets in her way.

READ TO THE PLACE WHERE OLIVIA BUILT A SKYSCRAPER SAND CASTLE.

 What can you conclude about Olivia's ability to make sand castles?

READ TO THE PLACE WHERE OLIVIA'S MOTHER TELLS HER IT IS TIME FOR A NAP. Encourage the students to look closely at the illustration of Olivia on the bed.

 What can you conclude about Olivia now?

CONTINUE TO THE END OF THE STORY. Pause occasionally to give partners time to talk and draw conclusions.

END OF STORY REFLECTION

Let's think about all of the conclusions we were able to draw about Olivia. Remember, these are things that the book doesn't tell us, but we can figure them out for ourselves. Who has a conclusion about Olivia?

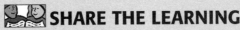

SHARE THE LEARNING
Focus on Drawing Conclusions

Tip for Share the Reading

🎭 Share the reading of this excerpt with the goal of drawing conclusions about Mr. and Mrs. Mallard, the setting, and the time of year. Possible conclusions to consider: It is spring and that is why they are thinking of building a nest. Foxes and turtles are predators for duck eggs and duck babies. Ducks eat grass and grains so there must be grass and grains nearby. It says they climbed out on the bank, so there must be water, and so on.

> *(excerpt from Make Way for Ducklings by Robert McCloskey)*
>
> "I like this place," said Mrs. Mallard as they climbed out on the bank and waddled along.
>
> "Why don't we build a nest and raise our ducklings right here? There are no foxes and no turtles and there is a lot of food. What could be better?"
>
> "Good," said Mr. Mallard, delighted that at last Mrs. Mallard had found a place that suited her.

Tip for Readers Theater Script

🎭 For emergent readers, read *Caterpillar Story* to them and talk about the life cycle of the caterpillar and butterfly. At each phase of the life cycle, talk about conclusions you can draw. For example, we could conclude that a butterfly egg is really tiny since a butterfly isn't very big. The text says, "I have to chew my way out of my egg." We can conclude that a caterpillar is inside since we can see a caterpillar in the next picture. Have emergent learners practice retelling the *Caterpillar Story* using the pictures. For developing readers, guide a conversation about conclusions and then engage learners in choral reading of the selection with a focus on reading with fluency and expression.

Caterpillar Story
By Linda Hoyt

After about five days of growing inside my egg, I am ready to hatch as a tiny caterpillar.

I have to chew my way out of my egg. It's hard work. Once I am out, I will eat my eggshell because I am very hungry.

I eat a lot. Soon I can't fit into my skin anymore. I need to shed my old skin and grow a bigger one. I don't sleep at all. I just eat and eat and eat. After four weeks, I shed my skin for the last time.

Under my last skin a shell has formed. I hang from a branch and wait for three more weeks.

When I come out, I am a beautiful butterfly!

EXTEND THE LEARNING

☆ Make a point to use the stem "I can conclude _____" frequently in daily classroom experiences. For example, you might look at the clock and say, "It is 10:55. I conclude that we need to get ready for lunch!" "I noticed that Alicia's cheeks were really red when she came in from recess. I can conclude that it must be pretty cold outside."

☆ In small group instruction, scaffold children in drawing conclusions about their reading selections.

☆ Draw conclusions about characters in a variety of Read-Aloud selections.

☆ Draw conclusions about nonfiction selections. This picture shows a chick pecking its way out of the egg. I conclude he has grown as much as he can while inside of the egg.

ASSESS THE LEARNING

➤ Confer with readers during independent reading to assess their ability to draw conclusions independently.

➤ Listen in on partner conversations when learners are drawing conclusions.

INFUSION OF FORMAL LANGUAGE
Test-style language

What *conclusion* can you draw about Olivia's sand castle?

  A. It isn't real.

  B. Her mother did it.

  C. It took a long time.

  D. Olivia is very good at building sand castles.

Which sentence best tells how Olivia's mother feels?

  A. You really wear me out, but I love you anyway.

  B. You need a nap.

  C. It is time to go to the beach.

  D. No, you cannot have five stories.

(excerpt from **Make Way for Ducklings** *by Robert McCloskey)*

"I like this place," said Mrs. Mallard as they climbed out on the bank and waddled along.

"Why don't we build a nest and raise our ducklings right here? There are no foxes and no turtles and there is a lot of food. What could be better?"

"Good," said Mr. Mallard, delighted that at last Mrs. Mallard had found a place that suited her.

Caterpillar Story

By Linda Hoyt

After about five days of growing inside my egg, I am ready to hatch as a tiny caterpillar.

I have to chew my way out of my egg. It's hard work. Once I am out, I will eat my eggshell because I am very hungry.

I eat a lot. Soon I can't fit into my skin any-more. I need to shed my old skin and grow a bigger one. I don't sleep at all. I just eat and eat and eat. After four weeks, I shed my skin for the last time.

Under my last skin a shell has formed. I hang from a branch and wait for three more weeks.

When I come out, I am a beautiful butterfly!

COMPARE AND CONTRAST
(STRUCTURE AND PLOT)

Goldilocks and the Three Bears

By James Marshall

INTERACTIVE READ-ALOUD
Model and Guide Practice

READ PAGES 1–2. Pause to think aloud. I found some things I can compare. I don't remember neighbors in the first version of this story. I also don't remember anyone calling Goldilocks "sweet." It is interesting when I compare the beginnings. In this one, Goldilock's mother has her promise not to go in the forest. That didn't happen in the other version.

 Turn to your thinking partner. What have you noticed about ways the stories are alike and different? Is there anything we should add to our chart?

READ TO THE PLACE WHERE THE BEARS GET ON THEIR BICYCLE AND RIDE AWAY. I am going to stop reading for a minute and think about ways I can compare this version of *Goldilocks* and the other version we read. I notice that in both books, the bears wanted to eat breakfast but it was too hot. I am going to add that to our chart under things that are the same.

 Turn to your thinking partner. Think about comparisons you can make. What is the same and what is different?

CONTINUE TO THE END OF THE STORY. Pause occasionally to give partners time to talk, to add comments to the chart, and appreciate the humor as they compare versions of this classic.

END OF STORY REFLECTION

Look at all of the comparisons we were able to make. Our chart shows lots of ways the stories are alike and different.

 Turn and talk to your partner. Think together to compare ways the stories were alike. What is an example of ways they were alike?

Then ... think together to compare ways in which the stories were different.

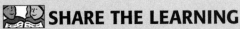 **SHARE THE LEARNING**
Focus on Compare and Contrast

Tip for Share the Reading

 Read the shared passage several times. Then lead a conversation comparing Goldilocks' behavior with the way people *should* act when visiting someone else's home. Have the students dramatize Goldilocks coming to the bears' house, and then dramatize visiting the home of a friend from school.

> A few minutes later Goldilocks arrived at the bears' house. She walked right in without even bothering to knock. On the dining room table were three inviting bowls of porridge. "I'm hungry," said Goldilocks, and she ate the whole bowl of porridge.

Tip for Readers Theater Script

 For emergent readers, engage readers with a brief retell of *Goldilocks and the Three Bears*, comparing their behavior, their voices, and the way in which they act. Read the script to the children and then create illustrations to support reading of the script. Encourage them to portray the characters in ways that help us compare and contrast their voices, their actions, and their thinking. For developing readers, assign roles, asking students to plan how to express the voice of the character as dramatically as they can so we can tell immediately if they are Papa Bear, Mama Bear, Baby Bear, or Goldilocks. Read the script dramatically adding physical actions if desired.

EXTEND THE LEARNING

☆ Guide conversations comparing structural elements of several familiar books. What similarities and differences do they notice in the settings, the problem/solution, the behavior of characters, the way passage of time is illuminated, and so on.

☆ Read two books and then develop a Venn diagram comparing the central character, the problem, or the setting in each.

☆ Connect compare/contrast to independent reading by having students select two books they can read by themselves and be ready to tell a partner about the ways the books are alike and different.

☆ Have the children read *Goldilocks Returns* by Lisa Campbell Ernst and compare the story lines.

ASSESS THE LEARNING

> Listen in as partners converse about comparisons between books.

> Confer with readers during independent reading asking them to compare attributes of books they are reading.

INFUSION OF FORMAL LANGUAGE
Test-style language

In comparing versions of *Goldilocks*, we notice that

A. the bears wear the same clothes.

B. Goldilocks is always very nice.

C. Goldilocks wishes she could be a bear.

D. there are differences in each story.

This story is mostly about:

A. A little girl who should stay out of other people's houses

B. The problems with hot porridge

C. Bears on bicycles

D. Danger in the forest

A few minutes later Goldilocks arrived at the bears' house. She walked right in without even

bothering to knock. On the dining room table were three inviting bowls of porridge. "I'm hungry," said Goldilocks, and she ate the whole bowl of porridge.

Goldilocks and the Three Bears

Readers Theater script by Linda Hoyt

Narrator 2:	Once upon a time there were three bears.
Narrator 1:	There was a papa bear . . .
Papa Bear:	"I'm the **BIG** bear."
Narrator 1:	A mama bear . . .
Mama Bear:	"I'm the **middle**-size bear."
Narrator 1:	and a little baby bear.
Baby Bear:	"I'm the **little** baby bear."
Narrator 2:	They sat down to eat breakfast.
Narrator 1:	The baby bear said,
Baby Bear:	"It's too hot!"
Narrator 2:	So they went for a walk.
Narrator 1:	A little girl named Goldilocks came to their house.
Goldilocks:	"Oh, what a cute house. I want to see inside."
Narrator 2:	She ate their porridge, broke the chair
Narrator 1:	And then fell asleep.
Papa Bear:	Someone ate our breakfast.
Mama Bear:	Someone broke our chair!
Narrator 2:	Goldilocks woke up,
Everyone:	And ran out the door.

Frederick
By Leo Lionni

FOCUS THE LEARNING

Introduction: When we compare things we see how they are alike and how they are different. Today, as I read *Frederick* by Leo Lionni, you will notice that there is a family of mice, but they are not all the same. Our job is to compare Frederick with the other mice and think about ways they are the same and ways that they are different.

INTERACTIVE READ-ALOUD
Model and Guide Practice

READ TO THE PLACE WHERE IT SAYS, "A CHATTY FAMILY OF FIELD MICE HAD THEIR HOME." I am trying to compare the mice by thinking about ways they are alike and different. They look alike. They are the same color and have similar ears. Those are two ways they are the same. When I look closely, I am noticing some differences. Notice how the mice in the top row have their eyes wide open and they look like they are a group. I see that there is one mouse alone. He is looking down and doesn't seem to be part of the group above. As I compare, I notice that they may look alike, but one mouse isn't part of the group.

READ THE NEXT PAGE. When I compare the mice now, I notice that four mice are working and Frederick is just sitting with his eyes closed. My comparison helps me understand that Frederick is different because he doesn't work.

READ THE NEXT PAGE.

 Think together. What are you noticing? What are the similarities and differences in the mice?

READ TO THE PAGE WHERE FREDERICK CLIMBS ON A BIG STONE AND BEGINS TO SPEAK.

 What do you notice now? How would you compare the mice now?

CONTINUE TO THE END OF THE STORY. Pause occasionally to give partners time to compare and contrast the behavior of the mice.

END OF STORY REFLECTION

Comparing and contrasting is an important skill. Let's compare more things we know about. Here are two pencils. They are alike in that they both have erasers. They are different in that the blue one is long and the red one is short.

 Think together. Find two things you can compare and tell how they are alike and how they are different.

Now let's think about characters in books. I am thinking about Goldilocks and Cinderella. They both have blonde hair. That part is alike. They are different in that Cinderella is a hard worker and tried to be nice. Goldilocks went into a house when she shouldn't and she broke things. Goldilocks wasn't a very nice person.

 Think together about two story characters you know. How are they alike and different?

SHARE THE LEARNING
Focus on Compare and Contrast (Characters and Setting)

Tip for Share the Reading

Read the selection fluently with expression. Then guide students in a discussion of similarities and differences in the mice. Read it again with the students participating in fluent, expressive interpretation of the text. They might enjoy alternating lines, reading in unison, trying echo reading, or reading in teams.

When the mice gather food,
Frederick gathers words.
When the mice work together,
Frederick is alone.
When the mice prepare for winter,
Frederick does, too.

Tip for Readers Theater Script

For emergent readers, enjoy "Frederick" as an echo poem: teacher reads and children echo. The children could then create illustrations that re-create the storyline. For developing readers, you might want to enjoy the script as a two-team experience. Team #1 reads one line and team #2 reads the next. With increased proficiency, partners can read the poem together for fluency and expression.

"Frederick"
Readers Theater adaptation by Linda Hoyt

Mice
Scampering
Gathering
Preparing for winter

Something to eat
Mental pictures for warmth
Spring will be here soon.

EXTEND THE LEARNING

☆ Read *Swimmy* by Leo Lionni and compare *Swimmy* and *Frederick*.

☆ Read a variety of Leo Lionni books and compare the themes and settings of each.

☆ Create a chart focused on comparisons of settings, characters, problems, situations, or authors.

☆ Have writers compare pieces of their own writing. How are they alike and different? What are the strengths of each?

ASSESS THE LEARNING

➤ Listen in as partners share comparisons to assess understanding.

➤ During small group instruction, have students compare characters, settings, problems, and other story elements.

➤ Confer with individuals during independent reading and assess ability to compare and contrast.

INFUSION OF FORMAL LANGUAGE
Test-style language

To *compare* the mice, it is important to notice that Frederick
   A. is lazy.
   B. looks the same.
   C. gathers words and images.
   D. is a hard worker.

When you *compare and contrast*, you
   A. find things that are similar.
   B. find things that are different.
   C. find things that are the same.
   D. All of the above.

When the mice gather food,

Frederick gathers words.

When the mice work together,

Frederick is alone.

When the mice prepare for winter,

Frederick does, too.

"Frederick"

Readers Theater adaptation by Linda Hoyt

Mice

Scampering

Gathering

Preparing for winter

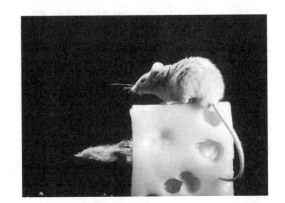

Something to eat

Mental pictures for warmth

Spring will be here soon.

IDENTIFY CAUSE AND EFFECT

If You Give a Mouse a Cookie

By Laura Joffe Numeroff

FOCUS THE LEARNING

Introduction: You will need a balloon filled with air and a pin, plus a rubber ball or some other safe object you can drop. Boys and girls, I am writing "Cause–Effect" on the board to help us think about a very important idea. When we do something, our action often causes something else to happen. If I poke this pin into this balloon, what will happen? Poking the pin will **cause** the balloon to burst. The explosion of the balloon is the **effect**, or result.

 If I hold this ball over my head and drop it to the floor, what will be the effect? What caused that effect?

INTERACTIVE READ-ALOUD
Model and Guide Practice

READ PAGES 1–5. Then pause to think aloud. I have found a lot to think about so far. Giving the mouse a cookie caused the mouse to ask for milk. Having milk caused the mouse to want a napkin. This is fun. I am going to read more.

READ PAGES 6–8.

 Turn to your thinking partner. Think together. What cause and effect have you noticed on these pages?

READ PAGES 9–12. I am going to stop reading for a minute and think about what has been happening. I am noticing that everything the boy does has an effect on the mouse and causes something to happen.

 Turn to your thinking partner. Tell each other what you have noticed about cause and effect.

CONTINUE READING TO THE END. Can you believe it! They are back to the milk and cookie. This story could keep going and going.

 What was your favorite part of this story? What caused that part to happen?

END OF STORY REFLECTION

I am going to write some of the cause and effect relationships we noticed on the board under our words "Cause" and "Effect." I am going to start with the cookie. I will write cookie under "Cause" and milk under "Effect" because the cookie made the mouse thirsty and he wanted milk.

 Turn and talk to your partner. What else can we write under "Cause" and "Effect"?

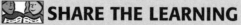

SHARE THE LEARNING
Focus on Identifying Cause and Effect

Tip for Share the Reading

Place the text on the overhead projector and read each paragraph aloud, encouraging the children to join in. After each paragraph, have partners discuss the cause and effect in each paragraph and then add their thinking to the Cause and Effect chart. For additional readings, have the children read the paragraphs with an emphasis on shifting their voices dramatically.

1. It has been raining for days and days. There are deep puddles everywhere and the rivers and creeks are full to the top.

2. The smells coming down the hall from the cafeteria were amazing. All morning the cooks had been busy making pizza for lunch, and the wonderful smell was making everyone hungry.

Tip for Readers Theater Script

For emergent readers: Read "If You Give a Mouse a Cookie" aloud and invite children to dramatize as they catch on. Distribute copies of the script and have them read along, then practice with partners. For developing readers, poems for two voices require a bit of practice but can be wonderful fluency builders. For a first experience, you may want to ask another teacher or a parent volunteer to read the poem with you, showing how sometimes your voices go together and sometimes just one of you will be reading. As the children catch on, read one part while the group reads the second part.

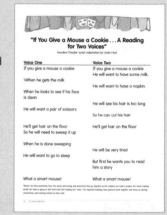

EXTEND THE LEARNING

☆ Help the children notice cause and effect relationships in daily living. Example: It is cold outside today. That will cause us to be sure to wear our coats. The effect of cold weather is we are wearing our coats. José fell down when he tripped on his untied shoelaces. The untied shoelaces caused José to fall down.

☆ During Read-Aloud, guided reading, and content area studies, watch for cause/effect relationships to point out to the children.

ASSESS THE LEARNING

➤ Ask individuals to respond individually to the paragraphs in Tip for Share the Reading to assess their ability to identify cause and effect relationships.

➤ Confer with readers during independent reading to see if they identify cause/effect relationships while reading independently.

INFUSION OF FORMAL LANGUAGE
Test-style language

What *caused* the mouse to ask for milk in this story?
  A. He likes milk.
  B. It was breakfast time.
  C. The cookie caused him to get thirsty.
  D. The boy wanted him to have it.

What would be most likely to happen after the end of this story?
  A. It would start all over again.
  B. The boy would send the mouse away.
  C. The mouse would have a big mess to clean up.
  D. The mom and dad would come home.

1. It has been raining for days and days. There are deep puddles everywhere and the rivers and creeks are full to the top.

2. The smells coming down the hall from the cafeteria were amazing. All morning the cooks had been busy making pizza for lunch, and the wonderful smell was making everyone hungry.

"If You Give a Mouse a Cookie . . . A Reading for Two Voices"

Readers Theater script adaptation by Linda Hoyt

Voice One	Voice Two
If you give a mouse a cookie	If you give a mouse a cookie
	He will want to have some milk.
\When he gets the milk	
	He will want to have a napkin.
When he looks to see if his face is clean	
	He will see his hair is too long
He will want a pair of scissors	
	So he can cut his hair
He'll get hair on the floor	He'll get hair on the floor
So he will need to sweep it up	
When he is done sweeping	
	He will be very tired
He will want to go to sleep	
	But first he wants you to read him a story
What a smart mouse!	What a smart mouse!

*Notice the lines sometimes have the voices alternating and sometimes they go together so the children can read in unison. For initial reading, divide the class or group in half with each half reading one "voice." For repeated readings, have partners work together and focus on pacing, smoothness, and creating interest as they read.

© 2007 by Linda Hoyt from *Interactive Read-Alouds, K–1* (Portsmouth, NH: Heinemann). This page may be reproduced for classroom use only.

IDENTIFY MAIN IDEAS AND SUPPORTING DETAILS

The Grouchy Ladybug
By Eric Carle

INTERACTIVE READ-ALOUD
Model and Guide Practice

READ THE NOTE ON THE TITLE PAGE ABOUT APHIDS. I am thinking about the main idea. I think the main idea of this is that it is good that ladybugs eat aphids because otherwise aphids would kill plants. Ladybugs are good.

 Do you agree? What are your thoughts about the main idea?

READ TO WHERE THE GROUCHY LADYBUG FLIES AWAY. Main idea? Hmm. I am thinking that it is really important to notice that this ladybug isn't just grouchy, she is kind of mean. That seems like a main idea to me.

 Think together. What are you thinking about this as a main idea?

READ TO THE PLACE WHERE SHE MEETS THE ELEPHANT. Isn't it interesting that the Grouchy Ladybug isn't learning anything. She is trying to fight with all of these animals, and it isn't making her life any better. And she still hasn't eaten any aphids.

 What are you thinking about for main ideas?

READ TO THE END.

 Think together. What is a main idea you can think of now? What changes has the Grouchy Ladybug made? Has she learned anything? Is there a main idea here?

END OF STORY REFLECTION

I am thinking about the main idea, the reason Eric Carle wrote the book and what the story was mainly about. I am going to start writing my thoughts about the main idea.

 While I begin to write, think together about a way I could write this that would really make sense.

I am writing, "A very grouchy ladybug learned that _____." Okay, readers. How should we finish the main idea?

SHARE THE LEARNING
Focus on Main Idea

Tip for Share the Reading

Read the selection to the students and use the picture to consider main ideas. Ask: what would be a good title for this piece? What main idea makes the most sense? Encourage partners to talk together about a main idea and then come to consensus as a group.

For some trees, winter is a time of rest. When the warm days of summer shift into cooler nights, leaves turn color and begin to fall. As the days continue to become colder, all the leaves fall away and the tree waits quietly in a blanket of snow.

The main idea is: _____

A good title would be: _____

Tip for Readers Theater Script

For emergent readers, enjoy "Five Little Ladybugs" as an echo poem: the teacher reads and children echo. As they gain confidence, have them chorally read along with you. For developing readers, you might consider having the students read the poem in unison, in partners, or individually.

"Five Little Ladybugs"
Readers Theater script adapted by Linda Hoyt

Five little ladybugs sitting on a leaf . . .
One flew away and then there were four.

Four little ladybugs sitting on a leaf . . .
One flew away and then there were three.

Three little ladybugs sitting on a leaf . . .
One flew away and then there were two.

Two little ladybugs sitting on a leaf . . .
One flew away and then there was one.

One little ladybug sitting on a leaf . . .
One flew away and then there were none.

EXTEND THE LEARNING

☆ Illustrate the main idea. Have children make drawings that show the main idea and share their thinking.

☆ Find main ideas in all areas of the curriculum, taking care to remember there can often be multiple main ideas.

☆ Find main ideas in small group instruction and independent reading.

☆ Use the *The Important Book* by Margaret Wise Brown to stimulate writing that opens and closes with the main idea.

☆ Create a graphic organizer that shows the main idea and lists supporting details.

ASSESS THE LEARNING

> Analyze illustrations of main idea to check for understanding.

> Have children identify main ideas in fiction and nonfiction selections.

> Confer with readers during independent reading to see if they can identify main idea independently.

INFUSION OF FORMAL LANGUAGE
Test-style language

The main idea of this selection is

  A. a grouchy ladybug was slapped by a whale.

  B. ladybugs eat aphids.

  C. two ladybugs had trouble getting along.

  D. a grouchy ladybug learned that being grouchy doesn't make life better—things are better when you are nice.

If more pages were added to the story, they would probably tell that

  A. the grouchy ladybug was still grouchy.

  B. the aphids were all eaten.

  C. the ladybugs became friends.

  D. the elephant came looking for the Grouchy Ladybug.

For some trees, winter is a time of rest. When the warm days of summer shift into cooler nights, leaves turn color and begin to fall. As the days continue to become colder, all the leaves fall away and the tree waits quietly in a blanket of snow.

The main idea is:

_____.

A good title would be:

_____.

"Five Little Ladybugs"

Readers Theater script adapted by Linda Hoyt

Five little ladybugs sitting on a leaf . . .

One flew away and then there were four.

Four little ladybugs sitting on a leaf . . .

One flew away and then there were three.

Three little ladybugs sitting on a leaf . . .

One flew away and then there were two.

Two little ladybugs sitting on a leaf . . .

One flew away and then there was one.

One little ladybug sitting on a leaf . . .

One flew away and then there were none.

RANK IMPORTANT VS. UNIMPORTANT INFORMATION

The Wednesday Surprise
By Eve Bunting

INTERACTIVE READ-ALOUD
Model and Guide Practice

READ PAGE 5. Then pause to think aloud. I am going to stop reading and think about what is important on this page. I think the surprise for Dad's birthday is important. "Surprise" is in the title, and on the first page it is talking about Dad's birthday "surprise." I think "surprise" is an important part of this book. I am going to look at the picture to see if there is something important there. There is a lady on the bench. She looks like the lady on the cover. It says on the first page that on Wednesdays Grandma comes to stay. I think that is important, too. I wonder if that is Grandma? I notice there is a bird on the sidewalk. The story hasn't talked about the bird and the bird isn't on the cover, so I am thinking that the bird is not very important to this story.

READ PAGES 6–12

 Put your heads together. Talk first about what you think is important, and then name something that is not very important to the story.

READ PAGES 15–20

 Turn to your thinking partner. Think together about this book. What is important?

CONTINUE TO THE END OF THE STORY. Pause occasionally to give partners time to talk.

END OF STORY REFLECTION

Wasn't that a wonderful surprise that Grandma and Anna had for Dad! Now that the story is over, it is time to think about the most important things in the whole book.

 Your turn. Decide together. What are the most important things in this book? Can you name something that was not so important?

SHARE THE LEARNING
Identifying Important Information Using the Key Word Strategy (Hoyt, 1999, 2003)

Tip for Share the Reading	Tip for Readers Theater Script

Read the selection about frogs once through, modeling fluent, interesting reading. Then show the children how you can read it a second time to search for the most important words or key words, in the passage. In the first sentence you might select *amphibians*. In the third you might select the phrase *sticky tongue*. Select only the most important words so the children understand that selecting too much is not helpful. After you and the children agree on the key words, cover the original text and use the key words to summarize what has been learned about frogs.

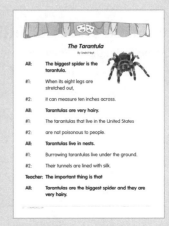

Read *The Tarantula* to the students. Guide children in a conversation about what is important in the passage. Once they have become familiar with the concepts, guide them in an echo reading of the script in which you read a line and the children repeat the line. Next, divide the students into two teams to read the script in parts. With each repeated reading, focus on fluency and expression so the text is read smoothly and with expressive voices.

EXTEND THE LEARNING

☆ Apply the Key Word strategy to wordless books, or focus the children on just looking at pictures, selecting a key word or two to highlight what is most important in a picture. Then use their key words to summarize their learning.

☆ Have partners apply the Key Word strategy in a variety of books. It works well to have them jot their key words on sticky notes or small squares of paper. After reading the words, they can then be arranged in an order that supports a retell of the content.

☆ Create a chart with headings labeled "Important" and "Not Important," and invite the children to help you complete it after reading a favorite selection.

ASSESS THE LEARNING

➤ Listen in as partners discuss important points from the reading selection.

➤ Confer with readers during independent reading to see if they can identify important ideas in their personal reading.

➤ Have students use key words to summarize their learning.

INFUSION OF FORMAL LANGUAGE
Test-style language

Which of the following is *most* important to the story?
  A. Grandma takes the bus.
  B. Dad brought Anna a rock.
  C. They decorated the house for the party.
  D. Grandma read a book called *Popcorn*.

This story is *mostly* about:
  A. Anna teaching Grandma to read
  B. A busy family
  C. Having a dad who travels
  D. Mom working late on Wednesdays

Key Words

Frogs are amphibians. That means that they can

live on land or in the water. When a frog is hungry,

his long sticky tongue snaps out to catch flies right

out of the air. Frogs make a wonderful sound that

you can often hear at night. Can you make the

sound of a frog?

The Tarantula

By Linda Hoyt

All: **The biggest spider is the tarantula.**

#1:   When its eight legs are stretched out,

#2:   it can measure ten inches across.

All: **Tarantulas are very hairy.**

#1:   The tarantulas that live in the United States

#2:   are not poisonous to people.

All: **Tarantulas live in nests.**

#1:   Burrowing tarantulas live under the ground.

#2:   Their tunnels are lined with silk.

Teacher: **The important thing is that**

All: **Tarantulas are the biggest spider and they are very hairy.**

REPRESENT TEXT GRAPHICALLY

A Pocket for Corduroy
By Don Freeman

INTERACTIVE READ ALOUD
Model and Guide Practice

READ TO THE PLACE WHERE LISA TELLS CORDUROY TO SIT STILL AND WAIT. I am thinking about this story map. I can write the title and author. I can also think about the setting. The setting is the place where the story takes place. I am going to write Laundromat in the box for Setting. Let's think about characters.

 Think together. Who are the characters? What should we write?

READ TO THE PLACE WHERE CORDUROY FALLS ASLEEP. I am going to stop reading and think about the events that have occurred so far. The first event was going to the Laundromat. I will write that on the chart, under Events. Let's look back through the pictures and think about important events.

 Talk to your thinking partner. Think together. What is important here? Which events should we write on our chart?

[Read to the end.] *We need to think about how the problem was solved.*

 Thinking partners. Put your heads together. What can we say about the solution for the problem? Were there any other events that are so important they should be added?

END OF STORY REFLECTION

Look at this great Story Map we have created. This really helps us to think about the most important parts of the story.

 If you were going to tell this story to someone who hadn't heard it, what would you want to say? Use the Story Map to think together about the important things to include in a retell of this story.

I am going to retell the story using the Story Map. Listen as I do and see if I have forgotten anything important.

Think together. How was my retell? Did I include the most important information? Is there anything else I should add?

Story Map
Title _____ Author_____
Setting   Characters

The Problem:
  Events
  •
  •
  •
  •
  •
  •

Solution

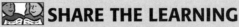

SHARE THE LEARNING
RepresentText with a Story Map

Tip for Share the Reading	Tip for Readers Theater Script

Tip for Share the Reading

Read *Foolish Puppies* aloud to model fluency. Then ask the children to join in as you read it a second time. Using the same Story Map format that you used with *A Pocket for Corduroy*, work together to complete a map for *Foolish Puppies*.

Foolish Puppies

Once upon a time there were three little puppies who didn't listen to their mother and went running out of their yard. They were having a wonderful time running and playing when they realized that they were lost. Next they saw a bakery and thought the nice man with the big white hat would help. He didn't want puppies in his bakery so he stamped his feet and told them to "shoo!"

Tip for Readers Theater Script

For emergent readers, engage them with "Good Morning, Little Bear" as a shared reading or partner reading. For developing readers, read the *Pocket for Corduroy* script straight through emphasizing fluent reading and dramatic interpretation. As you read, point to the portions of the Story Map that are being named within the text. Have readers join in chorally. Then meet in teams of three to build independence with the text and work on fluent, expressive oral reading.

"Good Morning, Little Bear"
By Linda Hoyt

Good morning, Little Bear.
Today's a sunny day.
Good morning, Little Bear.
Where should we go and play?
Good morning, Little Bear.
I'm so glad you're here with me.

EXTEND THE LEARNING

☆ During small group instruction, guide students in completing Story Maps.

☆ Model using a Story Map to plan a piece of fiction writing. Show the children how you plan characters, setting, problem, and solution before ever beginning to write. Create a draft while they watch. Then give the children a chance to create their own stories.

☆ Use Story Maps to represent stories shared during read-aloud time.

☆ Send a Story Map home and have children teach their parents how to fill it out after a bedtime story at home.

☆ Read *Knuffle Bunny* by Mo Willems, 2004 Caldecott Honor Book. It is a very similar story line to *A Pocket for Corduroy* that the children would have fun comparing and contrasting. Parallel Story Maps or Venn diagrams could be used to compare the two stories.

ASSESS THE LEARNING

> Listen in as children discuss selection of Problem, Setting, Solution, etc. in the Story Maps, to assess understanding.

> During small group instruction, collect the Story Maps that are created and assess them for individual understanding.

> Assess fiction writing created by students to assess story elements that may or may not be in place. Confer with the writers to help them compare their writing to the Story Map.

INFUSION OF FORMAL LANGUAGE
Test-style language

A Story Map helps us to represent:

  A. Everything in a story

  B. The most important parts of a story

  C. Our favorite parts of the story

  D. Funny things

The *setting* of this story is:

  A. Their house

  B. The street

  C. A laundromat

  D. The zoo

Foolish Puppies

Once upon a time there were three little puppies who didn't listen to their mother and went running out of their yard. They were having a wonderful time running and playing when they realized that they were lost. Next they saw a bakery and thought the nice man with the big white hat would help. He didn't want puppies in his bakery so he stamped his feet and told them to "shoo!"

The puppies were getting really tired and hungry. They didn't know what to do. Just then, their mother came running down the street. They were so happy to see her they followed her back home and never left the yard again without permission.

"Good Morning, Little Bear"

By Linda Hoyt

Good morning, Little Bear.

Today's a sunny day.

Good morning, Little Bear.

Where should we go and play?

Good morning, Little Bear.

I'm so glad you're here with me.

A Pocket for Corduroy

Readers Theater adaptation by Linda Hoyt

Narrator 1: Lisa and her mother went to the Laundromat with Corduroy, Lisa's bear.

Narrator 2: Lisa and Corduroy are **characters**.

Narrator 3: The Laundromat is the **setting.**

Narrator 1: Corduroy was supposed to sit still.

Narrator 2: But he didn't.

Narrator 3: He started looking all around the Laundromat for a pocket.

Narrator 2: That was a mistake.

Narrator 3: Corduroy climbed into a laundry bag and pretended it was a cave.

Narrator 2: Lisa couldn't find him anywhere and her mom said they had to leave.

Narrator 1: That was a **problem**.

Narrator 3: While they were gone, an artist put Corduroy in the dryer!

Narrator 1: He helped him get into dry clothes.

Narrator 2: And then he put him on top of a washing machine.

Narrator 3: When the Laundromat closed, Corduroy played in the soap flakes,

Narrator 1: Fell into a basket,

Narrator 2: And then fell asleep.

Narrator 3: Those are all **events**.

Narrator 1: Lisa went back the next morning and the manager found Corduroy in the basket.

Narrator 2: Lisa took him home

Narrator 3: And made him a pocket with his name and address inside.

Narrator 2: What a happy **solution**.

READ CLASSIC AND CONTEMPORARY WORKS

Mike Mulligan and His Steam Shovel
By Virginia Lee Burton

FOCUS THE LEARNING

Introduction: *Mike Mulligan and His Steam Shovel* by Virginia Burton is a "classic" story. As we enjoy this story today, you will need to think about why this book is a classic. Why do people still enjoy it so much, and what clues does this book give us about what life was like in 1939? Show pages 28 and 29 directing the children's attention to the fire engine, the cars, the wagon, and so on.

 Thinking partners, put your heads together as you look at these pages. What do you notice? What clues do you see that this is a classic?

INTERACTIVE READ-ALOUD
Model and Guide Practice

READ TO PAGE 9. I am thinking about the time in which this book was written. I see a lot of really old-fashioned looking cars and trucks. I am also noticing the art. The houses all look kind of alike. They look like they might have been drawn with crayons.

 Think together. What are you noticing? Are you finding clues that this is a classic? What are your ideas about why people still like this story?

READ TO PAGE 11. It says Mike Mulligan and Mary Anne made the landing fields for the airplanes. Does that mean that there weren't airports before that?

 Talk to your thinking partner. Think together. What do you think?

READ TO PAGE 15. Mary Anne is a steam shovel and no one wants her. They want gasoline shovels and diesel shovels. Do you know what our vehicles run on today? Do our cars run on steam?

 Share your thinking.

READ TO PAGE 20. This is pretty interesting. What do you think of this story? Will they be able to dig this in a day?

 Share your thinking.

CONTINUE TO THE END OF THE STORY. Pause occasionally to give partners time to talk about the story, share ideas on clues that it is a classic, and to talk about why they think people still like this story.

END OF STORY REFLECTION

OK. We know this is a classic story. For years people have loved this book. Let's put our heads together and think about why… Why do people like this so much?

Think together. Share your ideas.

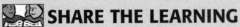
Tip for Share the Reading

Read the news article about the replica of Mary Anne that is now in California. Encourage the children to join in chorally reading the article. Help them to read with expression so their performance sounds fluent and interesting to a listener.

Mike Mulligan's Steam Shovel Comes to Willits, California

A group of volunteers, all lovers of the story of *Mike Mulligan and His Steam Shovel*, Mary Anne, raised enough money to purchase a steam shovel of their own. They searched until they found an old shovel similar to the one that became the furnace in the basement of the city hall in Poppersville.

The Willits steam shovel was built in 1932. It is 13.5 feet wide, 15 feet tall and weighs 15,000 pounds. It took four trucks to haul it to Willits where it is on display for children of all ages to enjoy.

Tip for Readers Theater Script

For emergent readers, enjoy *Mike Mulligan and His Steam Shovel* as an echo poem: teacher reads and children echo. The children then could create illustrations that re-create the story line. For developing readers, you might want to enjoy the poem as a two-team experience, alternating every other line. As they gain confidence, have students read the poem in partners and independently.

Mike Mulligan and His Steam Shovel
Readers Theater adaptation by Linda Hoyt

Mike Mulligan had a steam shovel.
Her name was Mary Anne.
He said she could dig a lot each day,
More than one hundred men!
But no one wanted steam shovels.
They liked the new machines.
Mike Mulligan and Mary Anne had to think and plan and dream.

They went on up to Poppersville
To help with a new town hall.
They had to dig it in one day
Or not get paid at all!

There was a happy ending . . .
Mary Anne did pass the test.
Now she and Mike are left in charge.
As a furnace, she's the best.

EXTEND THE LEARNING

☆ Gather other books by Virginia Lee Burton, such as *The Little House*, and consider the elements of her books that have helped them to live on in people's hearts.

☆ Look at examples of contemporary fiction and compare the art, the color printing, the paper used, and other elements that separate classic from contemporary selections.

☆ Ask your media specialist to find copies of fairy tales that were written many years ago, and compare contemporary versions of the same tales that have been written in the last ten years.

☆ Read *The Carrot Seed* and *The Happy Day* by Ruth Krauss and discuss why these are classics that are still loved today.

ASSESS THE LEARNING

> Listen in as partners talk about classics and assess their understanding of what it takes to become a classic and why it is important that we read classic and contemporary works.

> During small group instruction, read a classic selection, such as *The Carrot Seed* or *The Little House*, and have students explain why they think these are classics.

INFUSION OF FORMAL LANGUAGE
Test-style language

A *classic* story has been around for

  A. a few weeks.

  B. a little while.

  C. many years.

  D. since yesterday.

Virginia Burton captured our interest in Mary Anne by

  A. using personification, so Mary Ann had human qualities.

  B. creating a problem in the story.

  C. making the ending a surprise.

  D. All of the above.

Mike Mulligan's Steam Shovel
Comes to Willits, California

A group of volunteers, all lovers of the story of *Mike Mulligan and His Steam Shovel,* Mary Anne, raised enough money to purchase a steam shovel of their own. They searched until they found an old shovel similar to the one that became the furnace in the basement of the city hall in Poppersville.

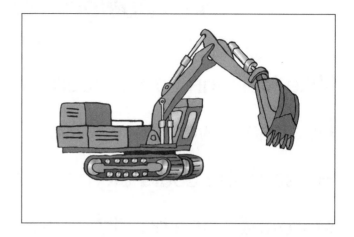

The Willits steam shovel was built in 1932. It is 13.5 feet wide, 15 feet tall and weighs 15,000 pounds. It took four trucks to haul it to Willits where it is on display for children of all ages to enjoy.

Mike Mulligan and His Steam Shovel

Readers Theater adaptation by Linda Hoyt

Mike Mulligan had a steam shovel.

Her name was Mary Anne.

He said she could dig a lot each day,

More than one hundred men!

But no one wanted steam shovels.

They liked the new machines.

Mike Mulligan and Mary Anne had to think and plan and dream.

They went on up to Poppersville

To help with a new town hall.

They had to dig it in one day

Or not get paid at all!

There was a happy ending . . .

Mary Anne did pass the test.

Now she and Mike are left in charge.

As a furnace, she's the best.

King Bidgood's in the Bathtub
By Audrey Wood

INTERACTIVE READ-ALOUD
Model and Guide Practice

Part of the fun of this book is that there is a repeating refrain. The Page, a helper to the king, comes out and cries, "Help! Help!" Then he says, "King Bidgood's in the bathtub, and he won't get out! Oh, who knows what to do?" I am going to model it for you. Listen carefully and then be ready to join me...Model reading the refrain with expression. Ready? "Help! Help! King Bidgood's in the bathtub and he won't get out! Oh, who knows what to do?" You've got it. We are ready to read for fun.

READ TO THE PAGE WHERE THE KNIGHT SAYS IT'S TIME TO BATTLE. This is so much fun. Did you notice the King's hand sticking through the curtain? What does he want?

 Think together. What does the King want? Predict together. Then we will peek and see.

READ TO THE PAGE WHERE THE KNIGHT WALKS AWAY DRIPPING AND THE PAGE IS CARRYING THE BATTLE TOYS. Look at the Knight! He has been in the bathtub. Look at his legs.

 Think together. What do you think?

READ TO THE PAGE WHERE THE QUEEN SAYS IT'S TIME FOR LUNCH.

 Talk to your thinking partner. Think together. What do you think will happen? Isn't this fun? Our purpose is reading for entertainment so we can read really fast and laugh and be a bit silly can't we . . .

CONTINUE TO THE END OF THE STORY. Pause occasionally to give partners time to enjoy, talk about their purpose for reading, and savor the fun factor.

END OF STORY REFLECTION

Our purpose was to have fun and we did! Now we need to think about how our purpose affected our reading. Did we read fast or slow? Did we take notes? Did we stop to laugh and think? What did we do that matched our purpose?

 Think together.

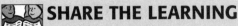 **SHARE THE LEARNING**
Focus on Purpose

Tip for Share the Reading

Remind the children that when we read for entertainment, there are often voices and characters we need to portray in our reading. Guide a conversation about how the Page, the Queen, and the King's voices might have sounded. Are they relaxed? Are they excited? Are they irritated? Read the passage with expression and an emphasis on the purpose of entertainment.

"Help! Help!" cried the girl when the dinner was served.

"King Dan's in the bathroom, and he won't come out.

"I don't know what to do?"

"Don't worry," cried the Prince when the lights were low.

"Hey, Dad, it's time to eat."

"No worries my son, I'm on my way."

"I don't want dinner in the tub!"

Tip for Readers Theater Script

Explain that the *purpose* is to read the directions and actually make Individual Cinnamon Bear Cookies. Ask children how they think their purpose will affect their reading. What will they do to be sure they follow all of the steps? Read the recipe to them. Then read it again chorally. For emergent readers, you might want to omit reading the ingredients list and focus on the steps of the recipe.

Recipe for Individual Cinnamon Bear Cookies
By Linda Hoyt

In a small cup, mix:
2 tablespoons of flour
2 teaspoons of oil
½ teaspoon of honey
¼ teaspoon of spice mix
¼ 1 teaspoon of brown sugar
¼ teaspoon of egg substitute

Mix well. Shape into a bear and bake at 350 degrees for 12 to 15 minutes.

Teacher note: Line a cookie sheet with parchment paper and write each child's name next to their individual cookie before baking to ensure that you are meeting health standards.

Ingredients List:	Spice Mixture for 28 Cookies
Flour	(mix in advance)
Oil	1 teaspoon nutmeg
Honey	¼ teaspoons cinnamon
Spice Mix	1 teaspoon cloves
Brown Sugar	¼ teaspoons ginger
Egg Substitute	¼ teaspoons baking soda

EXTEND THE LEARNING

☆ Read a nonfiction selection with a small group. Discuss their purpose for reading and talk about how they will adjust their reading to match their purpose.

☆ Read a newspaper article, a magazine article, and a riddle book to the students. Talk about purposes for reading each one.

☆ Have independent readers go through their personal reading collections and identify a purpose for each kind of text in their collection.

☆ Lead a conversation on purposes for writing. We write lists, write notes, letters, descriptions, directions, and so many other forms. Which forms are in their writing folders? Which forms might they be ready to try next?

ASSESS THE LEARNING

> Confer with readers about the books in their personal book collections for independent reading. Have them explain their purpose for reading each selection and how that purpose will affect their reading.

> During small group instruction, ask students to identify a purpose for reading.

INFUSION OF FORMAL LANGUAGE
Test-style language

In this story, it was *important* to understand that
  A. King Bidgood was in the bathtub.
  B. he didn't want to get out.
  C. lots of people tried to get him out.
  D. All of the above.

The *author's purpose* in this story was
  A. to teach us about kings.
  B. to make us want to take a bath.
  C. to entertain us.
  D. to show us how kings lived.

"Help! Help!" cried the girl when the dinner was served.

"King Dan's in the bathroom, and he won't come out.

"I don't know what to do!"

"Don't worry," cried the Prince when the lights were low.

"Hey, Dad, it's time to eat."

"No worries my son, I'm on my way."

"I don't want dinner in the tub!"

Recipe for Individual Cinnamon Bear Cookies

By Linda Hoyt

In a small cup, mix:

2 tablespoons of flour

2 teaspoons of oil

½ teaspoon of honey

½ teaspoon of spice mix

½ 1 teaspoon of brown sugar

½ teaspoon of egg substitute

Mix well. Shape into a bear and bake at 350 degrees for 12 to 15 minutes.

Teacher note: Line a cookie sheet with parchment paper and write each child's name next to their individual cookie before baking to ensure that you are meeting health standards.

Ingredients List:	**Spice Mixture for 28 Cookies**
Flour	(mix in advance)
Oil	1 teaspoon nutmeg
Honey	4 teaspoons cinnamon
Spice Mix	1 teaspoon cloves
Brown Sugar	4 teaspoons ginger
Egg Substitute	4 teaspoons baking soda

USE PICTURES TO SUPPORT COMPREHENSION

Farmer Duck
By Martin Waddell

INTERACTIVE READ-ALOUD
Model and Guide Practice

LOOK AT THE PICTURES ON THE FIRST TWO-PAGE LAYOUT AND COVER THE TEXT WITH YOUR HAND. I am looking at the picture. I can tell from looking at the picture that the man is in bed eating chocolates while reading the newspaper, and the duck is bringing him food! I remember from the cover that the duck was digging in the dirt. This duck does a lot! Just from the picture I can say that the man is probably lazy and the duck is working really hard. After you think together with your partner, I will read the words.

 Think together. What do we know now about the man and the duck?

TURN TO THE NEXT TWO-PAGE LAYOUT. Notice the farmer in the window and the duck in the mud with the cow.

 Talk to your thinking partner. Look at the picture. What can you learn from the picture? Read the text after they have talked about the picture. *Looking at the pictures is so helpful. The pictures really tell me what is happening. When I take time for the pictures, it is easier to figure out the words.*

TURN TO THE LAYOUT THAT SHOWS THE DUCK SAWING, DIGGING, WASHING DISHES, AND IRONING.

 Thinking partners. What can you learn from these pictures? Don't look at the words—try to learn from the pictures. After they chat, read the text.

TURN TO THE LAYOUT WHERE THE HENS ARE COMFORTING THE DUCK AND COVER THE TEXT WITH YOUR HAND. Look at this picture. The poor duck looks worn out. He is so tired he looks sleepy. I notice he is crying, too. Sometimes the word *weepy* is used when someone is crying just a little. I am going to read this page and see if it says he is sleepy and crying.

CONTINUE TO THE END OF THE STORY. Pause on each two-page layout to give partners time to talk about the pictures before reading the text. Talk often about words you can predict if you look at the pictures carefully.

END OF STORY REFLECTION
Let's use just the pictures and do a retell of this story. As I turn to each page, give yourself a minute to look at the pictures. Don't talk. Then, I will give you and your partner a minute to think together about what happened on each page and talk about what you would say in a retell based on the pictures. The pictures help us before reading, during reading, and after reading, too.

 **SHARE THE LEARNING**

Focus on Using Pictures

Tip for Share the Thinking	Tip for Readers Theater Script

 Engage partners in conversations about the picture. What do they think is happening? (Enlarge the image size to ensure that the children can see the details.) If they could select words that would be a good match for this picture, what would they be? Record their words and then engage in a shared writing experience to craft a text based on the picture. After the text is constructed, read it chorally to celebrate.

 For emergent readers: Guide the children in reading the illustrations for "I Can Read." Next, read the text to them as they follow along. Shift to partner and independent reading to build fluency.

For developing readers: Enjoy *Farmer Duck* as a choral reading experience followed by partner and independent reading to build fluency and expressive oral production.

EXTEND THE LEARNING

☆ During small group instruction, have students cover the text and take time with the pictures before attempting to read. You might want them to predict words they expect to see on the page before reading.

☆ Confer with independent readers to coach them on reading pictures before they read the words.

☆ As you share Big Books, draw children's attention to reading pictures as a helpful strategy before reading words.

☆ Use a wordless Big Book to emphasize pictures as tools for understanding. Use sticky notes to add text created by the children.

ASSESS THE LEARNING

> During small group instruction, have students cover the text and focus on the pictures before reading.

> Confer with individuals to see if they understand the role illustrations make in their comprehension and if they use pictures as a strategy.

> Have students create illustrations to communicate meaning, without adding words. Ask them to explain the meaning of their illustrations to assess their understanding of pictures as a communication system.

INFUSION OF FORMAL LANGUAGE

Test-style language

Illustrations are important. They help us to

A. think about what is happening.

B. understand characters.

C. understand the story.

D. All of the above.

Another name for this story might be:

A. *The Farmer Works Hard.*

B. *Animals Cause Trouble.*

C. *Farmer's Party.*

D. *The Animals Take Over.*

"I Can Read"

By Linda Hoyt

I can read.

I can read a book.

I can read.

I can read a clock.

I can read.

I can read a sign.

I can read.

I can read a smile!

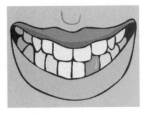

Farmer Duck

Readers Theater adaptation by Linda Hoyt

Everyone:	There once was a duck who was a very hard worker.
Narrator 1:	He lived with a lazy old farmer who stayed in bed,
Narrator 2:	Read the newspaper,
Narrator 3:	And ate chocolate
Everyone:	While the duck did all of the work.
Narrator 1:	The farmer would call,
Narrator 2:	"How goes the work?"
Narrator 3:	And the duck would answer,
Everyone:	"Quack."

Narrator 1:	The other animals loved the duck and wanted to help
Narrator 2:	So they had a meeting and made a plan.
Narrator 3:	"Moo! Baa! Cluck!"
Everyone:	They crept into the house in the middle of the night
Narrator 1:	And shook that lazy farmer right out of his bed.
Narrator 2:	"Moo! Baa! Cluck!"
Narrator 3:	They chased him down the lane,
Narrator 1:	through the field
Narrator 2:	and over the hill.
Narrator 3:	"Moo! Baa! Cluck!"
Everyone:	He never came back and the animals lived happily ever after.

Hattie and the Fox
By Mem Fox

FOCUS THE LEARNING

Summarizing is important. We summarize events in our lives, movies, and the books we read. Today we are going to read *Hattie and the Fox* by Mem Fox then summarize the story.

 Think together. Think about recess. What did you do during recess today? Summarize for each other.

INTERACTIVE READ-ALOUD
Model and Guide Practice

READ THREE PAGES OF TEXT, TO WHERE THE COW SAYS, "WHAT NEXT?" I am going to stop reading and think about summarizing this. I don't want to repeat what the animals said. For a good summary, I want to give the main ideas. Listen to this and see how you think I am doing. "Hattie the hen saw a nose in the bushes that worried her but the other animals didn't seem to care."

 Think together. How did I do? What did you think of my summary?

READ TO THE PLACE WHERE HATTIE SEES A NOSE, TWO EYES, AND TWO EARS BUT THE OTHER ANIMALS CONTINUE NOT TO BE BOTHERED.

 Talk to your thinking partner. How would you summarize this story so far?

READ TO THE PLACE WHERE HATTIE SEES THE WHOLE BODY AND FLIES INTO A TREE.

 What will you put in your summary now? What do you think the animals will do?

READ TO THE END OF THE STORY.

END OF STORY REFLECTION

What a great story! One of the ways we can practice good summaries is to act out a story. We will need Hattie, a cow, a goose, a pig, a sheep, a horse, and a fox. Have signs for the characters to wear as they enact the story. I am going to read the story again while our characters act it out.

I think we are ready to summarize. I am going to put the book aside, and we will use our memories to think of what happened. What should we include in our summary? Guide a conversation and assist children in planning a summary. Write their summary on a chart without looking in the book if possible. Engage the students in reading the summary with you while a new group of children acts out the summary.

SHARE THE LERNING

Focus on Summarizing

Tip for Share the Reading

Guide the children's attention to the photographs first and encourage them to talk about the moon and share any prior knowledge they may have. Then engage them as listeners as you read the selection. Read it again, inviting them to join in if they choose to. After the second reading, have partners consider what might be included in a summary of the passage. If desired, have children create illustrations and do a written summary of their learning.

It is amazing to think that spaceships and people have actually landed on the moon. Astronauts in special suits were able to walk on the moon and collect rocks from the moon. They learned that there is no air or water, no wind, and that nothing on the moon is alive.

Tip for Readers Theater Script

Provide a copy of *Hattie and the Fox* and animal illustrations for each student. Emergent readers can point to the animals as you read and summarize the selection. Then cut the page up and use their animals to do their own retells. Developing readers can use the animals to support oral retelling and then branch into a written reteling using the animals to support their summaries.

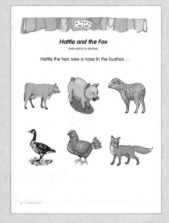

Hattie and the Fox

Hattie the hen saw a nose in the bushes ...

EXTEND THE LEARNING

☆ Have children use strips of sticky note material to mark VIPs (Very Important Points, Hoyt, 1999) in their reading resources. They then use the VIPs to support retells for partners.

☆ Have students create Paper Bag Theaters (Hoyt, 1999) for fiction summaries. They create illustrations for the setting and characters and then drop them into a paper bag. They pull illustrations from the bag to support their summary of a story.

☆ Rehearse nonfiction summaries to ensure that learners can summarize in a variety of genres.

☆ Have students use an Alphabox (Hoyt, 1999, 2002) to gather important words from a selection. Then use those words in a summary.

ASSESS THE LEARNING

> Listen in as partners summarize to assess understanding.

> During small group instruction, have students summarize orally so you can assess.

> Have students create an illustration and use it to support a summary.

INFUSION OF FORMAL LANGUAGE
Test style language

What was the *first* thing that Hattie did?
  A. She squawked.
  B. She talked to the cow.
  C. She told the animals about the nose in the bushes.
  D. She walked around.

Which statement is *not* true?
  A. Hattie scared the fox away.
  B. The animals didn't pay attention to Hattie.
  C. The sheep said, "Who cares?"
  D. The cow scared the fox away.

It is amazing to think that spaceships and people have actually landed on the moon. Astronauts in special suits were able to walk on the moon and collect rocks from the moon. They learned that there is no air or water, no wind, and that nothing on the moon is alive.

Hattie and the Fox

Hattie the hen saw a nose in the bushes …

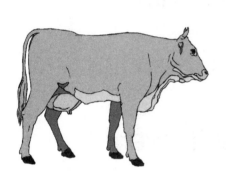  

DISTINGUISH REAL FROM MAKE-BELIEVE

The Very Hungry Caterpillar
By Eric Carle

FOCUS THE LEARNING

Introduction: I chose a book for today that is a favorite of children everywhere. It is called *The Very Hungry Caterpillar*. It was written by Eric Carle. As we read it today, we need to spend time thinking about the difference between real and make-believe. For example, if I said that my dog talked to me this morning, you would know that I was using make believe because dogs can't talk! If I said that my husband is so strong he can lift all of you in one hand, what would you say?

 Thinking partners, is that real or make-believe? How do you know?

As we read this book, we need to think about real caterpillars and what we know about them to decide if this book is real or make believe . . . or a little of both.

INTERACTIVE READ-ALOUD
Model and Guide Practice

READ PAGE 1. I am thinking about real and make-believe. I know that a caterpillar hatches from an egg and the egg is usually laid on a leaf. So I am thinking that this page could be real information.

READ PAGE 2. Hmm. We know that caterpillars hatch from eggs, but I wonder if it "pops" out or if it comes out slowly bit by bit like a chicken or a bird. I am wondering if there is a little bit of make-believe here.

 What do you think? Share your thinking. Is this real or make-believe?

READ THE PAGES WHERE HE IS EATING THROUGH THE VARIOUS FRUITS. What do you think? Would these foods be something that a caterpillar could find?

 Think together about this book. Are you thinking this is real or make-believe?

READ THE PAGES WHERE HE EATS CAKE, A PICKLE, AND SO ON. Oh, my...I think I am getting it.

 Would a caterpillar be able to find foods like these? Is this real or make-believe?

CONTINUE TO THE END OF THE STORY. Pause occasionally to give partners time to talk.

END OF STORY REFLECTION

Things a real caterpillar can do	Things that are probably make-believe

Read the story a second time, stopping often to record in a T chart such as the one above. Encourage the children to think about caterpillars and what they already know. (It would be very helpful to have access to a nonfiction book about caterpillars as you complete the chart.)

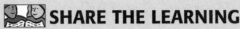 **SHARE THE LEARNING**

Focus on Real and Make Believe

Tip for Share the Thinking

Explain to your students that you are going to play a game called Thumbs-Up/Thumbs-Down. You will be naming storybook characters, people from school, items from real life, and things that can only happen in our imagination. Their job is to listen then give a "Thumbs-Up" if what you name is real or a "Thumbs-Down" if what you name is make-believe.

	Thumbs-Up (That's Real)	Thumbs-Down (That's Make-Believe)
Cinderella		√
The tree near the window		

Tip for Readers Theater Script

For emergent readers, read the two selections and guide the children in a conversation about real and make-believe. As they are ready, engage them in chorally reading the passages. For developing readers, begin with choral reading of the two passages and a conversation about real and make-believe. Then shift to partner reading and independent reading to support fluency and expression.

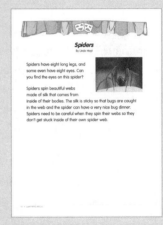

Spiders
By Linda Hoyt

Spiders have eight long legs, and some even have eight eyes. Can you find the eyes on this spider?

Spiders spin beautiful webs made of silk that comes from inside of their bodies. The silk is sticky so that bugs are caught in the web and the spider can have a very nice bug dinner. Spiders need to be careful when they spin their webs so they don't get stuck inside of their own spider web.

EXTEND THE LEARNING

☆ Read a variety of fiction and nonfiction titles to the children and discuss which are real and which are make-believe.

☆ Within fiction titles help children identify which events and situations could happen in real life and which can only happen in our imagination.

☆ Pair fiction and nonfiction on the same topic and encourage the children to use what they learned in the nonfiction selection to help them understand the fiction story.

☆ During small group instruction, guide children in considering real vs. make-believe.

ASSESS THE LEARNING

> Listen in as partners discuss elements of reality and make-believe in Read-Alouds.

> Confer with readers during independent reading to see if they can differentiate between fact and fiction.

> Use the Thumbs-Up/Thumbs-Down game as an assessment tool in small group instruction.

INFUSION OF FORMAL LANGUAGE
Test style language

Which of the following is *make-believe* in the book?

    A. The caterpillar came from an egg.

    B. The caterpillar was hungry.

    C. The caterpillar ate a leaf.

    D. The caterpillar ate chocolate cake.

Which of the following could a real caterpillar do?

    A. Eat a leaf

    B. Climb a mountain

    C. Talk to a dog

    D. Eat a candy bar

	Thumbs-Up (That's Real)	Thumbs-Down (That's Make-Believe)
Cinderella		√
The tree near the window		

Spiders

By Linda Hoyt

Spiders have eight long legs, and some even have eight eyes. Can you find the eyes on this spider?

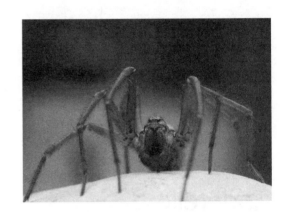

Spiders spin beautiful webs made of silk that comes from inside of their bodies. The silk is sticky so that bugs are caught in the web and the spider can have a very nice bug dinner. Spiders need to be careful when they spin their webs so they don't get stuck inside of their own spider web.

"Spider Meets a Pumpkin"

By Linda Hoyt

Once there was a happy spider
Hanging from a tree.

He spotted a pumpkin
And laughed with glee.

I love a good pumpkin
Smiling right at me.

We'll get to be friends
What fun that will be.

Story Elements

The story elements strand includes identifying events in a plot sequence, discerning author's purpose, tracking character development, developing a statement of theme for a text, and so on. There is also support for examining structural elements such as climax, setting, problem/solution, and the role of the narrator.

DISTINGUISH FICTION/NONFICTION

The Bremen-Town Musicians

By Ilse Plume

FOCUS THE LEARNING

Fiction books are those that are written for fun. They are not true stories. They didn't happen in real life. In these books the author can use his or her imagination, and almost anything can happen. Sometimes fiction books are a lot like real life. Sometimes we know they could never happen at all. But in all of them we read and enjoy and feel entertained. The book we are reading today is *The Bremen-Town Musicians* by Ilse Plume.

 Think together. As you look at this picture on the cover, how do you know right away that this book is fiction?

INTERACTIVE READ-ALOUD
Model and Guide Practice

READ TO THE PLACE WHERE THE DONKEY DECIDES TO BECOME A STREET MUSICIAN. Isn't this fun! In this fiction story, a donkey who is too old to work decides to use his bray to become a musican.

 Think together. What do you think? Could a real donkey do this? What clues are there that this is fiction? Be sure to look at the pictures!

READ TO THE PLACE WHERE THE DOG CHOOSES TO JOIN THE DONKEY ON HIS JOURNEY.

 Talk to your thinking partner. Think together. Do you think a dog and a donkey could make good music in the real world?

READ TO THE PLACE WHERE THEY JUMP INTO THE HOUSE AND SCARE THE ROBBERS. Is this fiction or nonfiction? Could this happen in real life?

 Talk to your thinking partner. What would it have sounded like when they all made noise? Would it have sounded like music?

CONTINUE TO THE END OF THE STORY. Pause occasionally to give partners time to talk about the story.

END OF STORY REFLECTION

Let's think about fiction. What makes a fiction story, fiction? Think with your partner for a moment, and then we will make a list, "Characteristics of Fiction." Guide a conversation about fiction elements so children can see that there are very distinct characteristics that identify fiction from nonfiction. Send them on a hunt in the classroom library, in their personal reading collections, or in the media center for books that fit all of the items on their "characteristics" lists.

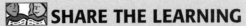

SHARE THE LEARNING
Distinguish Fiction from Nonfiction

Tip for Share the Reading

Read the excerpt to the children and guide a conversation about fiction. What happens in this passage that definitely can only happen in fiction? Reread the piece several times, inviting the children to join you chorally and read with expression.

"Hey, long ears, what do you see?" the 🐱 asked. The 🐴 explained, and the four friends quickly thought of a way to get rid of the robbers.

The 🐴 stood with his front hooves on the winowsill, the 🐕 jumped on the donkey's back, the 🐈 climbed upon the 🐕, and the 🐓 perched on the 🐈.

At the 🐴 signal they all made their music as loudly as they could. The 🐴 brayed, the 🐕 barked, the 🐈 meowed, and the 🐓 crowed.

Tip for Readers Theater Script

For emergent readers, enjoy *The Bremen-Town Musicians* as an echo poem: teacher reads and children echo. The children then could create illustrations that re-create the story line. For developing readers, you might want to enjoy the script as a three-team experience. With increased proficiency, small teams of three can read the poem together for fluency and expression.

The Bremen-Town Musicians
Readers Theater adaptation by Linda Hoyt

#1 There once was a donkey
#2 A dog
#3 A cat
#4 And a rooster.
All: Their masters thought they were too old to do any work.
#1 So they decided to go to Bremen-Town to become singers.
#2 On the way there
#3 They came to a house filled with robbers.
#4 They made a plan and
All: Sang with all their hearts.
#1 They were so loud, they frightened the robbers away.
#2 They liked the house
#3 So they decided to stay.
All They are probably still making music today.

EXTEND THE LEARNING

☆ Help children identify one fiction and one nonfiction selection. Help them prepare to explain how they know which one is fiction and which one is not.

☆ Find fiction/nonfiction partner books that are matched by theme. For example, a nonfiction book on bats and *Stellaluna*. Read the partner books to students and guide a conversation about fiction/nonfiction.

☆ Read a fiction selection that is purely fantasy and one that is realistic fiction. Help the children to compare them. Example: *The Wednesday Surprise* and *Chicken Little*.

☆ Model how writers create a piece of fiction by carefully planning a problem/solution, characters, setting, and events. You may want to plot the writing using a Story Map and even plan a few illustrations before you start drafting so children can see that nonfiction or fiction is planned from start to finish.

ASSESS THE LEARNING

➤ Listen in as partners discuss features of fiction to assess understanding.

➤ During small group instruction, have children work with fiction and nonfiction selections and show they can differentiate.

➤ Provide independent readers with opportunities to read fiction and nonfiction. Then take a running record in each to determine how well strategies are applied in each genre.

INFUSION OF FORMAL LANGUAGE
Test-style language

We know a story is *fiction* if the author
  A. only uses facts so that it is true.
  B. uses beautiful art.
  C. has a problem and a solution and uses imagination.
  D. has lots of pages.

The *purpose* of fiction is to:
  A. Explain something
  B. Entertain us
  C. Show what life is like
  D. Ask a lot of questions

"Hey, long ears, what do you see?" the 🐓 asked.

The 🫏 explained, and the four friends quickly

thought of a way to get rid of the robbers.

The 🫏 stood with his front hooves on the

windowsill, the 🐕 jumped on the donkey's back,

the 🐈 climbed upon the 🐕, and the 🐓

perched on the 🐈.

At the signal they all made their music as loudly

as they could. The 🫏 brayed, the 🐕 barked,

the 🐈 meowed, and the 🐓 crowed.

The Bremen-Town Musicians

Readers Theater adaptation by Linda Hoyt

#1   There once was a donkey

#2   A dog

#3   A cat

#4   And a rooster.

All: Their masters thought they were too old to do any work.

#1   So they decided to go to Bremen-Town to become singers.

#2   On the way there

#3   They came to a house filled with robbers.

#4   They made a plan and

All: Sang with all their hearts.

#1   They were so loud, they frightened the robbers away.

#2   They liked the house

#3   So they decided to stay.

All   They are probably still making music today.

Tops and Bottoms
By Janet Stevens

FOCUS THE LEARNING

Introduction: One of the jobs we have as readers is to think about the order in which things happen in a story. Today as we reread *Tops and Bottoms* by Janet Stevens, your job is to listen carefully and think about what happens first, second, third, and so on. (Post the words "first," "second," "third," "next," "then," "finally" and tell the children that these are words that help us when we think about the order in which events happen.)

INTERACTIVE READ-ALOUD
Model and Guide Practice

READ THE FIRST THREE PAGES. Then pause to think aloud. I am going to stop reading for a minute and think about what has happened so far. I am going to use some of our sequence words to tell what I remember: *First,* I remember that Bear has lots of land but he is lazy and sleeps all of the time. *Then,* I remember that Hare is poor and his children are hungry so he offers to become partners with Bear and do all of the work on the farm for half of the profit.

Turn to your thinking partner. How did I do? Do you want to add anything to my retell? Use some of our sequence words to tell what you remember.

READ UNTIL YOU GET TO THE PLACE WHERE BEAR REALIZES HE HAS BEEN TRICKED AND TELLS RABBIT TO PLANT THE FIELD AGAIN. I am going to stop reading for a minute and think about what has been happening and which of our sequence words I could use now. I can say that *first* the bear slept, *second* the Hare worked really hard and *next*…

Turn to your thinking partner. Think together about what happened next. Use the word "next" to tell what you remember.

READ UNTIL YOU GET TO THE PLACE WHERE BEAR WAKES UP AFTER THE SECOND HARVEST AND REALIZES HE HAS BEEN TRICKED YET AGAIN.

Turn to your thinking partner. We know so much more now. Think together about Hare and Bear and what has happened. Use our sequence words to share what you remember.

CONTINUE TO THE END OF THE STORY. Pause occasionally to give partners time to talk and use the sequence words to describe events.

END OF STORY REFLECTION
I am going to think about the order of ALL the events in this story. I am going to tell what happened using the sequence words to help me. "First," "second," "third…"

Turn and talk to your partner. Think together about the story and use sequence words to tell about the middle and the end of the story.

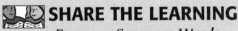 **SHARE THE LEARNING**
Focus on Sequence Words

Tip for Share the Reading

Place the text on the overhead projector and read it aloud with expression, emphasizing the sequence words that support the retell. On a second reading, have the children join you in reading, again placing special emphasis on the sequence words. Children could volunteer to stand in a line and do a shared retell using the cards and the sequence words.

> **First,** we learned that Bear was very lazy and had lots of money and lots of land.
>
> **Second,** we learned that Hare lived down the road and had a lot of very hungry children. **Third,** Hare asked Bear if he wanted to be partners and have Hare do all of the work. **Then,** Hare worked really hard while Bear just slept.
>
> **Next,** Rabbit woke Bear up to tell him his half of the crop was ready and Bear got really mad because_____ (Have partners finish.)

Tip for Readers Theater Script

For emergent readers, read *Tops and Bottoms* to the children asking them to visualize as you read and re-create the story in their heads. Read it again and have them dramatize the action or create visuals to support the script. For developing readers, have them meet in teams to practice reading their sections of the text so that all parts can then be brought together for a performance of the script that is fluent and expressive.

Tops and Bottoms
Readers Theater adaptation by Linda Hoyt

Team 1:	Once upon a time there was Bear
All:	Who just wanted to sleep.
Team 2:	Not far away lived a family of rabbits.
All:	They were very poor but they were good workers.
Team 1:	Mr. Rabbit asked Bear if they could be partners.
All:	And split the profits right down the middle.
Team 2:	Mr. Bear said yes,
All:	But did he learn a lesson!
Team 1:	Mr. Rabbit took all of the good parts
Team 2:	And left the rest for the bear.
Everyone:	Bear learned his lesson and planted his fields himself.

EXTEND THE LEARNING

☆ Have children draw and/or write about the story. Encourage them to use sequence words in their writing.

☆ Apply the sequence words to familiar classroom routines (e.g., washing hands for lunch).

☆ Engage in retells of familiar stories using the sequence words to assist retelling.

☆ Use a graphic organizer that emphasizes beginning, middle, and end to support understanding of story structure.

☆ Apply sequence words to other contexts such as the life cycle of a butterfly or the steps in planting seeds.

ASSESS THE LEARNING

➤ Listen closely for partners to use sequence words in their retellings.

➤ Analyze drawings and writing to see if there is evidence of understanding sequence and if the sequence words are used in writing.

INFUSION OF FORMAL LANGUAGE
Test-style language

The *first* event in this story was when
- A. Hare was working hard.
- B. Mrs. Hare said the children were hungry.
- C. Bear woke up.
- D. Bear was sleeping.

In the *last* scene of this story, which of the following is true?
- A. Bear was working.
- B. Mrs. Hare opened a vegetable stand.
- C. Hare bought back his land.
- D. All of the above.

First, we learned that Bear was very lazy and had lots of money and lots of land.

Second, we learned that Hare lived down the road and had a lot of very hungry children. **Third,** Hare asked Bear if he wanted to be partners and have Hare do all of the work. **Then,** Hare worked really hard while Bear just slept.

Next, Rabbit woke Bear up to tell him his half of the crop was ready and Bear got really mad because_____. (Have partners finish.)

Tops and Bottoms

Readers Theater adaptation by Linda Hoyt

Team 1:   Once upon a time there was Bear

All: Who just wanted to sleep.

Team 2:   Not far away lived a family of rabbits.

All: They were very poor but they were good workers.

Team 1:   Mr. Rabbit asked Bear if they could be partners.

All: And split the profits right down the middle.

Team 2:   Mr. Bear said yes,

All: But did he learn a lesson!

Team 1:   Mr. Rabbit took all of the good parts

Team 2:   And left the rest for the bear.

Everyone: Bear learned his lesson and planted his fields himself.

The Wednesday Surprise
By Eve Bunting

INTERACTIVE READ-ALOUD
Model and Guide Practice

We already read *The Wednesday Surprise*. I am going to look at this book again so we can think about its important parts: the beginning, the middle, and the end.

READ PAGE 5. I really like the beginning of this story. Eve Bunting, the author, gets me interested right away by making me wonder about the birthday surprise. The beginning is pretty easy to find because it will always be the first part of the book.

I am turning to the end of the book so I can think about the way Eve Bunting ended the story. She made the beginning special by making me wonder about the surprise. Let's think about her ending.

READ PAGES 24–32.

 Turn to your thinking partner. What do you think of her ending? What makes it a good ending for this story? How could you tell this was the end?

Let's think about the middle of the book. In the beginning, we wondered about the birthday surprise and why it was so special. In the end, they had the party and Grandma read for everyone. Now, we need to think about the middle. What was the middle mostly about?

 Turn to your thinking partner. Think together. What can we say about the middle of the book?

END OF STORY REFLECTION

I am going to use this Three Circle Map to help me remember the three important parts from this story. I will draw and write about the beginning in circle one. Then I will draw and write about the ending in the last circle. Last, I will come back and fill in the circle about the middle of the book. That helps me remember that the beginning and the end are like bookends: they keep everything together in a story.

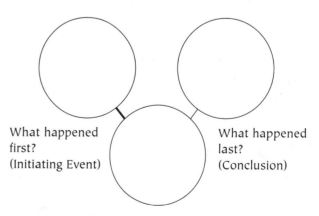

What happened first? (Initiating Event)

What happened last? (Conclusion)

What was it mostly about?

SHARE THE LEARNING
Focus on Beginning, Middle, End

Tip for Share the Thinking

Think out loud and model for the children how to record in the circles when thinking about an experience. You might highlight something you and the children did together or an experience you had away from school. Be sure to draw and write the beginning and ending first and then come back and record what happened in the middle. Model for the children how the notes and sketches you made can support you in turning this into a personal narrative that has a very clear structure.

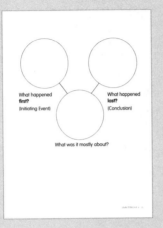

Tip for Readers Theater Script

For emergent readers, read *Rosie Gets Scared* to the children pausing to help them identify the beginning, the middle, and the end of the story. With repeated readings, invite them to join in chorally until they are ready to take over reading the sections marked "Children:" Make it clear that they will be reading the beginning and the end and that you will be reading the middle portion of the story. For developing readers, focus on fluency as they chorally interpret the beginning and end of the story. Encourage them to read with expression to convey the meaning of the selection. You might want to divide the group into three teams with one team reading the beginning, one reading the middle, and one team reading the ending.

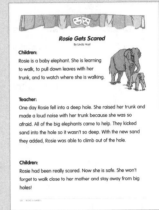

EXTEND THE LEARNING

☆ Give students personal copies of the Three Circle Map and have them record the beginning, middle, and endings of stories they are reading in guided or independent reading.

☆ Have partners use the Three Circle Map to record their thinking about another story.

☆ Act out the beginning, middle, and ending of a familiar story. Have actors identify which part of the story they are portraying by holding a sign that says "beginning," "middle," or "end."

ASSESS THE LEARNING

> Assess Three Circle Maps completed during guided reading to check for understanding.

> Confer with readers during independent reading to see if they understand the beginning, middle, and end of stories read independently.

> Assess a piece of writing children develop using the Three Circle Map for evidence of a clear beginning, middle, and end.

INFUSION OF FORMAL LANGUAGE
Test-style language

In the *beginning* of this story,
  A. Grandma was waiting for the bus.
  B. they decorated the house.
  C. They cooked dinner.
  D. Anna and Grandma were reading.

In the *ending* of this story,
  A. Dad blew out his birthday candles.
  B. they agreed it was a wonderful surprise.
  C. they cooked dinner.
  D. Anna read.

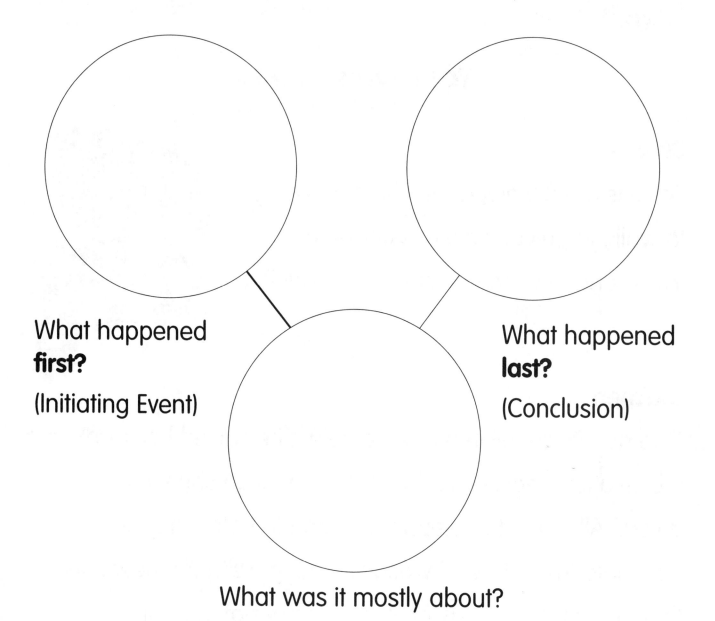

What happened **first?**

(Initiating Event)

What was it mostly about?

What happened **last?**

(Conclusion)

Rosie Gets Scared

By Linda Hoyt

Children:

Rosie is a baby elephant. She is learning
to walk, to pull down leaves with her
trunk, and to watch where she is walking.

Teacher:

One day Rosie fell into a deep hole. She raised her trunk and
made a loud noise with her trunk because she was so
afraid. All of the big elephants came to help. They kicked
sand into the hole so it wasn't so deep. With the new sand
they added, Rosie was able to climb out of the hole.

Children:

Rosie had been really scared. Now she is safe. She won't
forget to walk close to her mother and stay away from big
holes!

The Ghost-Eye Tree

By Bill Martin, Jr. and John Archambault

FOCUS THE LEARNING

A *climax* in a story is the place where things suddenly change. At the point of climax, we feel really involved with the story and are connecting to a character. Think about Little Red Riding Hood for a moment. Remember how the wolf ate the grandma and then he was going to eat Red Riding Hood? Remember how we wanted to know right away if she would be okay and were so happy when the woodcutter came and saved her? That was the climax of the story.

 Think together. What do you remember about the climax of Little Red Riding Hood?

INTERACTIVE READ-ALOUD
Model and Guide Practice

We are going to read *The Ghost-Eye Tree* by Bill Martin, Jr., and John Archambault. We are going to watch for the climax, the part where you feel really involved, a little nervous, and then the action changes and the story begins to end.

 Think together. What can you learn from the pictures?

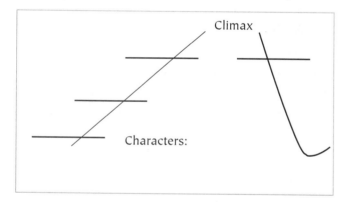

READ THE FIRST TWO PAGES. We know that the boy needs to go for milk. That isn't a climax. I like the phrase, "I dreaded to go . . . I dreaded the tree." That really fits with the dark scary looking tree. I can tell this boy really doesn't want to go. I think the climax is going to have something to do with the scary tree.

 What do you think?

READ TO THE PAGE WHERE IT LOOKS LIKE THE CHILDREN ARE DANCING. I can tell they are dancing because they are pretending not to be afraid. I am going to look at our Story Map and add some events. For event one I am going to say they left home with the bucket. I am thinking about the second event.

 Talk to your thinking partner. What should I write here?

READ TO THE PLACE WHERE THEY GET THE MILK AND ARE READY TO START HOME. For event three I can write "got the milk." This isn't a climax. We aren't worried and it isn't real exciting.

READ TO THE PLACE WHERE IT SAYS THE TREE REACHED OUT TO GET HIM. Oh, my. This is it! Are you nervous? Can you tell how scared the boy is? This is the climax! I am going to write it on our Story Map.

CONTINUE TO THE END OF THE STORY. Pause occasionally to give partners time to talk and to notice that after the climax, the story starts to feel less tense and the author builds toward an ending.

END OF STORY REFLECTION

That was such a great climax to the story. It was really scary, wasn't it! Especially where it said the arms of the tree reached out. Let's act out the climax. We need three people to work together to be the tree, and we need a boy and a girl. Ready? I will read the climax again while our helpers act it out.

SHARE THE LEARNING
Focus on Climax

Tip for Share the Reading

Read the climax expressively. Then ask the students to join in reading it chorally with you. If they were to create an illustration to go with this, what would they put in the picture? How could they make it clear that the boy and girl were really afraid? The climax signals a change in action. After the children ran home, how does the story change? What do they notice about the "falling action" as the story comes to an end?

My birthday cake
Here it comes
The candles are lit
The lights are out
Ready . . . take a big breath . . .
Blow out the candles
Happy Birthday!!!!

Tip for Readers Theater Script

Read *The Ghost-Eye Tree* reflecting the climax to the children, encouraging them to join in chorally. For emergent readers, have them turn the images on the script into puppets and place popsicle sticks on each so they can be used to retell the climax. For developing readers, support reading with expression and fluency to communicate the tension in the story line.

The Ghost-Eye Tree
Reader's Theater adaptation by Linda Hoyt

There it is . . .
I hear it . . .
Something is scratching under the porch . . .
Run!

Faster
Faster
Wow
That was scary!

EXTEND THE LEARNING

☆ During interactive writing, help the children to create a wordless book. Be sure it has several pages, one for each event, one page for the climax and one for the ending or falling action. Give them opportunities to tell their story for an audience and point out the climax they created.

☆ Keep a chart of Read-Alouds with climax structures. On the chart, list the title, a description of the climax, and some opinions about the climax. On a scale of 1-5, what would they rate this climax?

☆ Dramatize the climax in favorite fairy tales and folktales.

☆ During small group instruction in a fiction selection, have the children use their imaginations to orally create a climax that could be inserted into the book to make it more interesting.

ASSESS THE LEARNING

➤ Confer with individuals to assess ability to identify a climax in a story.

➤ During small group instruction, assess ability to identify events and a climax in a reading selection.

➤ Have children create an illustration of the climax in a story and see if they identified the correct part of the story.

INFUSION OF FORMAL LANGUAGE
Test-style language

In the climax of the story, the boy thought the tree
 A. reached for him.
 B. made noises.
 C. shook its arms.
 D. All of the above.

Halfway means:
 A. The beginning
 B. The end
 C. The middle
 D. A special place

My birthday cake

Here it comes

The candles are lit

The lights are out

Ready . . . take a big breath . . .

Blow out the candles

Happy Birthday!!!!

The Ghost-Eye Tree

Readers Theater adaptation by Linda Hoyt

There it is . . .

I hear it . . .

Something is scratching under the porch . . .

Run!

Faster

Faster

Wow

That was scary!

Joseph Had a Little Overcoat
By Simms Taback

FOCUS THE LEARNING

Good books and stories have at least one main idea. The main idea is like the glue that holds everything together. For example: If we had a recipe for chocolate chip cookies, the main idea would be to follow the steps to make the cookies. If we wanted to write a book about our school, then every page would need to be about our school, because our school is the main idea of our writing. We are going to read *Joseph Had a Little Overcoat* by Simms Taback and think together about the main ideas of the book. Let's start by looking at the cover. Look at the title and the illustration. We can tell a lot about the main idea just from the cover, can't we.

 What do you think is the main idea of this book? Be sure to notice the holes in Joseph's overcoat.

INTERACTIVE READ-ALOUD
Model and Guide Practice

READ THE FIRST PAGE. Look at the overcoat. On the cover it had holes and now it has patches over the holes. Read the second page. Look at the clever cutout in the book. When we turn the page, his old overcoat is now a jacket. I am thinking about main ideas here. I think a main idea is that Joseph liked his coat so much he didn't want to throw it away.

 Thinking partners. What are your thoughts about the main idea?

READ THE THIRD PAGE. Uh, oh. The jacket is old and worn now. Look at the cutout on the cow. When we turn the page, what do you think the cutout will show he has done?

 Think together. Do you have any new thoughts about the main idea?

CONTINUE TO THE END OF THE STORY. Pause occasionally to give partners time to predict what is coming and consider main ideas.

END OF STORY REFLECTION

Let's think about the main ideas we got from this book. We agreed that a main idea is that Joseph liked his coat a lot and didn't want to throw it away. Let's list our other main ideas as well.

If you were going to tell someone about this book, it would be important to include the main idea in your retell.

 Think together. To do a retell that included a main idea, what would you say? Think about how you could tell your parents about this story.

SHARE THE LEARNING

Focus on Main Ideas

Tip for Share the Reading

Read the selection to the children. Then guide a conversation about the main idea(s) of this selection. Have them read it again chorally to emphasize smooth, fluent expression. Have them create an illustration about the main idea.

"Your Heart"

Your heart needs to be strong. It pumps over and over and over again all through the day pushing blood around your body. To do all of that hard work, it needs to be strong and healthy. Put your hand over your heart. Can you feel it beating? Your heart keeps you alive.

Tip for Readers Theater Script

For emergent readers, enjoy "The Skunk" as an echo experience: teacher reads and children echo. The children then could create illustrations that re-create the story line. For developing readers, you might want to enjoy the script as a two-team experience, alternating every other line of print. With increased proficiency, partners can read the selection together for fluency and expression.

"The Skunk"
By Linda Hoyt

A skunk is usually peaceful.
It eats insects, berries, fruit, and seeds.
If a skunk gets angry or frightened,
Look out!
It will raise its tail.
The spray it sends out has a terrible smell that can last for weeks.

The main idea is that skunks _____
_____
_____

EXTEND THE LEARNING

☆ Read poetry and consider the main idea of each.

☆ Apply main idea thinking in science and social studies.

☆ During small group instruction, guide conversations around the main idea of a selection.

☆ Have writers plan the main idea for their writing before they begin a draft. Creating an illustration before they write will also help them stick to a main idea.

☆ Have children engage in an author study and keep track of the main ideas the author used in each book.

☆ Pause often in daily classroom experiences and have the children consider the main idea for what is happening. Example: The main idea of recess is to exercise and have fun. The main idea of lunch is to give our body nutrition and relax. The main idea of learning to tell time is so we can read a clock.

ASSESS THE LEARNING

> Listen in as partners discuss main ideas to assess understanding.

> During small group instruction, read and discuss main ideas to assess ability to transfer main idea thinking across many texts.

> Confer with readers during independent reading to assess ability to select main idea independently.

> Have writers jot down main ideas in a readers notebook so you can assess understanding.

INFUSION OF FORMAL LANGUAGE
Test-style language

One *main idea* is that Joseph
  A. could make new things out of something old.
  B. liked to dance.
  C. had a vest.
  D. went to the fair.

A word that means the opposite of *little* is:
  A. Small
  B. Medium
  C. Big
  D. Little pieces

"Your Heart"

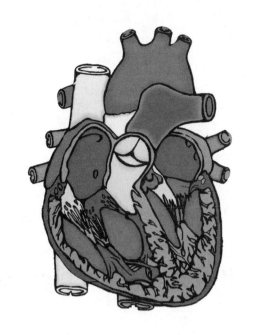

Your heart needs to be strong. It pumps over and over and over again all through the day pushing blood around your body. To do all of that hard work, it needs to be strong and healthy.

Put your hand over your heart. Can you feel it beating? Your heart keeps you alive.

"The Skunk"

By Linda Hoyt

A skunk is usually peaceful.

It eats insects, berries, fruit, and seeds.

If a skunk gets angry or frightened,

Look out!

It will raise its tail.

The spray it sends out has a terrible smell that can last for weeks.

The main idea is that skunks _____

_____

_____

The Art Lesson
By Tomie dePaola

FOCUS THE LEARNING

The setting of a story is the place or places where a story happens. In our school, we have many settings. We have our classroom, the playground, the kitchen, the office. As we read *The Art Lesson* by Tomie dePaola, our job will be to think about the settings in the story.

 Think together. What is your favorite setting in our school? What place do you especially enjoy?

INTERACTIVE READ-ALOUD
Model and Guide Practice

READ TO THE PAGE WHERE IT SAYS "TOMMY HUNG UP PICTURES IN HIS BEDROOM." Let's look at the pictures for this part one more time and think about the setting. I can see in this picture, Jeannie is doing cartwheels. It looks like she is outside. I am going to write "outside" as one setting. In this next picture Tommy is drawing, but it doesn't look like he is outside anymore. I think he is in a house. I will add that to our list of settings.

READ TO WHERE TOMMY IS AT THE BARBER SHOP, GROCERY STORE, AND GRANDMOTHER'S HOUSE.

 Think together. What settings have you noticed? What should we add to our chart?

CONTINUE TO THE END OF THE STORY. Pause occasionally to give partners time to talk and think about the various settings. Add to the list as you move through the book.

END OF STORY REFLECTION

There were a lot of settings in this book, weren't there? Let's read our list of settings and think together. Which setting do you think is most important to this story? Which setting is probably important to Tommy? Where do you think he is at the end of the story?

 Each of you is going to create an illustration representing one of the settings in this book. Share with your partner which setting you will draw and what you will include in your illustration.

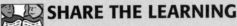 **SHARE THE LEARNING**
Focus on Setting

Tip for Share the Reading

Explain that we need to visualize settings in our head to understand a story more completely. Guide the children in sharing the reading of these settings in the story. With each, talk about the visualizations they can create in their minds. Encourage lots of detail then have them draw the settings.

Tommy put his pictures up on the walls of his half of the bedroom.

His mom put them up all around the house.

His dad took them to the barber shop where he worked.

Tommy's grandparents had his pictures in their grocery store.

Tip for Readers Theater Script

For emergent readers, look closely at the illustration and talk about the setting. Enjoy "Night Snow" as an echo poem: teacher reads and children echo. The children then could create illustrations that re-create the story line. For developing readers, you might want to enjoy the script as a shared reading followed by partner reading for fluency and expression.

"Night Snow"
By Linda Hoyt

Night snow
Chilly fingers
Stars are shining bright

Night snow
Chilly fingers
The tree will shine tonight

EXTEND THE LEARNING

☆ Read an array of fiction selections, and with each compare the settings.

☆ Engage children in retellings that include information about the setting.

☆ During interactive writing help students craft descriptions of settings from real experiences they have shared.

☆ Have children focus on setting as they craft an illustration before writing. Once they add detail to their setting, have them meet with partners and tell about their setting before they write.

☆ Consider the settings in nonfiction selections.

ASSESS THE LEARNING

➤ Listen in as partners identify settings to assess understanding.

➤ During small group instruction, have students identify settings.

➤ Assess an illustration about a personal experience to determine understanding of setting.

INFUSION OF FORMAL LANGUAGE
Test-style language

This story is *mostly* about:
   A. Tommy drawing pictures
   B. School
   C. Twin cousins
   D. His father taking his pictures to the barber shop

Why was Tommy so excited about getting art lessons?
   A. He liked the teacher.
   B. His mother told him to.
   C. He wanted to be a very good artist.
   D. They were a present.

Tommy put his pictures up on the walls of his half of the bedroom.

His mom put them up all around the house.

His dad took them to the barber shop where he worked.

Tommy's grandparents had his pictures in their grocery store.

"Night Snow"

By Linda Hoyt

Night snow

Chilly fingers

Stars are shining bright

Night snow

Chilly fingers

The tree will shine tonight

Strega Nona
By Tomie dePaola

FOCUS THE LEARNING

Introduction: In a good story we learn about people and animals who are in the story. When we notice the way characters act, the choices they make, and the kind of people they are, we can understand the story better.

Today we are going to read a wonderful book, *Strega Nona,* by Tomie dePaola. It will be our job to pay special attention to two of the characters, Strega Nona and Big Anthony. (Show the children a T chart labeled: Strega Nona ... Big Anthony.) As I read to you, we will be stopping often to write words that help us understand Strega Nona and Big Anthony.

Strega Nona	Big Anthony

INTERACTIVE READ-ALOUD
Model and Guide Practice

READ THE FIRST THREE PAGES. Then pause to think aloud, jotting words as you share them with the students. I am thinking about Strega Nona and words I can use to describe her. I am thinking I want to use the word *old* because that has been mentioned twice already. (Jot the word "old" under the heading "Strega Nona.") I am also thinking that I want to write "needs help" because she put up the sign asking for help.

READ UNTIL YOU GET TO THE PLACE WHERE STREGA NONA BLOWS THREE KISSES TO THE MAGIC PASTA POT. Now I am thinking of a lot more words. I can write that Big Anthony is "helpful" because he milked the goat. I can think of more words that describe Strega Nona, too.

 Turn to your thinking partner. What words can you think of to describe Big Anthony and Strega Nona? Think together!

READ UNTIL YOU GET TO THE PLACE WHERE BIG ANTHONY INVITES EVERYONE TO DINNER AT STREGA NONA'S HOUSE.

 Turn to your thinking partner. We know so much more now. What words can you use to describe Strega Nona and Big Anthony now? What should we add to our chart?

CONTINUE TO THE END OF THE STORY. Pause occasionally to give partners time to talk and suggest descriptors to add to the chart.

END OF STORY REFLECTION

Review the descriptors on the chart and show children how you can link several words to create a statement: The list for Strega Nona, has "old," "needs help," "magic," "nice," "bossy," and "_____." I am going to use two of our words to tell about Strega Nona.

"Strega Nona is a *nice* witch who needed help because she was getting *old.*"

How am I doing? Am I describing Strega Nona the way you would?

 Turn and talk to your partner. What words would you use to describe Strega Nona and Big Anthony? What would it sound like if you used several words like I did to tell about each of them?

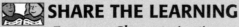

SHARE THE LEARNING
Focus on Characterization

Tip for Share the Reading	Tip for Readers Theater Script

Place the text on the overhead projector and read it aloud with great expression, making your voice shift clearly from speaker to narration. On a second reading, have the children join you with an emphasis on shifting their voices dramatically. As they become more dramatic, ask students

"String him up," the men of the town shouted.

"Now, wait," said Strega Nona. "The punishment must fit the crime." And she took a fork from a lady standing nearby and held it out to Big Anthony.

"All right, Anthony, you wanted pasta from my magic pasta pot," Strega Nona said, "and I want to sleep in my little bed tonight. So start eating."

And he did—poor Big Anthony.

to act the way the men of the town would have acted, moving their arms and looking angry. Then ask them to act like Strega Nona probably acted when she said these things.

Say something like: What does this passage tell us about the men of the town. How can we describe them? What words might we use to describe Strega Nona in this part of the story?

For emergent readers, read *Strega Nona* to them and have them act out the sequence of events. The children may enjoy joining in when you sing to the pasta pot. For developing readers, divide into three teams to enjoy the script. Focus on fluent interpretation as they read the selection.

Strega Nona
Readers Theater Adaptation by Linda Hoyt

Narrator 1:	Because Strega Nona was getting old, she needed someone to help her.
Narrator 2:	She hired Big Anthony.
Narrator 3:	His job was to sweep, wash dishes, and do the gardening.
Everyone:	The only thing he couldn't do was touch the pasta pot.
Narrator 1:	When Strega Nona had to go out of town,
Narrator 2:	Big Anthony tried to use the pasta pot even though he knew he shouldn't.
Everyone:	Bubbles, bubble, pasta pot, Boil me some pasta, nice and hot. I'm hungry and it's time to sup. Boil enough pasta to fill me up.

EXTEND THE LEARNING

Have children draw and write to show what they have learned about the characters in the story. Encourage them to draw the characters in a way that describes the character. (Example: Big Anthony looking really sad as he eats. The men of the town looking really angry, and so on.) Have the students use the character charts to support use of descriptive words in the labels for their illustrations and writing. Provide partner time so they can share their work.

ASSESS THE LEARNING

> Watch and listen closely as partners use words from the chart to describe characters.

> Analyze their drawing and writing to see if there is evidence of understanding of the characters.

> Have the students describe their parents, each other, characters from another book.

INFUSION OF FORMAL LANGUAGE
Test-style language

In this story, Big Anthony could be described as:
- A. Funny
- B. Smart
- C. Magic
- D. Foolish

In the scene where the pot was boiling over, the people of the town could best be described as:
- A. Happy
- B. Worried
- C. Helpful
- D. Sleepy

"String him up," the men of the town shouted.

"Now, wait," said Strega Nona. "The punishment must fit the crime." And she took a fork from a lady standing nearby and held it out to Big Anthony.

"All right, Anthony, you wanted pasta from my magic pasta pot," Strega Nona said, "and I want to sleep in my little bed tonight. So start eating."

And he did—poor Big Anthony.

Strega Nona

Readers Theater adaptation by Linda Hoyt

Narrator 1: Because Strega Nona was getting old, she needed someone to help her.

Narrator 2: She hired Big Anthony.

Narrator 3: His job was to sweep, wash dishes, and do the gardening.

Everyone: The only thing he couldn't do was touch the pasta pot.

Narrator 1: When Strega Nona had to go out of town,

Narrator 2: Big Anthony tried to use the pasta pot even though he knew he shouldn't.

Everyone: Bubbles, bubble, pasta pot,
Boil me some pasta, nice and hot.
I'm hungry and it's time to sup.
Boil enough pasta to fill me up.

Narrator 3:   The pot made so much pasta that Big Anthony was a hero.

Narrator 1:   Everyone ate a lot.

Narrator 2:   When they were full, Big Anthony sang:

Everyone: Enough, enough, my pasta pot

I have my pasta nice and hot.

So simmer down, my pot of clay

Until I'm hungry another day.

Narrator 1:   But he forgot to blow the three kisses and the pot kept bubbling.

Narrator 2:   The pasta poured out the door and ran down the street.

Narrator 3:   Just then, Strega Nona came home.

Narrator 1:   She sang the magic song,

Narrator 2:   stopped the pot, and

Narrator 3:   made Big Anthony eat all of the pasta!

Click, Clack, Moo: Cows That Type
By Doreen Cronin

FOCUS THE LEARNING

Introduction: Begin by reminding the children of a story they have heard recently in which the animals acted like people. Example: *Goldilocks and the Three Bears.* When animals act like people, it is called *personification.* With personification the author helps us to pretend that animals can talk, wear clothes, live in houses and do all of the things we do! We know it isn't true, but personification can make stories fun to read.

Today we are going to read a wonderful book, *Click, Clack, Moo: Cows That Type,* by Doreen Cronin. It will be our job to look for examples of personification, where the author has animals act like people.

INTERACTIVE READ-ALOUD
Model and Guide Practice

Introduce the book using the first page, which has only a typewriter and the title of the book. Show the typewriter and explain to the children that before computers, this machine is what people used to type letters and write books. Talk about the clicking noise made by a typewriter and explain that it was much noisier than a computer keyboard. Let's think about the title for a minute. I am wondering if the title is telling us that the author is using personification to have cows learn how to type! Can you imagine cows typing? How would they get their big hoof onto those little keys?

READ TO THE PAGE WHERE THE COWS WRITE FARMER BROWN A NOTE. Then pause to think aloud: I am thinking of the ways the author has used personification. First, she has the cows typing. Now they are writing a letter and asking for blankets! Would cows do that? Do cows know how to talk and read? No way! This is pretty funny. They are acting like people!

 Turn to your thinking partner. What do you think of cows that type and write notes?

READ THE NEXT TWO PAGES, UP TO THE COWS' SECOND NOTE. Strike? People sometimes go on strike when they are unhappy at work. That means that the people don't go to work until things change. Look how the author is using personification now!

 Turn to your thinking partner. What would happen if real cows went on strike and wouldn't give milk?

CONTINUE TO THE END OF THE STORY. Pause occasionally to think aloud about personification and giving partners time to talk.

END OF STORY REFLECTION

I am thinking about personification. It means that an author has animals act like people. Doreen Cronin used personification in a lot of ways in this book. Poor Farmer Brown really had some problems when the animals acted like people.

 Turn and talk to your partner. Think together about times the animals acted like people. What was your favorite?

SHARE THE LEARNING
Focus on Personification

Tip for Share the Reading

Place the text on the overhead projector and read it aloud with great expression, making your voice shift clearly from speaker to narration. On a second reading, have the children join you with an emphasis on shifting their voices dramatically. As they become more dramatic, ask students to act like the animals would have acted.

Say something like, *What personification can you find in this example from* Frog and Toad?

(excerpt from *Frog and Toad Are Friends*, by Arnold Lobel, p. 50)

Toad climbed out of the river. The water dripped out of his bathing suit and down onto his feet. The turtle laughed. The lizard laughed. The snake laughed. The field mouse laughed.

"What are you laughing at, Frog?" said Toad.

"I am laughing because you **do** look funny in your bathing suit," said Frog.

Toad picked up his clothes and went home.

Tip for Readers Theater Script

Read "Seal Baby" aloud emphasizing voices of the mother and the baby seal. Explain that this is another example of personification, as the seals are acting like people and talking to each other. For emergent readers, you may want to read it additional times, having the children echo you after you share each line. As learners are ready, have the children read just the part of the baby seal while you read the part of the mother seal. Then reverse roles. Have the children take the part of the mother while you take the part of the baby seal. Continue to emphasize expressive reading that reflects personification of the characters. When learners are ready, have partners read the script focusing on fluency and expression.

"Seal Baby"
By Linda Hoyt

Mother seal:	Hello my little one.
Baby seal:	Mama, where have you been?
Mother seal:	I have been searching for food so we won't be hungry.
Baby seal:	Mama, I'm cold.
Mother seal:	Hush little one. Come close and I will get you warm.
Baby seal:	Mama, I love you.

EXTEND THE LEARNING

Do a think-aloud and modeled write, showing how you can use personification in drawing and writing. Draw an animal wearing a skirt, hat, funny shoes and walking into a house or some other extreme example of personification. Use speech bubbles to show what the animal could be saying. After Watching you model, have the children draw and write to use personification. Provide partner time so students can share their work.

ASSESS THE LEARNING

> Confer with students as they draw and write to check understanding of personification.

> Ask learners to find examples of personification in their independent reading, small group reading experiences, and ongoing Read-Aloud experiences.

INFUSION OF FORMAL LANGUAGE
Test-style language

Personification means that animals act like they are:
  A. Mean
  B. Smart
  C. Magic
  D. People

On the second page in this book, the author wrote, "Cows that type? Impossible!"
Impossible probably means:
  A. Real
  B. Silly
  C. Cannot be true
  D. Sleepy

(excerpt from *Frog and Toad Are Friends*, by Arnold Lobel, p. 50)

Toad climbed out of the river. The water dripped out of his bathing suit and down onto his feet. The turtle laughed. The lizard laughed. The snake laughed. The field mouse laughed.

"What are you laughing at, Frog?" said Toad.

"I am laughing because you **do** look funny in your bathing suit," said Frog.

Toad picked up his clothes and went home.

"Seal Baby"

By Linda Hoyt

Mother seal: Hello my little one.

Baby seal: Mama, where have you been?

Mother seal: I have been searching for food so

we won't be hungry.

Baby seal: Mama, I'm cold.

Mother seal: Hush little one. Come close and I

will get you warm.

Baby seal: Mama, I love you.

Frog and Toad Are Friends: "The Swim"
By Arnold Lobel

FOCUS THE LEARNING

We are going to be reading "The Swim" with our friends Frog and Toad. Arnold Lobel is the author. In his books, Arnold Lobel has his characters talk frequently. You really feel like you are hearing their voices. But he also uses a "narrator" to tell us who is talking and explaining certain parts of the story. I have made signs that say "narrator," "Frog," "Toad," "turtle," and the names of the other animals. As I read to you, I will hold up the sign so you know who is talking.

 Thinking partners, look at the cover of Frog and Toad Are Friends. *Who do you think is talking?*

INTERACTIVE READ-ALOUD
Model and Guide Practice

Read page 40 using very different voices for Frog, Toad, and the narrator. Make a point to hold up the appropriate signs so the children have support in thinking about the speaker. You may want to stand in different places, one place for Frog, one for Toad, and one for the narrator.

 Thinking partners, how am I doing? Can you tell who is speaking? Are you noticing how important the narrator is . . . without the narrator, we wouldn't know who was speaking. Talk together.

READ TO PAGES 41–43. Highlight speakers and narration with signs and body position.

 Thinking partners. Did you notice that the narrator talked for a long time? Sometimes the narrator can help a story move along faster by telling what happened instead of having the characters talk a lot. What did you notice in that long narration?

CONTINUE TO THE END OF THE STORY. Pause occasionally to give partners time to talk about characters and the role of the narrator.

END OF STORY REFLECTION

Arnold Lobel writes great stories. He helps us understand his characters by having them talk ,and then he has the narrator explain more. I am trying to think like he does . . . Let's try to write like Arnold Lobel! Using a sheet of chart paper, start drafting a story featuring Frog and Toad. Be sure to include a bit of dialogue and a sentence or two of narration. Invite the children to help you think of what to write. It may be helpful to write Frog and Toad's voices in one color and the narration in another so the children have more visual support.

An example to consider:

One day Frog and Toad found a candy bar sitting on the front porch.

"I wonder how this got here?" Toad wondered.

"Wow. I wonder if my mom came by and left this for me?" said Frog.

They looked at the candy bar for a minute and then got a big grin on their faces.

"Let's eat it!" they called together and raced to the kitchen.

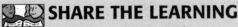

SHARE THE LEARNING
Focus on Narration

Tip for Share the Reading

Divide the group into "Toad" and "Frog." Read the passage aloud and have them just listen to the parts they will read. Then, begin a shared reading with you taking the role of the narrator and the children reading the parts of Frog and Toad. Talk about narration as the glue that holds the story together.

"Toad, Toad!" shouted Frog.

"Wake up, it's spring!"

"Go away!" yelled Toad.

"Toad, Toad!" shouted Frog.

"The sun is shining. The snow is melting. Wake up!"

"I am not here," said Toad. And Toad went back to sleep.

Tip for Readers Theater Script

Read Frog and Toad in "The Snake" to the children emphasizing changes in voice between Frog, Toad, and the narrator. As you read the script a second time, distribute a set of props and have children enact the events using the props. The props can then be used to support retelling of the story. For developing readers, divide them into teams representing each part. Have each team rehearse and prepare their part and present the script as a play, reading with expression and fluency.

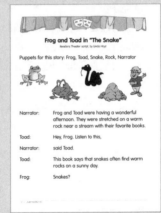

Frog and Toad in "The Snake"
Readers Theater script, by Linda Hoyt

Puppets for this story: Frog, Toad, Snake, Rock, Narrator

Narrator:	Frog and Toad were having a wonderful afternoon. They were stretched on a warm rock near a stream with their favorite books.
Toad:	Hey, Frog. Listen to this,
Narrator:	said Toad.
Toad:	This book says that snakes often find warm rocks on a sunny day.
Frog:	Snakes?

EXTEND THE LEARNING

☆ Search for narration in a variety of read alouds, and engage the children in working with you to dramatize character voices and narrator portions.

☆ Write narration and dialogue as a shared or interactive reading experience, showing how quotation marks work.

☆ Practice reading dialogue and narration with expressive voices that make the separation between character and narration more clear.

ASSESS THE LEARNING

➤ Listen in as partners read dialogue and narration to see if they can adjust their voices to reflect the differences.

➤ During small group instruction, read dialogue and narration to assess students' ability to differentiate.

INFUSION OF FORMAL LANGUAGE
Test-style language

In this story, it is *most important* to understand that
  A. Toad didn't want anyone to see his bathing suit.
  B. the animals were near the pond.
  C. Frog and Toad are friends.
  D. frogs don't wear bathing suits.

In this story, the word *shiver* means:
  A. Dance
  B. Wave your arms
  C. Shake with cold
  D. A small piece of wood

"Toad, Toad!" shouted Frog.

"Wake up, it's spring!"

"Go away!" yelled Toad.

"Toad, Toad!" shouted Frog.

"The sun is shining. The snow is melting.

Wake up!"

"I am not here," said Toad.

And Toad went back to sleep.

Frog and Toad in "The Snake"

Readers Theater script, by Linda Hoyt

Puppets for this story: Frog, Toad, Snake, Rock, Narrator

Narrator:	Frog and Toad were having a wonderful afternoon. They were stretched on a warm rock near a stream with their favorite books.
Toad:	Hey, Frog. Listen to this,
Narrator:	said Toad.
Toad:	This book says that snakes often find warm rocks on a sunny day.
Frog:	Snakes?

Narrator:	said Frog.
Frog:	What kind of snakes?
Toad:	It says that snakes are cold-blooded and most all of them like a warm rock on a sunny day.
Narrrator:	The friends went back to their reading. A few minutes later . . .
	Swish . . . .
	A head peeks up over the side of the rock, and Frog and Toad are looking into the face of the biggest snake they had ever seen.
Frog and Toad:	Run!
Narrator:	They yelled and jumped off that rock in a flash.

THEME/AUTHOR'S PURPOSE

When Sophie Gets Angry—Really, Really Angry...

By Molly Bang

FOCUS THE LEARNING

Have you ever been angry? Really, really angry? Being that angry is hard. It makes you feel mean. Sometimes we need to work really hard at controlling our feelings so we don't' say or do anything that isn't nice.

 What do you do when you are really, really angry? Share your thinking with your partner.

INTERACTIVE READ-ALOUD
Model and Guide Practice

READ TO THE PLACE WHERE IT SAYS SOPHIE IS REALLY ANGRY NOW. I am thinking about Sophie. Her sister got the gorilla. Her mom told her she had to share. I can see why she is upset...I wonder what she will do now.

 Think together. What do you think Sophie will do? What would you do with a problem like this?

READ TO THE PLACE WHERE IT SAYS SHE IS A VOLCANO READY TO EXPLODE. UH, OH! SOPHIE IS LOSING IT.

 Thinking partners, put your heads together. What should she do?

READ TO THE PLACE WHERE IT SAYS THE WIDE WORLD COMFORTS HER. Sophie is letting her feelings go, isn't she? She is learning that yelling and going crazy don't help.

 Thinking partners, think together about this. If you have feelings that are really strong and you need to get rid of them, what do you do?

READ TO THE END OF THE BOOK. Sophie is all calm now. She knows home is the best place to be. I hope she has learned about angry feelings and how to deal with them.

END OF STORY REFLECTION

Molly Bang, the author of this book, wanted us to learn from this story.

 Let's think together. What did the author want us to learn?

Invite individuals to share their thinking and create a list of possible messages the author had in mind. Help children understand that many books have a message and as readers we need to wonder what the author had in mind, what the purpose for the book might be...

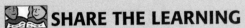 **SHARE THE LEARNING**

Focus on Theme/Author Purpose

Tip for Share the Reading

Remind the children that every author has some purpose when they write. So in every poem, storybook, and nonfiction selection, they need to think of the author's purpose and wonder if there is a theme or a message to be learned. Read the grizzly bear selection to them, and then

A grizzly bear is one of the strongest animals in the world. A full-grown male can be over eight feet tall and weigh 700 pounds. If you ever see a grizzly bear in the woods, don't run! Stand up tall, wave your hands, and talk loudly as you back away slowly.

A grizzly bear will eat almost anything for dinner.

The theme/author's purpose might be: _____

_____

guide a conversation about theme/author purpose for this piece. After the conversation, engage the children in a shared reading of the passage.

Tip for Readers Theater Script

Read "Friendship" to the children and guide a conversation about the author's purpose. What does the author want us to learn? What is the author's purpose? Is there a message here? Read the poem as an echo reading, with the students repeating each line after you

"Friendship"
By Linda Hoyt

Friendship must be cared for.
We need to give it thought.
Have you been a friend today
To someone that you know?

Have you done a little kindness?
Offered smiles and thoughtful looks?
Are you building up your friendships
While you learn and read from books?

read it. Then move to partner and independent reading of the poem. Have the children set goals for being good to friends.

EXTEND THE LEARNING

☆ After each read-aloud, guide a conversation about theme and author purpose. Encourage the children to consider why the author wrote the piece.

☆ During modeled writing, express your purpose for writing before you begin to make it clear that writers need to have a purpose.

☆ During writers workshop, have children state their purpose for their writing before they begin. Be sure they are thinking of an audience for their work.

☆ Read a variety of folktales and fairy tales to explore possibiities for theme and message in the stories.

ASSESS THE LEARNING

> Listen in as partners discuss theme and author purpose to assess understanding.

> During small group instruction, engage children in conversations about theme and author purpose to assess understanding.

> Assess writers' ability to state a purpose for their writing.

INFUSION OF FORMAL LANGUAGE

Test-style language

The most *important* purpose of this book is to

   A. tell a story.

   B. make us laugh.

   C. help us think about controlling our angry feelings.

   D. teach about climbing trees.

The *first* thing Sophie's sister did was

   A. sit in mom's lap.

   B. paint a picture.

   C. take the gorilla.

   D. run outside.

A grizzly bear is one of the strongest animals in the world. A full-grown male can be over eight feet tall and weigh 700 pounds. If you ever see a grizzly bear in the woods, don't run! Stand up tall, wave your hands, and talk loudly as you back away slowly.

A grizzly bear will eat almost anything for dinner.

The theme/author's purpose might be: _____

_____

"Friendship"

By Linda Hoyt

Friendship must be cared for.

We need to give it thought.

Have you been a friend today

To someone that you know?

Have you done a little kindness?

Offered smiles and thoughtful looks?

Are you building up your friendships

While you learn and read from books?

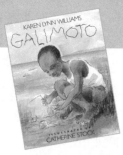

Galimoto

By Karen Lynn Williams

FOCUS THE LEARNING

Place the photograph that is in the Share the Reading section of this lesson on the overhead and explain to the children that a Galimoto is an African toy that children make themselves from pieces of leftover wire and other materials they can collect. We are going to read *Galimoto* by Karen Lynn Williams. Because this story takes place in Africa, you will want to look and listen closely to see what you can learn about life in Africa while we enjoy this story. The author of this book visited Africa and was so impressed by the Galimotos she saw there that she wanted to write a book so children all around the world could learn about them.

 Thinking partners, I am looking at the cover. I can see that Kondi, the main character in this story, has already started his Galimoto. Look closely. What do you see?

INTERACTIVE READ-ALOUD
Model and Guide Practice

READ THE FIRST PAGE. As I look at this, I notice several things that may help me learn about Africa and the village where Kondi lives. I notice that the children are all barefoot. It must be warm outside. I notice that there are chickens on the roof. We wouldn't see that here. I wonder if the roof is made of grass. I know in some countries where it is warm, they make their roofs of grass. I also notice that Kondi's special box has things he made himself.

 Think together. What are you noticing?

READ TO THE PLACE WHERE HE GETS WIRE FROM HIS UNCLE. I am noticing many things that help me know more about Africa. The names are different. There are ladies carrying sticks on their heads.

Think together. What have you noticed that may help you learn about Africa?

READ TO THE PLACE WHERE HE GETS YELLED AT FOR GOING TO THE FRONT DOOR OF THE FLOUR MILL.

This is really interesting. The ladies are carrying maize, which is corn, on their heads and waiting to have it ground into flour. How is that different from here? Where do we get our flour and our bread?

CONTINUE TO THE END OF THE STORY. Pause occasionally to give partners time to talk about their observations of cultural differences and the unfolding story line.

END OF STORY REFLECTION

Kondi worked really hard to gather what he needed for his Galimoto, didn't he? He had to wait and be very patient while he gathered and traded for the wire he needed, and then he still had to create his Galimoto. What differences did you notice between our life here and Kondi's life in his village?

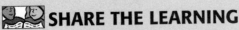 **SHARE THE LEARNING**

Focus on Understanding Culture

Tip for Share the Reading

Read the passage to the children and then guide them in a conversation. After talking about the picture, the Galimotos, and the culture of the African children, celebrate understanding by rereading the passage for fluency. Encourage children to talk about toys that are common in American culture.

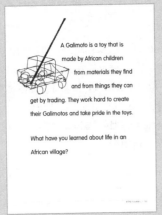

A Galimoto is a toy that is made by African children from materials they find and from things they can get by trading. They work hard to create their Galimotos and take pride in the toys.

What have you learned about life in an African village?

Tip for Readers Theater Script

For emergent readers, read *Galimoto* to them and have them talk about the *Galimotos* the African children create. For developing readers, engage them in a shared reading and then divide the script into parts that they can perform.

Galimoto
By Linda Hoyt

Narrator 1: A Galimoto is a toy
Narrator 2: created by children in Africa.
Narrator 3: They collect wire
Narrator 4: and other parts
Narrator 1: to make a Galimoto.
Narrator 3: They control their Galimoto with a long stick.
Narrator 3: It takes time and skill to bend the pieces
Narrator 4: into a shape that looks like a car or truck.
Everyone: How proud they must be of the Galimotos they create!

EXTEND THE LEARNING

☆ Read a range of stories about life in other cultures.

☆ Read nonfiction selections about other countries.

☆ Engage the children in researching toys from a variety of countries.

☆ Create illustrations and write summaries of *Galimoto*, highlighting what was learned about life in an African village.

ASSESS THE LEARNING

➤ Have children create illustrations reflecting their learning about life in Kondi's village. Assess their understanding of the cultural differences based on the illustration and their verbal explanation.

➤ After reading multicultural literature to the children, assess understanding of culture by meeting with small groups for conversations about the content.

INFUSION OF FORMAL LANGUAGE
Test-style language

The purpose of this story is to:
  A. Help us understand life in Africa.
  B. Appreciate how creative African children can be.
  C. Help us know what a Galimoto is.
  D. All of the above.

Which of the following is *not* true?
  A. Kondi was seven years old.
  B. He was looking for food.
  C. He wanted to make a Galimoto.
  D. He worked hard to gather supplies.

A Galimoto is a toy that is made by African children from materials they find and from things they can get by trading. They work hard to create their Galimotos and take pride in the toys.

What have you learned about life in an African village?

Galimoto

By Linda Hoyt

Narrator 1:   A Galimoto is a toy

Narrator 2:   created by children in Africa.

Narrator 3:   They collect wire

Narrator 4:   and other parts

Narrator 1:   to make a Galimoto.

Narrator 3:   They control their Galimoto with a long stick.

Narrator 3:   It takes time and skill to bend the pieces

Narrator 4:   into a shape that looks like a car or truck.

Everyone: How proud they must be of the Galimotos they create!

Inch by Inch
By Leo Lionni

FOCUS THE LEARNING

Introduction: Life is full of problems that we need to solve. If the zipper on my jacket gets stuck, I have a problem. I can solve it by carefully wiggling the zipper around until it comes loose and works again. If my pencil breaks, I have a problem. I can solve it by sharpening my pencil so it has a sharp point again. Many authors write stories that are focused on a problem and how a character solves the problem.

Today, we are going to read *Inch by Inch* by Leo Lionni. It will be our job to look for the problem in the story and see how it is solved. (On a piece of chart paper, create a T chart similar to the example below.)

Story	Problem	Solution(s)
Inch by Inch		
The Three Little Pigs		

INTERACTIVE READ-ALOUD
Model and Guide Practice

READ THE FIRST PAGE. Then pause to think aloud. Oh, my! The robin wants to "gobble up" the inchworm. That sounds like a problem for the inchworm. I am going to write this on the chart under "Problem" so I can remember that the inchworm has a problem that he will need to try to solve.

 Turn to your thinking partner. Think together about the inchworm. How should he solve his problem? The hungry robin wants to eat him up!

READ THE NEXT TWO PAGES. Then pause to think aloud. I am going to stop reading for a minute and think about the way the inchworm solved his problem. He was so smart! He offered to measure the robin's tail so the robin wouldn't eat him. (Jot his solution on the chart.) I am going to keep reading and see what else he does.

READ TO THE PLACE WHERE THE NIGHTINGALE ASKS THE INCHWORM TO MEASURE HIS SONG. Oh, my. The inchworm solved the problem with the robin and made lots of birds happy when he measured them. I think he has another kind of problem now. You can measure a tail or a beak, but how could an inchworm measure a song? (Add a notation about the nightingale under "Problem" on the chart.)

 Turn to your thinking partner. Think together. How could he solve this problem?

READ TO THE END OF THE STORY.

 Turn to your thinking partner. What did you think of the way inchworm solved his problem this time? What should we write on our chart?

END OF STORY REFLECTION

Point to the chart and think aloud: We know the inchworm had a problem. Birds wanted to eat him. We know he found a solution that was really smart. He measured things and measured his way away from the nightingale. Let's think about... (name another familiar story such as *The Three Little Pigs*).

 Turn and talk to your partner. Think together. What was the problem, and how was it solved in this other story? After you think together, we will write your ideas on our chart.

 **SHARE THE LEARNING**
Focus on Proble—Solution

Tip for Share the Reading

Place the text on the overhead projector and read it aloud with expression, making your voice shift clearly to show different speakers and narration. Explain that as a problem in a story develops, we need to show that in our voices when we read. Read the passage again, having the children join you with an emphasis on shifting their voices dramatically to show that the characters sound more dramatic as the problem is unveiled.

One morning, the nightingale met the inchworm.

"Measure my song," said the nightingale.

"But how can I do that?" said the inchworm. "I measure things, not songs."

"Measure my song or I'll eat you for breakfast," said the nightingale.

Then the inchworm had an idea.

Tip for Readers Theater Script

Engage the children in retells of the story with partners. In their retells, encourage them to include the problem and the solution. Some children may enjoy creating visuals to support their retell. Read "Inch by Inch" to them and have them use their props to enact the problem and solution pattern of the script.

For developing readers, engage them in chorally reading "Inch by Inch." As they are ready, have them present the script with fluent, expressive reading.

Inch by Inch by Leo Lionni
Reader's Theater Script adaptation by Linda Hoyt

Props: Robin, Inchworm, Another bird

A Problem:
One day a hungry robin saw an inchworm.
The robin was about to gobble the inchworm up.

A Solution:
The inchworm said, "Don't eat me. I can help you measure things."
So, the robin had the inchworm measure the bird's tail.

Another Problem:
Another bird said, "Measure my song or I'll eat you for breakfast!"
The inchworm didn't know how to measure a song.

A Solution:
He told the bird to sing and sing and sing.
Then the inchworm crawled away!

EXTEND THE LEARNING

☆ Have the children look through their independent reading books for problems and solutions.

☆ Select guided reading books with clear problem/solution structures and work with small groups to assess and extend understanding of problem/solution.

☆ Use the terms "problem" and "solution" throughout the learning day, applying the terms to daily challenges you and the children face.

☆ Engage students with the reader's theater script for this selection to develop fluency, to experience a "retelling" of the selection, or to generate artistic representations of the problem/solution structure.

ASSESS THE LEARNING

➤ Listen in during Turn and Talk conversations with additional stories to assess ability to identify problems and solutions.

➤ Confer with readers during independent reading to see if they understand and recognize problem/solution in independent reading stories.

➤ Have children draw and write about problems and how they are solved in a variety of stories.

INFUSION OF FORMAL LANGUAGE
Test-style language

In this story, the *problem* could best be described as:
   A. There were birds.
   B. The nightingale had a long song.
   C. The robin and the nightingale wanted to eat the inchworm.
   D. The inchworm was very smart.

The *solution* to the problem could best be described as:
   A. The birds were happy.
   B. The inchworm told the nightingale to sing.
   C. The inchworm measured the hummingbird.
   D. The inchworm measured birds and "inched" away from the nightingale.

One morning, the
nightingale met the
inchworm.

"Measure my song," said the nightingale.

"But how can I do that?" said the inchworm.
"I measure things, not songs."

"Measure my song or I'll eat you for
breakfast," said the nightingale.

Then the inchworm had
an idea.

Inch by Inch by Leo Lionni

Reader's Theater Script adaption by Linda Hoyt

Props: Robin, Inchworm, Another bird

A Problem:

One day a hungry robin saw an inchworm.

The robin was about to gobble the inchworm up.

A Solution:

The inchworm said, "Don't eat me. I can help you measure things."

So, the robin had the inchworm measure the bird's tail.

Another Problem:

Another bird said, "Measure my song or I'll eat you for breakfast!"

The inchworm didn't know how to measure a song.

A Solution:

He told the bird to sing and sing and sing.

Then the inchworm crawled away!

CIRCULAR/CUMULATIVE STRUCTURE

If You Give a Mouse a Cookie
By Laura Joffe Numeroff

FOCUS THE LEARNING

You will need several blocks, books, or other items you can stack. When things are cumulative, that means that they build on each other. For example, when I stack these blocks up, each one is resting on the one that came before. If I pull out the one on the bottom, the whole stack will fall over. We are going to read *If You Give a Mouse a Cookie*, by Laura Numeroff, which is a cumulative, or circular, story. You will see how the story is like our stack: everything is built on what came before.

INTERACTIVE READ-ALOUD
Model and Guide Practice

READ PAGES 1–5. Then pause to think aloud. Do you see what is happening? With each thing the mouse asks for, the boy needs to give him something else. This is what makes the story cumulative.

READ PAGES 6–8.

 Turn to your thinking partner. What have we added to our cumulative story on these pages?

READ PAGES 9–12.

What is new now in our cumulative story?

 Turn to your thinking partner. Tell each other what you have noticed about cumulative or circular structure.

CONTINUE READING TO THE END.

 What was your favorite part of this story? In what part of our cumulative story did your favorite part appear?

END OF STORY REFLECTION

Let's make a list of the cumulative events in this story.

First, the boy gave a mouse a cookie,

Then he …

Now that we have our list of the cumulative events, let's read them together.

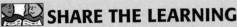

SHARE THE LEARNING
Focus on Circular/Cumulative Structure

Tip for Share the Reading

Place the text on the overhead projector and read each paragraph aloud, encouraging the children to join in. Have them create illustrations with arrows between each picture to show how the events are linked together.

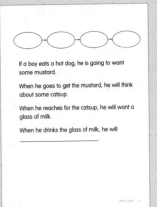

If a boy eats a hot dog, he is going to want some mustard.

When he goes to get the mustard, he will think about some catsup.

When he reaches for the catsup, he will want a glass of milk.

When he drinks the glass of milk, he will _____.

Tip for Readers Theater Script

Read "If You Give a Rooster Some Peanuts" to the children and engage them in planning ways for the script to continue. Read the script chorally, adding text and drawings to support the ending the children create.

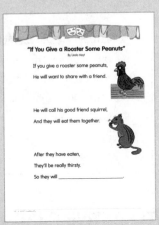

"If You Give a Rooster Some Peanuts"
By Linda Hoyt

If you give a rooster some peanuts,
He will want to share with a friend.

He will call his good friend squirrel,
And they will eat them together.

After they have eaten,
They'll be really thirsty.
So they will _____.

EXTEND THE LEARNING

☆ Read a variety of cumulative stories. Laura Numeroff has written many titles using this structure. You might also enjoy *A House is a House for Me*, by Mary Ann Hoberman, or *The House That Jack Built*.

☆ Have children write a cumulative or circular story as a class book. Create a list of the linking events. Then have individuals take responsibility to illustrate and write their page for the class book.

ASSESS THE LEARNING

➤ Ask children to identify stories with cumulative structure within an array of books that have many different organizational patterns.

➤ Confer with readers to assess understanding of cumulative structure.

INFUSION OF FORMAL LANGUAGE
Test-style language

Before the mouse wanted a straw, he ate a:
- A. Cookie
- B. Banana
- C. Cheese
- D. Peanut

After the mouse drank the milk, he wanted:
- A. More milk
- B. A straw
- C. A napkin
- D. Another cookie

After the mouse drank the milk, he wanted:
- A. More milk
- B. A straw
- C. A napkin
- D. Another cookie

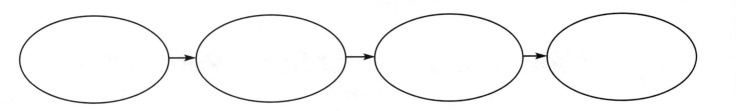

If a boy eats a hot dog, he is going to want some mustard.

When he goes to get the mustard, he will think about some catsup.

When he reaches for the catsup, he will want a glass of milk.

When he drinks the glass of milk, he will

_____.

"If You Give a Rooster Some Peanuts"

By Linda Hoyt

If you give a rooster some peanuts,

He will want to share with a friend.

He will call his good friend squirrel,

And they will eat them together.

After they have eaten,

They'll be really thirsty.

So they will _____.

Vocabulary/ Literary Language

Standards in this strand encourage learners to observe the power of precise vocabulary; to identify and appreciate rhythm, rhyme, onomatopoeia, alliteration, and literary language; and to discern the meanings of unfamiliar words through context clues. Transitional words and words with multiple meanings are also highlighted in this strand.

Owen
By Kevin Henkes

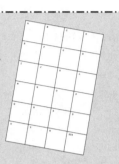

FOCUS THE LEARNING

Introduction: As we read *Owen* by Kevin Henkes today, we are going to be noticing and thinking about the wonderful words Kevin Henkes uses in his writing. When authors choose their words carefully, it makes the story more interesting and helps us understand what is happening. I am going to put up this Alphabox (Hoyt, 1999) and use it to collect wonderful words as I read.

INTERACTIVE READ-ALOUD
Model and Guide Practice

READ PAGE 1. Then pause to think aloud. I am going to stop reading and think about the word "fuzzy." It says that Owen has a fuzzy yellow blanket. I really like that word. I know that fuzzy can mean hairy, furry, fluffy. Thanks to that great word, I can really picture Owen's fuzzy yellow blanket. I am going to put fuzzy in the Alphabox.

 Think together. Can you think of something that is fuzzy like Owen's blanket?

READ PAGE 2. Listen to the way Kevin Henkes plays with the words on this page. "Upstairs, downstairs, in-between. Inside, outside, upside down." That is so much fun. Let's do it together and add some hand motions! What wonderful words he chose. Should I choose any of these for the Alphabox?

READ TO THE PLACE WHERE OWEN'S PARENTS TELL HIM TO PLACE FUZZY UNDER HIS PILLOW FOR THE BLANKET FAIRY.

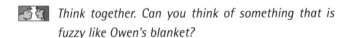 *Turn to your thinking partner. Think together about the words you are hearing. Are there any wonderful words we should put in the Alphabox?*

READ TO WHERE OWEN IS IN THE DENTAL CHAIR. I am going to stop again. These words are wonderful. It says that Fuzzy is "torn and ratty" and that Owen became "invisible." It also said Fuzzy was "essential."

 Turn to your thinking partner. What might those words mean? Should we add any to the Alphabox? Which ones do you like the best?

CONTINUE TO THE END OF THE STORY. Pause occasionally to think aloud, add words to the Alphabox, and give partners time to talk.

END OF STORY REFLECTION

Let's look at our Alphabox and think about the wonderful words we collected from this book. Let's read the words together. Then you can tell your partner which ones you like the best. Read the words chorally.

Turn to your thinking partner. Which ones do you like best? Why?

SHARE THE LEARNING
Focus on Vocabulary

Tip for Share the Reading

Help the children use the Alphabox words to consider possibilities for completing the cloze passage. Encourage them to talk about options for each blank, word meanings, and even to add more words to the Alphabox as they think of wonderful words to explore. Read the com-

> Fuzzy was a _____, _____
> blanket that Owen loved very much.
> He _____ it and _____ it
> everywhere. He wore it. He _____
> with it. He sucked and _____ and
> twisted it. When Owen put Fuzzy on his
> head, he thought he was
> _____.

pleted passage with expression and, when appropriate, add dramatic actions.

Tip for Readers Theater Script

For emergent readers, read "How to Make a Peanut Butter Sandwich" to the children emphasizing the verbs as you read. Well-chosen verbs are the engines of sentences and can help us visualize what is happening. Read the directions again, acting out each verb and inviting

How to Make a Peanut Butter Sandwich
By Linda Hoyt

First you **select** a piece of bread that is really soft and fresh.

Then you **gather** a knife, a plate, and a jar of rich, brown peanut butter.

Take a moment to **inhale** the wonderful smell as you **twist** off the lid of the jar.

Slide your knife into the wide opening of the jar and **scoop** out a mound large enough to coat your bread.

Starting at one edge, **smooth** the peanut butter across the surface of the bread.

Stretch your mouth open and **sink** your teeth into the first gooey, peanut-filled bite.

Mmmm.

the students to act them out with you. As students are ready, have them read the directions in partners and then look at some of their own writing to see if they can make some of their verbs more interesting.

EXTEND THE LEARNING

☆ Challenge the children to listen for great words when they are talking and reading. Add their words to the Alphabox.

☆ Make a point to use words from the Alphabox in daily conversations with students. When you use one, point it out and ask them to clap. Challenge the children to use the Alphabox words when they talk to each other.

☆ Model a piece of writing in which you pull words from the Alphabox to include in your writing. Show the children how you use it as a tool to use wonderful words in your writing.

☆ Encourage children to select a wonderful word to take home and celebrate with their family. They can put their wonderful word on a card and show their parents how they can use it in conversation.

ASSESS THE LEARNING

> Listen to partners attempt to use target vocabulary from the Alphabox. Are they able to use the words correctly?

> Confer with readers during independent reading to draw attention to strong vocabulary choices in the text or to talk about other words an author might have selected to make the writing more interesting.

> Assess children's writing to monitor inclusion of well-chosen words.

INFUSION OF FORMAL LANGUAGE
Test-style language

When Kevin Henkes said that Fuzzy was *essential*, he probably meant that

  A. Fuzzy was really a mess.

  B. Fuzzy smelled bad.

  C. Fuzzy was torn.

  D. Fuzzy was very important to Owen.

Owen's mother *snipped* and sewed Fuzzy. *Snipped* means:

  A. Cut

  B. Washed

  C. Tore up

  D. Wiped

Fuzzy was a _____, _____

blanket that Owen loved very much.

He _____ it and _____ it

everywhere. He wore it. He _____

with it. He sucked and _____ and

twisted it. When Owen put Fuzzy on his

head, he thought he was

_____.

How to Make a Peanut Butter Sandwich

By Linda Hoyt

First you **select** a piece of bread that is really soft and fresh.

Then you **gather** a knife, a plate, and a jar of rich, brown peanut butter.

Take a moment to **inhale** the wonderful smell as you **twist** off the lid of the jar.

Slide your knife into the wide opening of the jar and **scoop** out a mound large enough to coat your bread.

Starting at one edge, **smooth** the peanut butter across the surface of the bread.

Stretch your mouth open and **sink** your teeth into the first gooey, peanut-filled bite.

Mmmm.

Where the Wild Things Are
By Maurice Sendak

INTERACTIVE READ-ALOUD
Model and Guide Practice

READ TO THE PLACE WHERE MAX WAS SENT TO HIS ROOM. I am going to stop and think about the word "mischief." I am going to write "mischief" on our chart. We can tell by the pictures that Max is pounding nails into walls to make a tent. Ooh! I don't imagine most parents would want him to do that. He is chasing the dog with a fork. Not good, Max! Then he tells his mom he will eat her up! I am thinking that mischief might mean trouble, problems, naughtiness. I am going to write these ideas on the chart and now I am going to try the sentence on page 1 replacing "mischief" with each of the other words we listed.

 Partners, what do you think? Do those words mean the same as mischief? How did you know?

READ TO THE PLACE WHERE MAX IS SAILING IN THE BOAT. Here is another wonderful word. It says "an ocean tumbled" by with a private boat for Max. "Tumbled" belongs on our chart for sure.

 Think together. What might "tumbled" mean? We will write your ideas on the chart and then try them in the sentence.

READ TO THE PLACE WHERE THE WILD THINGS ROAR THEIR TERRIBLE ROARS. Here is another terrific word for our chart, "gnashed."

 What might gnashed mean? Think together. Then we will try your ideas in the sentence.

READ TO THE END STOPPING FREQUENTLY TO ENJOYING LOOKING AT PICTURES AND SENTENCES TO DETERMINE WORD MEANINGS. Words to watch for: "terrible," "tamed," "blinking," "rumpus," "wild," "roared," "private."

END OF STORY REFLECTION

We found lots of wonderful words in this book, and we were able to use the pictures and the sentences around the words to think about their meaning. Let's think about the words we wrote on our chart and select some to act out! After you have time to think together, we will have some of you act out your words from the chart while the rest of us guess which words you are sharing.

 Turn and talk to your partner. What was your favorite word on the chart? What clues helped you to know what it meant? How might you act it out?

SHARE THE LEARNING
Focus on Using Context Clues

Tip for Share the Reading

Place the text on the overhead projector. Then read the passage to the children. Read it a second time asking them to think of all the words they can that would make sense in the blanks. Explain that they need to use the meaning of the passage and what they remember from the story to help them select words. Use the boxes to record all of their ideas.

> Max's private boat took him across an ocean and left him in the place of the wild things. They were roaring terrible roars and _____ their terrible teeth. Max wanted them to be good so he used a magic trick to tame them. After the wild things learned how to be good, Max had a wild _____ and they all made a lot of _____.

Tip for Readers Theater Script

For emergent readers, read the Brown Bear variation, "Max, Max, What Do You See?", to them and have them think about word(s) they could fill in the blanks that would make sense. Support the addition of the word(s) they select and have them create a supportive illustration. Perform their readers theater for fluency and fun. For developing readers, show the song on an overhead, as a chart, or provide copies that the children can illustrate. For developing readers, sing "Max" so that they become familiar with the lyrics. Then give them personal copies to enjoy over time.

"Max, Max, What Do You See?"

Group 1: Max, Max, What Do You See?
Group 2: I see mom _____ at me.

Group 1: Max, Max, What Do You See?
Group 2: I see wild things _____ at me.

Group 1: Max, Max, What Do You See?
Group 2: I see a dinner that's just for me.

EXTEND THE LEARNING

☆ Create cloze passages in their guided reading books by putting sticky notes over key words then having the students use context and think before uncovering the word.

☆ Have children create cloze passages for each other by covering words with sticky notes and then trading books.

☆ Use "oral cloze" during Read-Alouds. As you read along, leave a word off the end of a sentence and have the children talk about words that would make a good ending to the sentence. As they get better, omit a noun or verb from the middle of the sentence. After finishing the sentence, have the children think of nouns or verbs that could have made sense in that spot.

☆ Support the children in remembering that illustrations are vitally important context clues and should be used as a support when trying to determine word meaning.

ASSESS THE LEARNING

> Listen in as partners converse about word meanings and the contextual clues they are using to determine meaning.

> Confer with readers during independent reading to see if they can determine the meaning of unknown words using contextual clues.

> During small group instruction, guide conversations around interesting vocabulary to assess learner's ability to use context as well as phonics for word solving.

INFUSION OF FORMAL LANGUAGE
Test-style language

In *Where the Wild Things Are,* the word *mischief* means:
  A. Good
  B. Trouble
  C. Silly
  D. In charge

The books says Max tamed the Wild Things. *Tamed* means:
  A. Wild
  B. Sit down
  C. Made them mind him
  D. Magic

Max's private boat took him across an ocean and left him in the place of the wild things. They were roaring terrible roars and _____ their terrible teeth. Max wanted them to be good so he used a magic trick to tame them. After the wild things learned how to be good, Max had a wild _____ and they all made a lot of _____.

"Max, Max, What Do You See?"

Group 1:   Max, Max, What Do You See?

Group 2:   I see mom _____ at me.

Group 1:   Max, Max, What Do You See?

Group 2:   I see wild things _____ at me.

Group 1:   Max, Max, What Do You See?

Group 2:   I see a dinner that's just for me.

"Max"

Readers Theater script adaptation by Linda Hoyt

(Sing to the tune of "Take Me Out to the Ball Game")

Max was sent to his bedroom

For making mischief and such.

He pounded a nail in the living room wall

And chased the dog with a fork!

Max was sent to his bedroom

Where he had quite a dream.

He dreamed that he sailed on an ocean blue

To the land where the Wild Things Roam.

Max was sent to his bedroom.

He finally woke up from his dream—

His dinner was waiting and smelled really good.

Now he's ready to smile and be good.

LITERARY/FIGURATIVE LANGUAGE LEADS

Owl Moon, Blueberries for Sal, Goldilocks and the Three Bears, Farmer Duck, Stellaluna, The Mitten

FOCUS THE LEARNING

I brought several of my favorite books to share. As we look at these books today, we are going to think about the words authors use when they start a story. I am going to use this chart to write ideas for great ways to start a story. This will help us remember to look at story beginnings and also to think about this when we write our own stories.

 Think together about some of our favorite stories. Think about Cinderella, Little Red Riding Hood, The Three Little Pigs. *What do you remember about the way they start?*

INTERACTIVE READ-ALOUD
Model and Guide Practice

I am going to start with *Owl Moon*. Listen carefully. I am only going to read the first page. "It was late one winter night…" Isn't this interesting. Jane Yolen started by telling us when her story happened. She focused on the time of day and the time of year. If I was going to write a story about what we are doing right now, I could say, "It was early one winter day at _____ (name of school)."

It was late one winter night.	Time of day. Time of year. Description.

 Think together. I am going to read that one more time. Listen to the words Jane Yolen used. How does her opening help us get ready to read the story?

READ THE FIRST LINE FROM *BLUEBERRIES FOR SAL*. Isn't this interesting! This starts, "One day," and then it tells us where they went. I am going to write that on our chart. Isn't this interesting. Two of our authors have started with when the story is happening. One added where it was happening. If I was going to write a story about what we are doing right now, I could use what I am learning about starting a story and say, "It was early one winter day at _____ (name of school) on _____ (name the street)."

It was late one winter night.	Time of day. Time of year.
One day, Little Sal went with her mother to Blueberry Hill.	Time of day. Where.

READ THE FIRST LINES FROM "GOLDILOCKS AND THE THREE BEARS."

 Think together. What did you notice about the beginning of this story? Did you notice the author added a little humor?

CONTINUE READING LEADS. Pause to add information to the chart, recast your sentence about the school to reflect the author's style, and give the children time to talk about their observations.

END OF STORY REFLECTION

We learned a lot about the way some authors use words to start their stories.

 Think together for a moment. If you were going to start a story about going out for pizza, how would you want your story to start? Look at our chart and think about the books we have been looking at. How would you start?

Do a modeled write using an interesting lead that includes time, place, and something interesting to hook the reader. Think outloud as you draft so the children can see you looking at the chart or at one of the books and thinking about your lead.

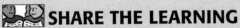

SHARE THE LEARNING
Focus on Literary/Figurative Language Leads

Tip for Share the Reading

Read the passage fluently with expression. Then guide a conversation about the words this author used to start the story. Is this a story that makes them want to read more? What made them feel like that? If they were to add this story to the chart, what would they say about the

One night, just as I was falling asleep. Waaaaaaa! The baby started to cry. I covered my ears. I pulled my pillow over my head. I even put my stuffed bunny on my head. But nothing worked. Waaaaa! That baby was really upset.

opening? Did they like the addition of "sound words?" Could they use sound words in a story of their own?

Tip for Readers Theater Script

For emergent readers, read "Blankets" to them and talk about the beginning. There is only one word, "fuzzy," yet it gives us a really good picture in our mind about the blanket. Read it again and have the children visualize the blanket as the poem unfolds.

"Blankets"
By Lynette Brent

Fuzzy
Comfortable
Blankets keep us warm.

Safe
Restful
Blankets feel good.

Pretty
Soft
Blankets hold a baby.

Big
Fun
Blankets make a tent.

Encourage them to talk about their own blankets. Engage the children in a shared reading of the poem. Then, as they are ready, have partners try reading together.

EXTEND THE LEARNING

☆ During small group instruction, compare the words authors use to begin stories.

☆ During Read-Alouds, continue comparing the words authors use to start their stories.

☆ During writers workshop, confer in small groups to talk about interesting words they might use to begin their writing.

☆ Guide an interactive writing group in looking at the chart about story openings. Then, craft a piece of writing together.

☆ Meet with individuals to revise story openings.

☆ Have children create illustrations based on just the first page of a story. See how much detail they are able to include.

ASSESS THE LEARNING

> During small group instruction, have children point out the beginning of the selection and share thinking about the way the author chose to begin.

> Confer with readers about the beginnings of books they are reading for independent reading.

> Confer with writers to assess ability to use varied openings in their writing.

INFUSION OF FORMAL LANGUAGE
Test-style language

Jane Yolen wrote, "It was late one winter night." Her lead told us:

  A. About the time of year

  B. About the time of day

  C. That it was late

  D. All of the above.

In the beginning of a story, many authors choose to tell about:

  A. The time

  B. The place

  C. The problem

  D. All of the above.

One night, just as I was falling asleep.

Waaaaaaa! The baby started to cry. I

covered my ears. I pulled my pillow over

my head. I even put my stuffed bunny

on my head. But nothing worked.

Waaaaa! That baby was really upset.

"Blankets"

By Lynette Brent

Fuzzy

Comfortable

Blankets keep us warm.

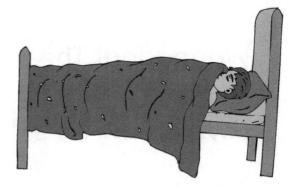

Safe

Restful

Blankets feel good.

Pretty

Soft

Blankets hold a baby.

Big

Fun

Blankets make a tent.

Chicken Little
By Steven Kellogg

FOCUS THE LEARNING

Alliteration is a strategy that many writers use to give their writing a little touch of humor and interest. An example is *Lilly's Purple Plastic Purse*. Do you notice all of the "P" words? Today as we read *Chicken Little* by Steven Kellogg, we will be watching for alliteration, places where words start with the same letter of the alphabet.

INTERACTIVE READ-ALOUD
Model and Guide Practice

READ TO THE PAGE WHERE FOXY LOXY IS IMAGINING DRUM-STICKS FOR DINNER. I found some alliteration! It says "plump pair" of drumsticks. Say that with me. "Plump pair of drumsticks."

 Turn to your thinking partner. What beginning sound do you hear in "plump pair?"

READ TO THE POINT WHERE FOXY LOXY IS LOOKING IN THE COOKBOOK. I FOUND SOME MORE ALLITERATION. Listen. "Simmered in spices and sauce." I am going to write it so you can look at the alliteration. Let's read it together. Isn't alliteration fun.

READ TO THE PLACE WHERE FOXY LOXY SAYS HE WILL AVOID A SCUFFLE.

 The last sentence on this page has alliteration at the end. Listen carefully as I read that sentence again. Talk to your thinking partner. Can you find the alliteration?

CONTINUE TO THE END OF THE STORY. Pause occasionally to give partners time to notice and talk about alliteration. Some alliteration to notice: "resist reading the recipes"; "Hippo Hefty"; "flattened the fleeing fox"; "green-bean gruel."

END OF STORY REFLECTION

This book is so much fun! Let's think together about our favorite alliteration.

 Turn to your partner. Which alliteration was your favorite?

Let's create some alliteration of our own. Example: Mrs. Hoyt hops to the heater.

SHARE THE LEARNING
Focus on Alliteration

Tip for Share the Reading

Plant a little pumpkin seed.
Push it in the ground.
Pour a little water.
Pull a little weed.
Plenty of pretty pumpkins.
Enough to go around.

Read the poem fluently, dramatizing with hand motions as you read. Invite the children to join in chorally. Place the poem on the overhead projector and read it again, tracking under the line of print as children read along with you. Invite children to draw lines under the words that start with "P." Then read the poem again emphasizing alliteration and the "P" words.

Tip for Readers Theater Script

"Bubbles"
By Linda Hoyt

Bright
Blue
Balls
Floating in the air.
Bursting balls of soap film
Popping everywhere.

Blow bubbles with the children. Then read the poem "Bubbles" to them. Invite them to join in chorally, emphasizing the alliteration in the poem. As children gain confidence in reading the selection chorally, provide copies of the script for them to illustrate and read with partners.

EXTEND THE LEARNING

☆ Read *Animalia* by Grahame Base to enjoy wonderful alliteration together.

☆ Describe classroom objects and people using alliteration: This is a Big Book. The ball is bouncing. Tony has tomatoes in his sandwich. The chunky chalk. The plastic pencil box.

☆ Reread favorite class poems and check for alliteration.

☆ During small group instruction, look for opportunities to add alliteration using sticky notes.

☆ During writers workshop, encourage writers to add alliteration to their titles and descriptions.

☆ Model a piece of writing and demonstrate adding alliteration to your descriptions.

☆ Have children create illustrations of alliterations: Red robins. Bouncing bunnies. Bursting bubbles.

ASSESS THE LEARNING

> Have children create illustrations to show understanding of an alliteration.

> Confer with readers during independent reading to see if they can identify alliteration in a poem.

INFUSION OF FORMAL LANGUAGE
Test-style language

Alliteration means that the author has used words that
  A. he likes.
  B. are funny.
  C. start with the same letter of the alphabet.
  D. match the picture.

"Foolish fowl" is an example of:
  A. Silly talk
  B. Chicken language
  C. Poetry
  D. Alliteration

Plant a little pumpkin seed.

Push it in the ground.

Pour a little water.

Pull a little weed.

Plenty of pretty pumpkins.

Enough to go around.

"Bubbles"

By Linda Hoyt

Bright

Blue

Balls

Floating in the air.

Bursting balls of soap film

Popping everywhere.

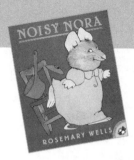

Noisy Nora

By Rosemary Wells

FOCUS THE LEARNING

Rhyming words can be a lot of fun. We know poems can rhyme, and sometimes books can rhyme as well. In *Noisy Nora* by Rosemary Wells the whole book is based on rhyming and it still tells a great story.

 Think together. What do you remember about rhyming? Can you think of two words that rhyme?

INTERACTIVE READ-ALOUD
Model and Guide Practice

Since we have already read this story, today we are going to put on our special listening ears and listen for rhymes that Rosemary Wells used to tell her story. Read the first three pages. I heard some rhyming already. Father played with Kate so Nora had to *wait*. Let's say that together. Do you hear how "Kate" and "wait" rhyme? The ends of the words sound the same.

READ TO THE POINT WHERE NORA DROPS THE MARBLES ON THE FLOOR. I am going to stop. I heard a rhyme. Then she slammed the door and dropped the marbles on the floor.

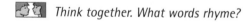 *Think together. What words rhyme?*

We have had some great rhyming words so far. We have had "Kate "and "wait" and "door" and "floor." Read to the place where her sister calls her dumb.

 Talk to your thinking partner. Can you name the rhyme?

CONTINUE TO THE END OF THE STORY. Pause occasionally to give partners time to talk about rhyming words they hear.

END OF STORY REFLECTION

Poor Nora. She was really frustrated that no one had time for her. But didn't we have fun with the rhymes.

What were your favorite rhymes in the book? When you share your ideas, we will all say them together.

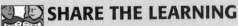 **SHARE THE LEARNING**
Focus on Rhyming

Tip for Share the Reading

Read the poem aloud for the children, tracking under the print as you go. Invite children to act it out as you read it a second time. On a third reading, show the children that the last line in each group is the very same. Have them chorally read the last line while you read the preceding line. As they are ready, have them chime in on the entire poem.

"Five Little Ducks"

5 little ducks sitting on a door
1 flew away and then there were 4.

4 little ducks sitting in a tree
1 flew away and then there were 3.

3 little ducks looking at you
1 flew away and then there were 2.

2 little ducks sitting in the sun
1 flew away and then there was 1.

Tip for Readers Theater Script

Read "Hello" to the children and encourage them to act it out. With subsequent readings, have them join in chorally, read with partners, read independently while continually focusing on fluent interpretation of the rhyming pattern.

"Hello"
By Linda Hoyt

Hello, Pretty Bird.

Hello, Little Fly.

It's time to get going.

The sun's in the sky.

EXTEND THE LEARNING

☆ Finger plays and poems are great supports to rhyming. Be sure to point out the rhymes that are often present in our everyday favorite selections.

☆ Read Caldecott winner, *In the Small, Small Pond* by Denise Fleming, and look for the rhymes.

☆ Read *Chicken Little* by Steven Kellogg and have fun with the rhyming names.

☆ Sing lots of songs with rhymes.

☆ Read Dr. Seuss books and celebrate the rhyming patterns.

☆ Have children illustrate and label words that are rhyming pairs.

ASSESS THE LEARNING

> Confer with individuals to determine their ability to identify rhyming patterns.

> Guide small groups in reading poems and identifying the rhymes.

INFUSION OF FORMAL LANGUAGE
Test-style language

Select a word that *rhymes* with *door*:
  A. Doll
  B. Fur
  C. Drip
  D. Floor

Why was Nora noisy?
  A. She wanted attention.
  B. She was looking for food.
  C. She was hungry.
  D. She was in the kitchen.

"Five Little Ducks"

5 little ducks sitting on a door

1 flew away and then there were 4.

4 little ducks sitting in a tree

1 flew away and then there were 3.

3 little ducks looking at you

1 flew away and then there were 2.

2 little ducks sitting in the sun

1 flew away and then there was 1.

"Hello"

By Linda Hoyt

Hello, Pretty Bird.

Hello, Little Fly.

It's time to get going.

The sun's in the sky.

Brown Bear, Brown Bear, What Do You See?

By Bill Martin, Jr.

FOCUS THE LEARNING

Introduction: Rhyming is so much fun. When things rhyme, the ends of the words sound a lot alike. Let's play with a rhyme.

> Clickety-clack, clickety-clack
> Tunnel ahead, everything's black.
> Clickety-clack, clickety-clack
> Train is rolling down the track.

Did you notice the rhymes, the words with the endings that sounded a lot alike? I am going to read it again. Listen to the endings of the words.... Did you hear it this time? (Clack, black, track) I am going to write these on the board so you can see that they also look a lot alike. While I am writing, let's play with some rhymes. "cat…hat…sat…"

 Think together. What else would rhyme?

Let's play with more rhymes. I am going to say a word. Then you and your partner need to think together to see if you can come up with another word that rhymes. "Man."

 Think together. What might rhyme?

How about "boom?"

 Think together. What rhymes with that?

INTERACTIVE READ-ALOUD
Model and Guide Practice

I am going to read *Brown Bear, Brown Bear, What Do You See?* by Bill Martin, Jr., straight through. Listen for the rhyme and have fun with the rhythm of the language. Be ready to say something to your thinking partner when I finish.

 Turn to your partner. What rhyme(s) did you hear? What did you notice?

END OF STORY REFLECTION

Bill Martin, Jr., and his partner, John Archambault, wrote another book that rhymes. It is called *Chicka Chicka Boom Boom.* Listen to the opening line: "A told B and B told C, I'll meet you at the top of the coconut tree."

 What rhyme did you hear?

Chicka Chicka Boom Boom! Will there be enough room?

 What rhyme did you hear now?

SHARE THE LEARNING
Focus on Rhyme (Interpret)

Tip for Share the Reading

Read the nursery rhymes aloud placing emphasis on the rhyming words as you read. As the children are ready, invite them to share the reading with you. Identify the rhyming words you can find in the rhymes.

Jack and Jill went up the hill
To fetch a pail of water.
Jack fell down and broke his crown
And Jill came tumbling after.

Tip for Readers Theater Script

For "Ladybug" to carry meaning, be sure that children understand that ladybugs eat aphids and that their wings are protected by their hard outer shell which must be opened before they can fly. Read the poem aloud with expression, emphasizing the rhyme structure. Have children identify the rhyming words and consider actions they could use to dramatize the poem. As learners gain confidence, have them read in unison, in partners, or by trading off and reading every other line.

"Ladybug"
By Linda Hoyt

Ladybug, ladybug
Hungry for a treat

Then she finds an aphid
That's what she likes to eat

Ladybug, ladybug
Looking at the sky

Opens up her shell then . . .
Spreads her wings to fly.

EXTEND THE LEARNING

☆ Play with rhyming words while lining up.

☆ Begin a collection of rhyming poetry to display on charts for children to read.

☆ Read widely from poetry showing children that sometimes it rhymes and sometimes it doesn't.

☆ Read *Whiskers & Rhymes* by Arnold Lobel (Mulberry Books, 1985).

☆ Have fun with silly limericks and poetry by Jack Prelutsky and Shel Silverstein.

ASSESS THE LEARNING

> At the end of guided reading experiences, spend 30 seconds playing with rhymes to assess who can and can't identify the rhyme.

> During independent reading, confer with individuals and ask them to provide rhymes to words you designate.

> Have children read several poems and identify those with rhymes and those without.

INFUSION OF FORMAL LANGUAGE
Test-style language

Which of the following pairs of words rhyme?

A. Pan/Pat
B. Run/Ran
C. Fat/Cat
D. Me/Met

Which of the following words rhymes with *spot?*

A. Spoil
B. Spit
C. Hot
D. Pond

Jack and Jill went up the hill

To fetch a pail of water.

Jack fell down and broke his crown

And Jill came tumbling after.

Humpty Dumpty sat on a wall.

Humpty Dumpty had a great fall.

All the king's horses and all the king's men.

Couldn't put Humpty Dumpty together again.

"Ladybug"

By Linda Hoyt

Ladybug, ladybug

Hungry for a treat

Then she finds an aphid

That's what she likes to eat

Ladybug, ladybug

Looking at the sky

Opens up her shell then . . .

Spreads her wings to fly.

We're Going on a Bear Hunt

By Michael Rosen

FOCUS THE LEARNING

Introduction: Have you ever listened to a faucet drip or to big, slow drops of rain coming down? Do you remember the sound? I am going to write "Drip, Drop, Drip, Drop" on this large piece of paper so we can say these yummy words together. I can think of more words that sound like rain dropping. "Plip, Plop, Plip, Plop." Do you notice how the words sound just like water dripping when we say them slowly? Let's add those to our chart, too. *We're Going on a Bear Hunt* by Michael Rosen is filled with wonderful words that make interesting sounds. When they go through water, they say, "Splash, splosh!" Going through gooey mud, they are going to say, "Squelch squerch!" Can't you just visualize what is happening!

 Think together about wind blowing. What words and sounds could we use to sound like blowing wind? As you think of ideas, I will write them down.

INTERACTIVE READ-ALOUD
Model and Guide Practice

READ TO THE POINT WHERE THE TEXT SAYS "SWISHY SWASHY." I am thinking about walking through tall grass and how the grass bends and waves and sticks to me as I walk through. Swishy swashy, swishy swashy…That is just how it sounds. Let's say those great words together and make it sound like we're pushing our way through tall grass.

READ TO THE PLACE WHERE THEY ARE WADING THROUGH WATER. Let's think about water and what it sounds like when it splashes.

 Think together…Have you ever splashed in a bathtub or a swimming pool? What did it sound like? Practice saying "Splash splosh, Splash splosh" so it sounds like water splashing.

READ TO THE PAGE WHERE THEY ARE IN THE MUD. Let's pretend our feet are in ooey, gooey mud and pull each one out slowly. As you pull your foot out and step down, we can say, "Squelch squerch, squelch squerch."

CONTINUE TO THE END OF THE STORY. Pause occasionally to give partners time to talk about the wonderful words that help us understand the sounds being made. You may want to have the children develop hand motions for each sound pairing as well.

END OF STORY REFLECTION

That was so much fun! I loved all of those terrific words and the sounds they made. Let's think about sound words we can add to our chart. Then we can read our chart like a poem! These wonderful words have what is called *onomatopoeia*. That means that we are using words to imitate natural sounds.

 Think together. I am going to say more wonderful words. Your job is to think together. What might make these sounds? And, are there any of these sounds we should add to our chart?

Thumpety thump	Swoosh
Ding Dong	Boom
ZZZZZ	Bang
Zoom	Clip Clop, Clip Clop
	Splat

SHARE THE LEARNING

Focus on Onomatopoeia

Tip for Share the Reading

Read the ono-matopoeia poem fluently with expression at least twice. As you read, ask the children to visualize a little chick trying to get out of the shell. What do they think is happening on each line? How do the ono-matopoeia words help them to know? Ask the students to join you in a shared reading that might include unison reading, trading every other line, dramatizing, and so on.

Peck, Peck

Crunch, Crunch

Peep!

Peck, Peck

Crunch, Crunch

Peep! Peep! Peep!

Tip for Readers Theater Script

For emergent readers, enjoy "Frogs" as an echo poem: teacher reads and children echo. Then have them dramatize and really focus on making their voices imitate the real animal. For developing readers, you might want to enjoy the script as a two-team experience. Team One reads line 1 and Team Two reads line 2 ensuring they pause to give the other team a chance to read their line. With increased proficiency, partners can read the poem together for fluency and expression.

"Frogs"
By Linda Hoyt

Team One:	Big frogs
Team Two:	Little frogs
Team One:	Leaping frogs
Team Two:	Sleeping frogs
Team One:	Croak! Croak!
Team Two:	Peep!
Team One:	Gr-r-ump!
Team Two:	Ribbit . . .
Together:	Splash!

EXTEND THE LEARNING

☆ Read *It Could Always Be Worse* by Margot Zemach, and insert onomatopoeia words to go with each animal and situation.

☆ Read *Rosie's Walk* by Pat Hutchins and insert onomatopoeia words for each problem the fox encounters.

☆ Insert onomatopoeia words in the leads of children's writing. Start pieces with great words like, "Zap," "Crunch," "Zing," "Zoom," "Snap," "Pop" to liven up their writing pieces.

☆ Look for poetry with onomatopoeia. Example: "Choo Choo Choo. The train runs up the track. Choo Choo Choo. The train comes running back." Talk to the children about the sound. What makes the choo sound? What sound might the wheels make?

☆ Look for onomatopoeia in *How the Grinch Stole Christmas* by Dr. Seuss, *Umbrella* by Taro Yashima, and *Sky Dogs* by Jane Yolen.

ASSESS THE LEARNING

> Assess writing samples to monitor the children's ability to insert onomatopoeia words into their writing.

> Confer with children to see if they can identify onomatopoeia in a text.

> During guided reading, ask students to think of onomatopoeia words they could add to better explain the sounds that relate to the story.

INFUSION OF FORMAL LANGUAGE

Test-style language

Onomatopoeia means:

A. Acting silly

B. Acting things out

C. Words that imitate real sounds

D. Writing big words

Which of the following use *onomatooeia*?

A. Rat-a-tat-tat

B. Hissss

C. Baaa

D. All of the above.

Peck, Peck

Crunch, Crunch

Peep!

Peck, Peck

Crunch, Crunch

Peep! Peep! Peep!

"Frogs"

By Linda Hoyt

Team One: Big frogs

Team Two: Little frogs

Team One: Leaping frogs

Team Two: Sleeping frogs

Team One: Croak!   Croak!

Team Two: Peep!

Team One: Gr-r-ump!

Team Two: Ribbit . . .

Together: Splash!

The Snowy Day
By Ezra Jack Keats

FOCUS THE LEARNING

Authors help us know what is happening by using words that tell us *when* things are happening. These words help us figure out the order of events in a story. Here is an example: "First, I asked you to come to the rug. Then you pushed in your chairs and walked nicely. After that you sat on the carpet and turned to face me. Now you are listening very carefully so you will be ready to read. Soon I am going to open this book and begin." Did you notice the words I was using?

Partners, think together. What did you notice about the words I was using? Which words helped you think about the order in which things happened?

Today as we read *The Snowy Day* by Ezra Jack Keats we are going to be listening for special words that are called *transition* words.

INTERACTIVE READ-ALOUD
Model and Guide Practice

READ TO THE PLACE WHERE HE GOES OUTSIDE. Let's think about the transition words we have heard. I noticed "One winter morning." I also noticed "After breakfast." These helped me know when. It is one morning in winter, after breakfast. I am going to write "one winter morning" and "after" on our chart of transition words.

READ TO THE POINT WHERE HE IS DRAGGING HIS FEET SLOWLY. Here is another transition word. It says, "Then, he dragged his feet." Because of the word "then," I know this happened next. I am going to add "then" to our chart.

READ TO THE PLACE WHERE HE MAKES A SNOWMAN. I am going to read this page again. I want to think about "so" and if this is a transition word. I think it is! It helps me know that after he couldn't play with the big boys, he found something he could do. So he made a snowman.

Talk to your thinking partner. Think together. Can you use some of the transition words on our list and retell what has happened so far?

CONTINUE TO THE END OF THE STORY. Pause occasionally to give partners time to talk about transition words. Be sure to notice "then," "while," "before," "but when," and "after."

END OF STORY REFLECTION

Display signs that say "First," "Next," "Then," and "Finally." Model a retell of story time using the cards. "First, we came to the rug. Next, we sat down. Then…" Have partners practice doing a retell of *The Snowy Day* using the transition words on the signs. Invite group members to come forward to hold the cards and retell the story using transition words.

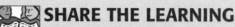

SHARE THE LEARNING
Focus on Transition Words

Tip for Share the Reading

Read the passage to the children emphasizing the transition words. Invite them to dramatize the action as you hold up cards showing the transition words. With repeated readings, invite the children to join in chorally.

One winter morning Peter woke up and saw snow. It was everywhere. **Then** he put on his snowsuit and went outside. **Next** he made footprints in the snow. **Soon** he made a snowman and a snow angel. **After that** he went inside and got ready for bed. **When** he woke up the next day, it had snowed and he got to go outside again!

Tip for Readers Theater Script

For emergent readers, have them use the puppets to support a retell. Encourage them to use transition words such as *first, next, then,* and *finally.* For developing readers, read the Play Dough recipe to them, holding up objects and ingredients as you name them. Use transition words as you demonstrate the steps in the recipe. Have a student dramatize the steps as you read the steps a second time. As soon as students are ready, have them follow along chorally as you read the recipe. Have partners work together to create the play dough. Children might also enjoy taking the recipe home to make with their parents.

Making Play Dough
By Linda Hoyt

First, you need to get:
Flour
Salt
Oil
Food coloring
A mixing bowl

Then, you need to get:
Measuring spoons
Measuring cups
A big spoon

Because you have everything, you are ready to mix the dough.

First, pour ⅓ cup water

Then, add 1 cup of salt

Now, you need 1 cup of flour

Next, add 1 teaspoon of oil plus ⅓ teaspoon of oil

Finally, add a bit of food coloring and mix well.

Because all of this is done, you can have fun!

EXTEND THE LEARNING

☆ Post a chart of transition words in a visible place and encourage children to listen for them in Read-Aloud, notice them in their own books, and to use them in their writing. (Example: *before, after, now, first, then, finally, next, after, but, soon, once, now, right before, whenever, one day, so, suddenly, because, one day*)

☆ Look for transition words in books about life cycles.

☆ Read *The Carrot Seed* by Ruth Kraus, and insert transition words on sticky notes.

☆ Look at procedural ("how to") books and recipes, and look for transition words.

☆ Interactively create a set of directions using transition words.

☆ Read then follow the directions in a recipe noticing the transition words and numbers.

☆ Have writers deliberately include transition words in their personal narratives.

ASSESS THE LEARNING

> Have children create illustrations in spaces labeled, *first, next, then, finally.* Assess their ability to correctly present a sequence from a book or real-life event.

> During small group instruction, assess children's ability to point out transition words in print.

INFUSION OF FORMAL LANGUAGE
Test-style language

In this story, the *first* thing that happened was:
   A. Peter woke up.
   B. He played in the snow.
   C. He put on his snowsuit.
   D. He made a snowman.

The *last* thing that happened was:
   A. He went to bed.
   B. It snowed.
   C. He went to play in the snow with his friend.
   D. He had a dream.

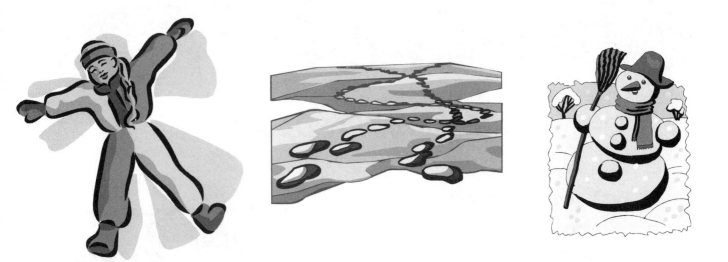

One winter morning Peter woke up and saw snow. It was everywhere. **Then** he put on his snowsuit and went outside. **Next** he made footprints in the snow. **Soon** he made a snowman and a snow angel. **After that** he went inside and got ready for bed. **When** he woke up the next day, it had snowed and he got to go outside again!

Making Play Dough

By Linda Hoyt

First, you need to get:
    Flour
    Salt
    Oil
    Food coloring
    A mixing bowl

Then, you need to get:
    Measuring spoons
    Measuring cups
    A big spoon

Because you have everything, you are ready to mix the dough.

First, pour ½ cup water

Then, add ½ cup of salt

Now, you need 1 cup of flour

Next, add 1 teaspoon of oil plus ½ teaspoon of oil

Finally, add a bit of food coloring and mix well.

Because all of this is done, you can have fun!

Literary Elements and Devices

Literary elements and devices, such as point of view, foreshadowing, repetition, and exaggeration, get at the heart of the way an author structures a text to effectively tell a story. Standards in this strand involve readers in more complex story structures and more sophisticated language devices such as simile/metaphor and allusion.

Click, Clack, Moo: Cows That Type
By Doreen Cronin

FOCUS THE LEARNING

I am going to tell part of a story you might know. Can you figure it out? "I was tired, so I tried three beds. One was too hard, one was too soft, and one was just right! Some bears live in this house and they might be home soon."

 Talk to your thinking partner. What is the story, and who is telling it?

That's right—it's *Goldilocks and the Three Bears!* Did you notice that the way I told it was like having Goldilocks tell the story? I told it from her point of view. Point of view describes *who* is telling a story. Usually, Goldilocks doesn't tell the story! We just heard the story from a different point of view. We are going to read *Click, Clack, Moo: Cows That Type* by Doreen Cronin and think together about point of view.

INTERACTIVE READ-ALOUD
Model and Guide Practice

LOOK AT THE COVER. I love the title! *Click, Clack, Moo* sounds funny. Look at the cow—I wonder what the cow is typing. Maybe the story tells the cow's point of view.

 Talk to your thinking partner. If the story were from the cow's point of view, what do you think the cow would say?

READ TO THE PLACE WHERE FARMER BROWN SEES THE FIRST NOTE FROM THE COWS. Farmer Brown sees a note. Who wrote the note? That will tell you the point of view!

How can you tell who wrote the note? What do the cows want?

READ TO WHERE FARMER BROWN CRIES, "NO MILK TODAY!" I think the point of view changed.

Talk to your thinking partner. What does this story look like when we are reading the cows' point of view? How did the point of view change here?

READ TO THE PLACE WHERE FARMER BROWN TYPES. I never thought about how cows must feel in a cold barn! Here's another note. Most of the notes are from the cows' point of view.

Who typed this note? How did the point of view change here?

READ TO THE END. Now the story could be called "Click, clack, quack!" Let's think about the point of view at the end of the story.

Thinking partners, talk about the end of the story. Who typed this note? How did the point of view change this time?

END OF STORY REFLECTION

I was surprised that the ducks typed a note! I wonder what Farmer Brown will do next.

What were the different points of view in this story? How could you tell when the point of view changed? What did the author do to help you figure it out?

I am going to talk about the point of view of this note. (Turn to the note that Farmer Brown typed.) This note is from Farmer Brown's point of view.

Think together. How do you know this note tells Farmer Brown's point of view? How did Farmer Brown feel when he typed this note? What if the story didn't have these typed notes? How would it be different?

SHARE THE LEARNING
Talk About Point of View

Tip for Share the Reading

Read *No Eggs* aloud to model fluency. Then ask the children to join in as you read it a second time. Ask children to identify the point of view of the story. What clues help them figure out who is telling the story?

No Eggs

We were cold in our barn. The cows found an old typewriter and started writing notes to Farmer Brown. They asked for blankets. The cows would not give milk until we got blankets. We would not lay eggs until Farmer Brown got us blankets.

Tip for Readers Theater Script

Read the "Five O'Clock News" script. Emergent readers can read the "All: Click, Clack, Moo!" noticing how the moo shifts from very quiet to louder as the script progresses. Developing readers can read the parts of the news anchor, cows, hens, and the duck. Hold up a sign to signal when each part begins. Ask children to talk about point of view.

"Five O'Clock News"
by Lynnette Brent and Linda Hoyt

Newsman:	We have breaking news at the farm of Farmer Brown.
All:	Click, clack, **moo!**
Cows:	We were cold in the barn.
All:	Click, clack, **moo!**
Hens:	We were cold, too.
All:	Click, clack, **moo!**
Newsman:	Farmer Brown has cows that are typing notes.
All:	Click, clack, **moo!**
Cows and hens:	We asked for blankets.
All:	Click, clack, **moo!**
Newsman:	And Farmer Brown doesn't like it.

EXTEND THE LEARNING

☆ Work with the students to tell the story from Farmer Brown's point of view.

☆ Pairs of children can work together to retell a familiar story from a different point of view. How would *Jack and the Beanstalk* be different if the giant told the story?

☆ Read *Diary of a Worm* by Doreen Cronin (Joanne Cotler, 2003). Ask: What do we learn about worms by reading this point of view? How is this story different from other books about animals?

☆ Read *Giggle, Giggle, Quack* (Simon & Shuster, 2002), the sequel to *Click, Clack, Moo*. Children will enjoy finding out what happens when Farmer Brown goes on vacation.

☆ Read a variety of fairy tales and folktales. Then dramatize and retell them from different points of view.

ASSESS THE LEARNING

> Listen in as children talk about point of view with learning partners. Assess children's ability to find clues to figure out the point of view.

> Ask children to identify the points of view of other texts that they have read in class.

> Ask children to choose a piece of text that they have written and discuss that piece's point of view.

INFUSION OF FORMAL LANGUAGE
Test-style language

The *point of view* of a story describes
  A. the most important part of the story.
  B. who is telling the story.
  C. what happens in the story.
  D. where the story takes place.

This story is told mostly from the *point of view* of:
  A. the ducks.
  B. the hens.
  C. the cows.
  D. Farmer Brown.

No Eggs

We were cold in our barn. The cows found an old typewriter and started writing notes to Farmer Brown. They asked for blankets. The cows would not give milk until we got blankets. We would not lay eggs until Farmer Brown got us blankets.

"Five O'Clock News"

By Lynnette Brent and Linda Hoyt

Newsman: We have breaking news at the farm of Farmer Brown.

All: Click, clack, **moo**!

Cows: We were cold in the barn.

All: Click, clack, **moo**!

Hens: We were cold, too.

All: Click, clack, **moo**!

Newsman: Farmer Brown has cows that are typing notes.

All: Click, clack, **moo!**

Cows and hens: We asked for blankets.

All: Click, clack, **moo!**

Newsman: And Farmer Brown doesn't like it.

All:	Click, clack, **moo!**
Newsman:	Farmer Brown wants the animals to stop typing and act like animals.
All:	Click, clack, **moo**!
Duck:	I traded the typewriter for blankets.
All:	Click, clack, **moo!**
Newsman:	The cows and hens were happy.
All:	Click, clack, **moo!**
Newsman:	Now, the ducks want a diving board.
	What should Farmer Brown do?
All:	Click, clack, **quack!**

Rosie's Walk
By Pat Hutchins

FOCUS THE LEARNING

Imagine going to visit your grandmother. You open the door, and you can smell something baking—a sweet chocolaty smell. You can't see any ingredients, but you can smell chocolate chip cookies. It's a hint you are going to have a yummy snack later. Authors do the same thing sometimes. They don't give you cookies, but they give a hint about something that is going to happen. When an author gives you a hint about what will happen later, that's called *foreshadowing*. If you see dark clouds, what do you think might happen later? That's right—there might be rain! The clouds *foreshadow* the rain.

INTERACTIVE READ-ALOUD
Model and Guide Practice

LOOK AT THE COVER. I see two animals on the cover—the chicken and the fox. We know foxes and chickens are usually friends. I think foxes eat chickens! I wonder if the chicken knows a fox is watching her.

READ THE ENTIRE BOOK TO CHILDREN, STOPPING TO SAVOR THE PICTURES. Then return to the beginning of the book to discuss foreshadowing. The fox tried to catch Rosie. Thank goodness, he never did! Lots of funny things happened to the fox. Let's look at the pages again and think about hints the author gives us about what will happen. We are looking for foreshadowing.

Let's look at the page with the words "across the yard."

🐿🐓 *Thinking partners, what do you see in the picture that foreshadows what happens to the fox next?*

Let's look at the page with the words "past the mill." Look carefully at the illustration.

🐿🐓 *Talk with your partner about foreshadowing on these pages. You might remember what happened to the fox. What details on these pages hint at what will happen?*

Discuss the clues that children point out. Encourage them to use the term foreshadowing as they discuss hints the author provided.

END OF STORY REFLECTION

Work with children to create a chart with two columns: "Foreshadowing"/"What Happens." Children can help you complete the chart about foreshadowing and events in *Rosie's Walk*.

Foreshadowing	What Happens
A rake is on the ground.	The fox steps on the rake, and it hits him in the head.

SHARE THE LEARNING
Focus on Foreshadowing

Tip for Share the Reading

Guide the children in looking through the pages again. Their goal is to warn the fox (foreshadow the action) using the stems provided. As they look at the pictures, have the children decide what to say to the fox to warn him what is coming. Example: "Look out, fox! There's a (wet pond, haystack you'll sink in, flour bag over your head, wagon with wheels, angry bees)." After the children create their warnings for the fox, engage them in sharing the reading of the warnings.

> Look out, Fox!
>
> Look out, Fox! There's a _____
>
> Look out, Fox! Don't step on _____
>
> Look out, Fox! You are going to _____
>
> Look out, Fox! Here come the _____
>
> Look out, Fox! _____

Tip for Readers Theater Script

Have the children place Rosie and the Fox on popsicle sticks so they can use them like puppets. As you read "Rosie's Walk" aloud, have the children use their puppets to dramatize the prepositions that are featured in the script. As they become familiar with the script, have them join in on the lines, "Where does Rosie walk?" Developing readers can read the parts to focus on fluency and dramatic interpretation. Children will enjoy acting out the way that Rosie walks and considering where else chickens might walk.

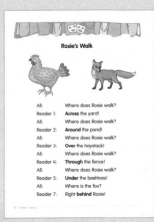

Rosie's Walk

All:	Where does Rosie walk?
Reader 1:	**Across** the yard!
All:	Where does Rosie walk?
Reader 2:	**Around** the pond!
All:	Where does Rosie walk?
Reader 3:	**Over** the haystack!
All:	Where does Rosie walk?
Reader 4:	**Through** the fence!
All:	Where does Rosie walk?
Reader 5:	**Under** the beehives!
All:	Where is the fox?
Reader 7:	*Right* **behind** Rosie!

EXTEND THE LEARNING

☆ Share with children other books that include foreshadowing. You might read *The Little House* or *Mike Mulligan and the Steam Shovel*, both by Virginia Lee Burton. What hints does the author give about what might happen next?

☆ Share a nonfiction text with children and ask them how they might use sticky notes to add foreshadowing. Using a nonfiction text about a chicken egg, for example, you could add foreshadowing focused on the egg. (Example: The baby chick might feel a bit crowded as he grows, but he will be coming out soon.)

☆ Have the children create illustrations that foreshadow events in *Rosie's Walk*.

☆ Create a chart such as the one in the "End of Story Reflection" for a Booklinks book.

ASSESS THE LEARNING

> Listen in as children discuss foreshadowing with their learning partners. Children should be able to link the foreshadowing hint with the outcome.

> Assess children's contributions to the foreshadowing chart.

> Assess illustrations created to show foreshadowing to check for understanding.

INFUSION OF FORMAL LANGUAGE
Test-style language

Foreshadowing gives the reader

  A. a hint of what will happen next.

  B. clues about something that already happened.

  C. a clear picture of where the story takes place.

  D. information about what a character in the story is like.

In *Rosie's Walk*, the author uses foreshadowing when

  A. a goat stands in the field.

  B. two frogs sit on rocks near a pond.

  C. a rake is on the ground where the fox will step.

  D. Rosie walks into her coop at the end of her walk.

Look out, Fox!

Look out, Fox! There's a _____.

Look out, Fox! Don't step on _____.

Look out, Fox! You are going to _____.

Look out, Fox! Here come the _____.

Look out, Fox! _____.

Rosie's Walk

All:	Where does Rosie walk?
Reader 1:	**Across** the yard!
All:	Where does Rosie walk?
Reader 2:	**Around** the pond!
All:	Where does Rosie walk?
Reader 3:	**Over** the haystack!
All:	Where does Rosie walk?
Reader 4:	**Through** the fence!
All:	Where does Rosie walk?
Reader 5:	**Under** the beehives!
All:	Where is the fox?
Reader 7:	Right **behind** Rosie!

A Chair for My Mother
By Vera B. Williams

FOCUS THE LEARNING

Introduction: Authors, like Vera B. Williams, sometimes use a strategy called *flashback* to help us understand why characters do things or why something is very important in a story. Flashback means that the author pauses in the middle of a story to explain something that happened before the story started. Let's listen to *A Chair for My Mother* again and try to find the flashback.

INTERACTIVE READ-ALOUD
Model and Guide Practice

READ PAGE 1. Then pause to think aloud. I am thinking about flashback. I don't think this is a flashback because it is telling what is happening now. The little girl is at the diner helping.

READ PAGES 2–3. I am going to stop reading for a minute. I don't think this is flashback either. We are still learning about putting coins in the jar.

READ PAGE 4.

 I think this might be it. Turn to your thinking partner. Do you think this could be the beginning of the flashback? Why?

READ PAGE 5.

This is it! I can tell this is the flashback because it sounds like the beginning of a whole new story and we are in the middle of the book! This is like getting two stories in one.

READ PAGES 6–7.

 Share with your partner what you learned so far in the flashback.

READ THE PAGE NEXT TO THE PICTURE OF THE JAR FULL OF COINS. I think the flashback is over and we are back to the story about saving money in the jar. The first line says, "That was last year." That tells me that the flashback is over. I am going to finish the story and think how the flashback helped me understand this story better.

END OF STORY REFLECTION

 Turn and talk to your partner.

What did you learn in the flashback? How did the flashback help you understand this story? Would the story have been as good without the flashback?

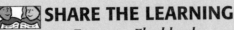

SHARE THE LEARNING
Focus on Flashback

Tip for Share the Reading

🖍️ Explain to the students that you are going to share another story that includes a flashback. Place the text on the overhead so the students can read along and visually identify the flashback. Reread for fluency practice by dividing into three oral reading teams: Anya, the friend, and narrator.

> Anya and her friend were planting flowers in her garden, pushing the tiny seeds into the soil and watering carefully so the flowers would be sure to grow. As they worked, Anya began to tell a story.
>
> "When I was a little girl, I spent wonderful times with my grandmother in her garden. She loved flowers and took great joy in caring for them. I remember how the sun would shine in and the soil would feel warm on my fingers and how the scent of the blooms was like a sweet perfume in the air. Oh, how I loved picking flowers with grandma.
>
> Her friend smiled and said, "Is that why you are working so hard to create a beautiful garden of your own?"
>
> Anya replied, "I know my grandma would be proud of me for planting this garden."

Tip for Readers Theater Script

📖 There are two scripts to enjoy with "A Chair for My Mother." One of the scripts reflects the flashback from the story. The other script reflects the story line without the script. For emergent readers, you might read the two scripts and guide them in a conversation about the differences they notice, encouraging them to act out portions of the script that they find to be especially meaningful as they consider the role of the flashback in the story. Emergent learners might also create illustrations to support the readers theater scripts. For developing readers, you might have teams rehearse and then present each of the scripts practicing reading with fluency and expression.

A Chair for My Mother (with flashback)
Readers Theater adaptation by Linda Hoel

Narrator 1:	My mother works as a waitress
Narrator 2:	at a diner.
Narrator 3:	Sometimes I get to work there too.
Narrator 4:	I earn money for filling catsup and peeling onions.
Narrator 2:	At the end of the day,
Narrator 3:	I put half my money into a big jar.
Narrator 1:	My mom puts in the change from her tips.
Narrator 4:	Sometimes we have a lot of change.
Narrator 2:	Sometimes there isn't much at all.
Narrator 3:	When the jar is full,
Narrator 1:	We are going to buy a beautiful soft chair.
Narrator 4:	We don't have any soft furniture because
Narrator 2:	Last year all of our furniture burned up in a fire.

EXTEND THE LEARNING

☆ Demonstrate an oral retell of a familiar event from school and insert a flashback into the middle.

☆ Model a piece of writing in which a flashback is placed in a speech bubble in the illustration.

☆ Model writing a personal narrative and place a flashback in the middle to show children how you plan a main story and use the flashback to explain something more fully.

☆ Have the children look through their independent reading books for examples of flashback and give them a chance to share with partners.

ASSESS THE LEARNING

➤ Listen to partners do retells of favored memories, and consider how these stories might be woven into personal narratives as flashbacks.

➤ Confer with readers during independent reading to see if they understand and recognize flashbacks.

Anya and her friend were planting flowers in her garden, pushing the tiny seeds into the soil and watering carefully so the flowers would be sure to grow. As they worked, Anya began to tell a story.

"When I was a little girl, I spent wonderful times with my grand-mother in her garden. She loved flowers and took great joy in caring for them. I remember how the sun would shine in and the soil would feel warm on my fingers and how the scent of the blooms was like a sweet perfume in the air. Oh, how I loved picking flowers with grandma.

Her friend smiled and said, "Is that why you are working so hard to create a beautiful garden of your own?"

Anya replied, "I know my grandma would be proud of me for planting this garden."

A Chair for My Mother (with flashback)

Readers Theater adaptation by Linda Hoyt

Narrator 1:   My mother works as a waitress

Narrator 2:   at a diner.

Narrator 3:   Sometimes I get to work there too.

Narrator 4:   I earn money for filling catsup and peeling onions.

Narrator 2:   At the end of the day,

Narrator 3:   I put half my money into a big jar.

Narrator 1:   My mom puts in the change from her tips.

Narrator 4:   Sometimes we have a lot of change.

Narrator 2:   Sometimes there isn't much at all.

Narrator 3:   When the jar is full,

Narrator 1:   We are going to buy a beautiful soft chair.

Narrator 4:   We don't have any soft furniture because

Narrator 2:   Last year all of our furniture burned up in a fire.

Narrator 3:	We are lucky that grandma and our cat got out in time.
Narrator 1:	But now we live in a really empty apartment.
Narrator 4:	Our neighbors and friends brought us what they could.
Narrator 2:	We know we are really lucky.
Narrator 3:	That was last year.
Narrator 1:	Finally, our jar of coins is full.
Narrator 4:	We have enough money to buy a chair.
Narrator 2:	Grandma felt like Goldilocks
Narrator 3:	when we went shopping and tried lots and lots of chairs.
Narrator 4:	Finally we found the chair we were dreaming of.
Everyone:	Grandma and mother and I all love to sit in it.

A Chair for My Mother (without flashback)

Readers Theater adaptation by Linda Hoyt

Narrator 1: My mother works as a waitress

Narrator 2: at a diner.

Narrator 3: Sometimes I get to work there too.

Narrator 4: I earn money for filling catsup and peeling onions.

Narrator 2: At the end of the day,

Narrator 3: I put half my money into a big jar.

Narrator 1: My mom puts in the change from her tips.

Narrator 4: Sometimes we have a lot of change.

Narrator 2: Sometimes there isn't much at all.

Narrator 3: When the jar is full,

Narrator 1: We are going to buy a beautiful soft chair.

Narrator 1: Finally, our jar of coins is full.

Narrator 4: We have enough money to buy a chair.

Narrator 2: Grandma felt like Goldilocks

Narrator 3: when we went shopping and tried lots and lots of chairs.

Narrator 4: Finally we found the chair we were dreaming of.

Everyone: Grandma and mother and I all love to sit in it.

Quick as a Cricket
By Audrey Wood

FOCUS THE LEARNING

It is fun to compare things. In *Quick as a Cricket*, Audrey Wood uses similes to compare lots of different things. Let's practice to get ready for our book. We could say (name a child)_____'s hair is as dark as midnight. _____'s hair is as bright as sunshine. _____'s eyes are as blue as the sky. _____'s eyes are as dark as chocolate pudding. (name an animal) _____ is as speedy as a racecar.

Think together. I want to say, "_____ is as gentle as a lamb." Partners, whose name should I use? Who is really gentle?

INTERACTIVE READ-ALOUD
Model and Guide Practice

READ THE FIRST PAGE ABOUT THE CRICKET. Did you notice the simile? I'm as quick as a cricket. Could we say someone is as quick as a rocket? As quick as a fire truck?

Think together. If you wanted to say someone is quick. What could you say?

READ TO THE POINT WHERE IT SAYS "SLOW AS A SNAIL." Let's think about similes. What else is really slow? How about, "Slow as catsup coming out of a new bottle." "Slow as a turtle." Let's turn our ideas into a simile. Have you ever watched a worm crawl? We could say a worm is as slow as . . .

Think together. How could we finish that?

Let's think of things that are fast. A fly is as fast as a _____.

CONTINUE TO THE END OF THE STORY. Pause occasionally to give partners time to talk about similes and to create their own in response to the book.

END OF STORY REFLECTION

We have used so many similes! Let's write some of them down. We decided that a fly is as fast as _____. Brian rides his bike as fast as a _____. Help me think—I want to write our similes down so we can remember them.

SHARE THE LEARNING
Focus on Simile and Metaphor

Tip for Share the Reading

Read each line to the children and have them dramatize the meaning of each line. As they are ready, invite them to read along and share the reading.

I'm as small as an ant.

I'm as strong as an ox.

I'm as quiet as a mouse.

I'm as loud as a lion.

I'm as wiggly as a worm.

I'm perfect just like I am.

Tip for Readers Theater Script

Read "Me" to the children as they follow along with the pictures. Provide repeated experiences with the similes in the script having children read in unison and in partners to support fluency and expression.

"Me"
By Linda Hoyt

I'm as sad as a baby.

I'm as fast as a racer.

I'm as brave as a firefighter.

I'm as bright as the fireworks up in the sky.

EXTEND THE LEARNING

☆ Have the children create illustrations for the similes they created while interacting with *Quick as a Cricket*.

☆ Use similes throughout the classroom day. "You need to be quick as a cricket while you wash your hands for lunch!" "Let's be quiet as mice while we walk down the hall."

☆ Model a piece of writing using a simile in the writing.

☆ During interactive writing, help the children generate and write similes.

☆ Create similes for favorite characters in stories. "Goldilocks was as scared as a mouse when she ran out the door after the bears came home." "Cinderella was as fast as a deer when she ran out of the ball at midnight."

ASSESS THE LEARNING

> Assess children's illustrations for understanding of simile.

> After a Read-Aloud, help the children create similes about characters and setting. Assess their ability to show relationships and make comparisons through similes.

INFUSION OF FORMAL LANGUAGE
Test-style language

Finish the *simile*: A worm is as slow as a _____.

  A. bird

  B. dog

  C. snail

  D. deer

Which of the following is a *simile*?

  A. You are fast.

  B. You are really fast.

  C. You run really fast.

  D. You're as fast as a cheetah!

I'm as small as an ant.

I'm as strong as an ox.

I'm as quiet as a mouse.

I'm as loud as a lion.

I'm as wiggly as a worm.

I'm perfect just like I am.

"Me"
By Linda Hoyt

I'm as sad as a baby.

I'm as fast as a racer.

I'm as brave as a firefighter.

I'm as bright as the fireworks up in the sky.

Goodnight Moon

By Margaret Wise Brown

FOCUS THE LEARNING

(Tip: The children will need to be familiar with the stories for *Cinderella, The Three Bears, The Three Little Pigs* plus the nursery rhymes "Hey, Diddle Diddle" and the "Three Little Kittens.")

"When I was scrubbing floors, making beds, and cooking, I felt like Cinderella!" Remember how in the story Cinderella's sisters and her stepmother made her do a lot of work? When I said I felt like Cinderella, you could probably tell that I had a lot to do. I made an allusion. An *allusion* in a story is a hint of another story. Allusions help us to make connections between stories that we already know and the one we are reading.

INTERACTIVE READ-ALOUD
Model and Guide Practice

LOOK AT THE COVER. This looks like a warm, cozy room! Someone must be going to bed and saying "goodnight" to the moon. I see a picture on the wall over the fireplace.

 Talk to your thinking partner. What do you see in the picture? Can you figure out the allusion?

READ UP TO THE THREE LITTLE BEARS SITTING ON CHAIRS. Look at this picture. There's another allusion here to a story that most of you know. What story do you know that has three bears? When you figure that out, you'll know the author's allusion!

 Thinking partners, talk about the bears in the picture. What story do you know that has three bears like this?

READ UP TO THE PAGES THAT SAY "GOOD NIGHT KITTENS" AND "GOOD NIGHT MITTENS." Listen to this rhyme: "Three little kittens, They lost their mittens, And they began to cry."

 Thinking partners, what is the allusion in this part of the story?

READ TO THE END. The little bunny in the bed says "Good night" to a lot of different things, even to the pictures in the room! I like to say "good night" before I go to bed, too.

 Thinking partners, talk about the different things that the bunny says "good night" to.

END OF STORY REFLECTION

In this story, there are many allusions. There are parts of "Hey, Diddle, Diddle," "Goldilocks and the Three Bears," and "Three Little Kittens."

 Think together. Which allusion was your favorite?

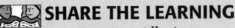

SHARE THE LEARNING
Focus on Allusion

Tip for Share the Reading

Use a piece of paper to cover the transparency so only one line shows at a time. Read each line to the children and ask partners to talk together about the allusion in each line. Celebrate each line with a quick retell of the story or rhyme that is alluded to or by reciting the nursery rhyme.

1. My bed is so messy it looks like Goldilocks was here!

2. That cow is jumping around so much it looks like it could jump over the moon.

3. Look at that house of bricks. It looks strong enough to keep out a big, bad wolf.

4. I lost my mitten. I feel like one of the little kittens!

Tip for Readers Theater Script

Children will enjoy a choral reading of a nursery rhyme they talked about while reading *Goodnight Moon.* You might read the narrator lines and ask emergent readers to read the lines marked "*Kittens.*" Create a sign that says "Kitten" to remind children when it is their turn to read. Developing readers can read the narrator lines. Discuss with children how these lines should be read—nursery rhymes should be read with excitement and fun!

"Hey Diddle Diddle"
Readers Theater script by Linda Hoyt

Hey diddle diddle,

The cat and the fiddle,

The cow jumped over the moon,

The little dog laughed to see such sport,

And the dish ran away with the spoon.

EXTEND THE LEARNING

☆ Work with children to create a list of rhymes and stories that most of them know well. Children can select from the list to create another picture that might be on the bunny's wall in *Goodnight Moon.*

☆ Read another story to children that has allusions to other stories. In David Weisner's *The Three Pigs,* for example, the three pigs "leave" the book to interact with characters from other stories. What allusions to other stories can children identify with?

☆ Read the *True Story of the Three Little Pigs* and find the allusions in it.

☆ Read *Sleeping Ugly* by Jane Yolen and invite the children to watch for allusions.

☆ Create a list of characters that children know well, and/or provide sentence stems for them to complete. (Examples: I was as scared as *Little Miss Muffet when she saw the spider.* When I couldn't find my hat, I felt like *Little Bo Peep looking for her sheep.*) Use the allusions in a natural way throughout the learning day.

☆ Read Janet Stevens' *And the Dish Ran Away with the Spoon* and search for allusions.

☆ Read *The Tortoise and the Hare* then *Tops and Bottoms* by Janet Stevens, and find the allusion in each.

ASSESS THE LEARNING

> As children discuss allusion with thinking partners, listen in to be sure that they can figure out which other stories are being referred to or hinted at.

> Assess children's understanding of allusion by assessing the illustration they create for the Bunny's room in *Goodnight Moon.*

INFUSION OF FORMAL LANGUAGE
Test-style language

An *allusion* is
  A. a character in a story.
  B. a hint of another story.
  C. a bad allergy.
  D. the person who wrote a story.

Goodnight Moon has allusions to:
  A. *Hansel and Gretel*
  B. *The Three Little Pigs*
  C. *Jack and the Beanstalk*
  D. *Goldilocks and the Three Bears*

---

1. My bed is so messy it looks like Goldilocks was here!

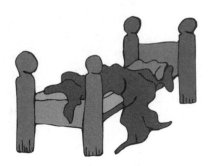

2. That cow is jumping around so much it looks like it could jump over the moon.

3. Look at that house of bricks. It looks strong enough to keep out a big, bad wolf.

4. I lost my mitten. I feel like one of the little kittens!

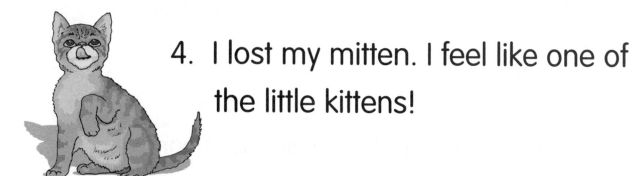

"Hey Diddle Diddle"

Readers Theater script by Linda Hoyt

Hey diddle diddle,

The cat and the fiddle,

The cow jumped over the moon,

The little dog laughed to see such sport,

And the dish ran away with the spoon.

Have You Seen My Duckling?
By Nancy Tafuri

INTERACTIVE READ-ALOUD
Model and Guide Practice

READ PAGE 1. Then pause to think aloud. As I look at the adjoining page with the butterfly, I can infer that the single duckling is headed after the butterfly. I can infer the duck-lings in the nest are pointed in the same direction because they are watching the baby ducks swim away. I notice the mother duck isn't in the picture. I can infer that if she was there, she would bring that baby duck back to the nest.

READ PAGES 2–5. There aren't any words on these pages. I need to look closely at the pictures and think about what is happening. Here comes Mother Duck. She is putting her head into the nest. I can infer that she is counting her ducklings. I can infer that the chicks are quacking at her. (Be sure the children notice the baby chick at the top of each page.)

 Turn to your thinking partner. What do you think is happening? Infer together, what might the chicks be saying?

READ PAGES 6–9. (Keep looking for the single duckling hidden in each picture.) "Have you seen my duckling?" That is such an important line. The Mother Duck must be really worried. If I was that mother, I would ask everyone I could find if they had seen my duckling. I can infer she wants to find her baby.

 You know what to do. Think together. What do you infer is happening?

READ TO PAGE 11. (Mother Duck talks to the turtle.) Did you notice the repetition? The sentence on this page is exactly the same as the previous page. Why do you think the author chose this line to repeat? Let's turn the page and see if we find the sentence again.

CONTINUE READING TO PAGE 17 (THE MULTICOLORED BIRD FAMILY). Stop on each two-page layout to emphasize the repetition of the sentence, infer what is happening, and look for the missing duckling.

 If you could talk to the mother duck, what would you say to her? What should she do?

TURN TO PAGES 18–19 THEN 20–21 TO SHOW THE TURTLE IN LINE WITH THE DUCKLINGS. What can you infer is happening here? Why is the turtle in line with the ducklings?

END OF STORY REFLECTION

Nancy Tafuri didn't use very many words in this book, and she repeated the same sentence several times. How were we able to know what was happening? How did the repeated sentences help our thinking?

 Turn and talk to your partner.

SHARE THE LEARNING
Focus on Repetitive Language

Tip for Share the Reading

Place the text on the overhead projector and read it aloud with expression. Guide a conversation focused on the repeated lines in this poem. Invite the children to read the poem with expression and dramatic action. For additional readings, you might perform this as an echo reading or start with a whisper and get a bit louder on each line.

"Rainy Day"
I do not like a rainy day.
The streets are wet and the sky is gray.

I do not like a rainy day.
Puddles form and get in my way.

I do not like a rainy day.
I want to go but Mom says, "Stay."

I do not like a rainy day.
I wish I could go out and play.

Tip for Readers Theater Script

If possible, bring in real balloons for the children to examine for size, color, and shape. For emergent readers, enjoy "Balloons" as an echo poem: teacher reads and children echo. The children then could create illustrations for each kind of balloon in the poem. For developing readers, you might want to enjoy the script as a two-team experience. Team one reads line one; then team two reads the next line. With increased proficiency, partners can read the poem together for fluency and expression. You may want to consider writing repetition poems as part of your interactive writing or writers workshop.

Balloons
A Repetition Poem by Linda Hoyt

Big balloons
Small balloons

Red balloons
Blue balloons

Yellow balloons
Green balloons

Floating, swirling, great balloons!

EXTEND THE LEARNING

☆ Read a variety of selections with repetition of language. Examples: *Rain Makes Applesauce* by Julian Scheer, *Brown Bear, Brown Bear What Do You See?* By Bill Martin, Jr., *Mrs. Wishy Washy* by Joy Cowley.

☆ Have the children create worldless books that are supported by a repetitive word, phrase, or sentence that appears on each page.

☆ Encourage students to use repetitive language in their writing to emphasize important ideas.

☆ Write list poems that use repetitive words. Example:

Rain

Dripping

Slicking

Turning dirt to mud

Rain

ASSESS THE LEARNING

➤ Analyze the wordless books with repetitive text to check for understanding.

➤ Have readers read *Mrs. Wishy Washy* or another book with repetitive language and identify the repetitive portions.

INFUSION OF FORMAL LANGUAGE
Test-style language

The story is *mostly about*
  A. animals.
  B. a pond.
  C. a missing duckling.
  D. counting ducks.

Repetition means
  A. the same words used several times.
  B. boring writing.
  C. the same characters.
  D. something is missing.

"Rainy Day"

I do not like a rainy day.

The streets are wet and the sky is gray.

I do not like a rainy day.

Puddles form and get in my way.

I do not like a rainy day.

I want to go but Mom says, "Stay."

I do not like a rainy day.

I wish I could go out and play.

Balloons

A Repetition Poem by Linda Hoyt

Big balloons

Small balloons

Red balloons

Blue balloons

Yellow balloons

Green balloons

Floating, swirling, great balloons!

Rotten Ralph

By Jack Gantos

FOCUS THE LEARNING

"I'm so tired, I could sleep for a whole year!" Think about what I just said. Could I really sleep for a whole year? No, no one could sleep for a whole year! I was exaggerating. When you exaggerate, you make something bigger than it actually is. If I try to lift a heavy box and say "This box weighs a ton!" we know the box doesn't *really* weigh a ton. It's just a very heavy box. Authors exaggerate sometimes, too. Let's read *Rotten Ralph* by Jack Gantos to look for exaggeration.

INTERACTIVE READ-ALOUD
Model and Guide Practice

LOOK AT THE COVER. Ralph must be the cat sitting on the bed. What has he done? He ripped the head off that doll! He really is rotten! No wonder the girl looks so mad.

READ TO PAGE 6. Look at what Ralph is doing! I think this must be an exaggeration. I know cats that do some bad things, like scratch furniture and chase birds, but I have never seen a cat that would saw off a branch and hurt his owner!

 Thinking partners, talk about exaggeration in this story. How is Ralph different from other cats? Do you really think a cat can be so mean?

READ THROUGH PAGE 22. At various points, stop and discuss the ways in which the author exaggerates Ralph's behavior.

 Thinking partners, talk about exaggeration. What does Ralph do that makes him worse than a real cat would be? Why do you think the author exaggerates?

READ TO PAGE 40.

 Talk with your partner about Ralph. What lesson has he learned?

END OF STORY REFLECTION

Ralph does so many bad things! The author exaggerates about Ralph—in real life, cats don't do things like Ralph does.

 Think together about exaggeration you noticed in the story. Get ready to share your thinking.

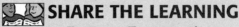 **SHARE THE LEARNING**
Focus on Exaggeration

Tip for Share the Reading

Let children know you are going to read about another exaggerated character, Paul Bunyan. Paul Bunyan is a famous character in tall tales. Tall tales are full of exaggerations! Put the story on the overhead as you read it for children. Read one sentence at a time, and ask the children to identify the exaggerations in the story.

Paul Bunyan

Paul Bunyan was so big, his head touched the clouds.

Paul's clothes were so big, he used wagon wheels for buttons.

Paul's mouth was so big, he used a shovel for a spoon.

Paul's feet were so big, people could live in his shoes.

Tip for Readers Theater Script

The readers theater script describes some of the rotten things that Ralph does! Read *Rotten Ralph* to the children. Engage them in dramatizing Ralph's exaggerated adventures as you read to them. Have the children join in on the refrain "Rotten Ralph!" Practice with children how they might say these lines—are they mad? Frustrated? Or do they think Ralph is funny? That will affect how they say the lines. Engage developing readers in reading the narrator lines.

Rotten Ralph
Readers Theater adaptation by Lynette Brent

Narrator One:	Ralph made fun of Sarah's dancing.
ALL:	Rotten Ralph!
Narrator Two:	Ralph cut down a branch.
ALL:	Rotten Ralph!
Narrator Three:	Ralph ate Sarah's cookies.
ALL:	Rotten Ralph!
Narrator Four:	Ralph put soap in dad's pipe.
ALL:	Rotten Ralph!
Narrator One:	Ralph smashed his bike.
ALL:	Rotten Ralph!
Narrator Two:	Ralph chased birds.
ALL:	Rotten Ralph!
Narrator Three:	Ralph tied balloons on a dog.
ALL:	Rotten Ralph!
Narrator Four:	Ralph said he was sorry.
ALL:	That's better, Ralph.

EXTEND THE LEARNING

☆ Children might enjoy reading other stories about Ralph, such as *Worse than Rotten, Ralph* and *Rotten Ralph's Rotten Christmas.*

☆ Work with children to create a list of exaggerations they hear all the time such as *I told you a million times not to do that!* or *I almost died laughing.*

☆ Read *Cloudy with a Chance of Meatballs* and look for exaggeration.

☆ As children write on their own, have them consider the effect of adding an exaggeration. Some exaggerations make a point or make a story funnier. But not all exaggerations add more to the story. Help children use exaggerations appropriately in their work.

ASSESS THE LEARNING

➤ As children discuss exaggerations in *Rotten Ralph*, assess understanding.

➤ Give children sentence stems that they can complete with exaggerations. Some sample stems include "I'm so hungry, I _____." "I'm so tired, I _____." "It was so cold out that _____." "It was raining so hard that _____."

INFUSION OF FORMAL LANGUAGE
Test-style language

An *exaggeration* is
  A. something that happened before the story.
  B. a character who is hard to like.
  C. making something sound bigger than it really is.
  D. a funny sentence in a story.

Which of these is an exaggeration?
  A. I'm very hungry.
  B. It's time to eat a big dinner!
  C. I'm so hungry I could eat a horse.
  D. Hamburgers are my favorite food!

Paul Bunyan

Paul Bunyan was so big, his head touched the clouds.

Paul's clothes were so big, he used wagon wheels for buttons.

Paul's mouth was so big, he used a shovel for a spoon.

Paul's feet were so big, people could live in his shoes.

Rotten Ralph

Readers Theater adaptation by Lynette Brent

Narrator One: Ralph made fun of Sarah's dancing.

ALL: Rotten Ralph!

Narrator Two: Ralph cut down a branch.

ALL: Rotten Ralph!

Narrator Three: Ralph ate Sarah's cookies.

ALL: Rotten Ralph!

Narrator Four: Ralph put soap in dad's pipe.

ALL: Rotten Ralph!

Narrator One: Ralph smashed his bike.

ALL: Rotten Ralph!

Narrator Two: Ralph chased birds.

ALL: Rotten Ralph!

Narrator Three: Ralph tied balloons on a dog.

ALL: Rotten Ralph!

Narrator Four: Ralph said he was sorry.

ALL: That's better, Ralph.

Genre

Genre categories—fiction, nonfiction, fairy tale, drama, and so on—each have a particular kind of content or structure. Exploring the standards in this strand, learners begin to understand the distinguishing features of various genres and learn what to expect from each.

DISTINGUISHING FEATURES OF GENRES

An Array of Fiction and Nonfiction Selections
By Linda Hoyt

FOCUS THE LEARNING

You will need fiction selections with illustrations on the cover as well as nonfiction books that have a photo on the cover, a table of contents, headings, and labels. You might want to use Big Books if they are available.

Information books look different than books that are stories. They have important parts that help us to understand what we are learning and to find information quickly.

 Think together. You look at a lot of information books. How can you tell if a book is a story or if it is an information book, just by looking at it?

INTERACTIVE READ-ALOUD
Model and Guide Practice

Let's start with the cover. Here is a fiction book. It has a title and the author's name. Here is a nonfiction book. It has a title and the author's name, too. So far, the covers are not very different except that the fiction book has a drawing on the cover and the information book has a photograph on the cover.

 Think together. Can you tell by the cover which one is nonfiction? How do you know?

SHOW THE TABLE OF CONTENTS PAGE. A table of contents is very helpful in an information book. We can use the table of contents to find things quickly. Let's look at this table of contents and think about what we might like to learn. This will also show us which page in the book we should turn to. Select a heading and turn to the correct page in the book.

OPEN TO A PAGE WITH LABELS. Notice these labels on the picture. Fiction books don't have labels, but information books do. We use labels to help us learn more. I am going to read the labels on this page.

 Talk to your thinking partner. Think together about what you learned from the labels.

OPEN TO A PAGE WITH HEADINGS. Do you see the headings at the top of the page? These are really important. Headings are like a title for just this section. They tell us what the section is going to be about. I am going to read just the heading.

 Think together. All you heard was the heading. What do you think this page is going to be about?

CONTINUE TO THE END OF THE SELECTION. Pause occasionally to point out headings, labels, page numbers, and so on.

END OF STORY REFLECTION

We learned about telling the difference between a fiction story and a nonfiction book. We learned that there are features that distinguish these two kinds of books.

 We are going to list some of the ways you can tell a fiction book from a nonfiction book. Think together. What should be on our list?

CREATE A CHART LISTING THE CHILDREN'S IDEAS.

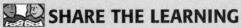 **SHARE THE LEARNING**
Focus on Distinguishing Features of Genre

Tip for Share the Thinking

Place the diagram of the dog on the overhead and have the children help you place labels on the drawing. Add labels for body parts such as tail, eye, ear, foot, knee, back, nose, etc. Then model a piece of writing about the dog and try to use some of the labels in your writing. When

you use a word that had appeared as a label, bold it so it is darker print and explain that those are "boldface" words to help us remember that they are important. Finally, add a heading then reread the writing to enjoy your shared creation and to talk about the nonfiction features you were able to incorporate.

Tip for Readers Theater Script

Assemble a nonfiction book by cutting the page into quarters and then stapling the left margin so it opens like a book. Guide the children in looking at the features of this nonfiction selection. Point out the title, table of contents, headings, labels, and page

numbers. Read "Leaves, Leaves, Leaves" to the students. Then engage them in sharing the reading as they become more comfortable with the content. As they become more proficient, have them read independently for fluency.

EXTEND THE LEARNING

☆ Read a series of poems to the children and talk about the features of poems. How can you distinguish a poem from a story? From a nonfiction book?

☆ Have children create nonfiction illustrations then add labels and a heading to their work. Assemble all of the pages together in a book, adding a table of contents to help locate each child's work.

☆ Read an array of fairy tales and talk about the distinguishing features such as presence of magic, a problem/solution structure, royalty, and so on.

☆ Look at recipe books, brochures, and a wide array of nonfiction texts and talk about the distinguishing features. What are the features of a recipe?

☆ Read and sing "The Wheels on the Bus" and other favorite songs. What are the features of a songbook?

☆ During small group instruction, have children sort books according to their types and talk about distinguishing features that enable them to tell an information book from a story, from a songbook, set of directions, and so on.

☆ Confer with readers during independent reading about distinguishing features of various genre.

ASSESS THE LEARNING

➤ Assess illustrations to determine level of understanding of nonfiction text features.

➤ During small group instruction, assess individual ability to distinguish one genre from another.

INFUSION OF FORMAL LANGUAGE
Test-style language

Information books often have:

  A. Headings

  B. Labels

  C. A table of contents

  D. All of the above.

Headings help us

  A. laugh.

  B. write.

  C. know what a section is about.

  D. learn about the author.

Heading:

_____

Leaves

Leaves

Leaves

This book belongs to

_____

Table of Contents

Colors

yellow

brown

red

Leaves come in many colors.

page 3

Patterns

lines

circles

Leaves come in many patterns.

page 4

Q is for Duck
By Mary Elting and Michael Folsom

FOCUS THE LEARNING

You will need an array of nonfiction books.

We know that nonfiction books are true. They are about real things, real people, and real places. Sometimes they have photographs so we can see exactly what something looks like. Other times, nonfiction books may have sketches and illustrations that look a lot like a storybook. *Q is for Duck* is one of those kinds of nonfiction books. The information is true, so it is nonfiction, but the illustrations look a lot like a story. As we read *Q is for Duck* by Mary Elting and Michael Folsom, listen to the pattern and think about what you know.

INTERACTIVE READ-ALOUD
Model and Guide Practice

READ THE SECTION FOR "A." This pattern is really great. This is an alphabet book about real things. I like the way we have to think a bit to find the connection to the letter of the alphabet. We need to use a lot of prior knowledge to figure out the pattern.

 Think together. Have you ever heard this book before?

READ THE SECTION FOR "B." We know this one, don't we!

 Why would "B" be a good letter dog?

CONTINUE TO THE END OF THE BOOK. Pause frequently to have partners think together about the relationship between the letter and the animals.

END OF STORY REFLECTION

We have been learning about the difference between fiction and nonfiction books. The pictures in *Q is for Duck* look like fiction but it isn't! This book is full of real information about animals.

 What was your favorite part of Q is for Duck*? Did you learn anything new in this book?*

SHARE THE LEARNING
Focus on Nonfiction

Tip for Share the Thinking

Place the picture of the lamb and the sentence stems on the overhead. Guide the children in crafting a piece of writing using the format of *Q is for Duck*. Read the completed piece for fluency and expression.

_____ is for lamb because a lamb _____.
_____ is for lamb because a lamb _____.
_____ is for lamb because a lamb _____.
_____ is for lamb because a lamb _____.
_____ is for lamb because a lamb _____.

Tip for Readers Theater Script

Read "Little Turtle" to the children and remind them that poetry can be nonfiction, too. Have the children use the pictures to tell what they learned about turtles from listening to the poem. Read the poem again, inviting children to read chorally with you. As they become more comfortable, they might enjoy reading the script with a partner trading every other line, reading independently, or even making tape recordings of themselves reading the script to self-assess fluency.

"Little Turtle"
By Linda Hoyt

This is a little turtle
He lives in a shell

He climbs on the rocks
And he swims really well

Turtles have soft bodies
Protected by their shells

They love to eat insects
And little bugs as well.

EXTEND THE LEARNING

☆ Have the children use the *Q is for Duck* format to write about themselves, a parent, another student, or a unit of study in science or social studies.

☆ Provide experience with a wide array of nonfiction formats such as directions, descriptions, poetry, and biography.

☆ Have children do lots of nonfiction writing to learn to express information in interesting ways.

☆ Look at recipe books, brochures, and a wide array of nonfiction texts and talk about author's purpose for each kind of nonfiction.

☆ Have children create a class Big Book related to a unit of study. Insert a table of contents so each child's page is easy to find. Place a photocopy of each child on the page he or she created.

☆ Support nonfiction reading during small group instruction.

ASSESS THE LEARNING

➤ Confer with individuals during independent reading to assess ability to differentiate between fiction and non-fiction.

➤ Assess understanding of nonfiction genre by analyzing each child's informational writing.

INFUSION OF FORMAL LANGUAGE
Test-style language

Nonfiction books are:
  A. True
  B. False
  C. Funny
  D. Only about animals

This book was *mostly* about:
  A. Camels
  B. Ducks
  C. People
  D. Animals

_____ is for lamb because a lamb _____.

_____ is for lamb because a lamb _____.

_____ is for lamb because a lamb _____.

_____ is for lamb because a lamb _____.

_____ is for lamb because a lamb _____.

"Little Turtle"

By Linda Hoyt

This is a little turtle

He lives in a shell

He climbs on the rocks

And he swims really well

Turtles have soft bodies

Protected by their shells

They love to eat insects

And little bugs as well.

Rumpelstiltskin

By Paul Zelinsky

FOCUS THE LEARNING

Long ago people didn't have television, radio, computers, or even very many books. For entertainment they told stories and tried hard to remember them so they could pass them along to others. Folktales and fairy tales are stories that were told over and over again and eventually were written down and turned into books. I am going to name some fairy tales and folktales. Give me a thumbs-up when I name a story that you remember . . . *Cinderella, Little Red Riding Hood, Goldilocks and the Three Bears, Snow White.* One of the ways you can identify a folktale or fairy tale is on the cover. It will say, "Retold by _____." That tells us that this story is not one the author made up. It is an old story that was told over and over again. Today we are going to read *Rumpelstiltskin* retold by Paul Zelinsky.

INTERACTIVE READ-ALOUD
Model and Guide Practice

READ PAGES 1–2. Then pause to think aloud. I am thinking about the miller's daughter. How terrible for her. She didn't tell a lie—her father did. What will she do?

 Turn to your thinking partner. We know this is a fairy tale. It isn't true. How do you think she will get out of this?

READ TO THE PLACE WHERE RUMPLESTILTSKIN TAKES HER NECKLACE AND SPINS THE STRAW INTO GOLD. There is magic here, isn't there? Real people can't spin straw into gold. This is like in *Cinderella* when the Fairy Godmother uses her magic wand to turn the pumpkin into a carriage. Fairy tales always have at least a little magic or magical people such as a fairy or an elf.

READ TO THE PLACE WHERE RUMPLESTILTSKIN TAKES HER RING AND SPINS FOR A SECOND NIGHT.

 Thinking partners, what do you think will happen?

CONTINUE TO THE END OF THE STORY. Pause occasionally to give partners time to talk to consider what makes a fairy tale different from other stories.

END OF STORY REFLECTION

What a fairy tale that was! There was a lot of magic, a king and a queen . . . and some really big problems to solve.

 Thinking partners, if you were to retell this tale, what would you want to say?

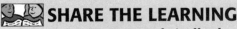

SHARE THE LEARNING
Focus on Fairy Tale/Folktale

Tip for Share the Reading

Read the passage with expression. Have the children retell the events or act them out. Explain that this story has many elements of a fairy tale. It has magic, a prince and princess, and a problem and a happy ending. Read the passage again, inviting the children to join in chorally.

A Frog Tale by Linda Hoyt

Once upon a time there was a frog. He had a great pond where he could swim, play in the mud, and snap up flies with his long sticky tongue. One day a princess came to his pond. She was really sad so he hopped up into her lap and put his little frog arms around her to make her feel better. She leaned down and kissed the frog to say thank you. All of a sudden, there was a puff of smoke and the frog turned into a handsome prince!

Tip for Readers Theater Script

Have emergent readers use the props to retell *Jack and the Beanstalk* after you read it to them. Have them work in partners so each person gets to talk. Read it again, having them use their props to enact the story as you read. On a third reading, invite those who are ready to share the reading of the selection with you.

Jack and the Beanstalk
Retold by Linda Hoyt

Teacher: Once upon a time there was a boy named Jack.
Children: He was very poor.
Teacher: His mother asked him to take their old cow and trade it for food.
Children: Jack traded the cow for three magic beans.
Teacher: His mother was furious and threw the beans out the window. That night a huge beanstalk grew far up into the clouds.
Children: In the morning
Teacher: Jack climbed the beanstalk and found himself in the castle of a giant! There were beautiful things everywhere, so Jack took a goose that could lay golden eggs and climbed down
Children: to give it to his mother.
Teacher: The giant was furious and came after Jack. As the giant climbed down the stalk to get his goose back,
Children: Jack cut down the beanstalk.
The End

EXTEND THE LEARNING

☆ Read *The Frog Prince* and *The Frog Prince Continued*.

☆ Read and dramatize *Snow White, Cinderella, The Princess and the Pea,* or *Rapunzel*.

☆ Guide small groups in reading folktales and fairy tales.

☆ Ensure children are including folktales and fairy tales in their independent reading selections.

☆ Illustrate favorite folktales and fairy tales.

☆ Create puppets for a tale and "tell" it for an audience.

☆ Have the children read *Goldilocks Returns* by Lisa Campbell Ernst and compare the story line with the original *Goldilocks*.

ASSESS THE LEARNING

➤ Listen in as partners talk about fairy tales and folktales to determine quality of undertanding.

➤ During small group instruction, have children identify key elements of a folktale or fairy tale.

INFUSION OF FORMAL LANGUAGE
Test-style language

Rumpelstiltskin knew how to:
  A. Get into locked rooms.
  B. Fly a wooden spoon.
  C. Spin straw into gold.
  D. All of the above.

The queen was afraid that Rumplestiltskin would
  A. want more straw.
  B. take her baby.
  C. fly his spoon in the castle.
  D. dance around a fire.

A Frog Tale by Linda Hoyt

Once upon a time there was a frog. He had a great pond where he could swim, play in the mud, and snap up flies with his long sticky tongue. One day a princess came to his pond. She was really sad so he hopped up into her lap and put his little frog arms around her to make her feel better. She leaned down and kissed the frog to say thank you. All of a sudden, there was a puff of smoke and the frog turned into a handsome prince!

Jack and the Beanstalk

Retold by Linda Hoyt

Teacher: Once upon a time there was a boy named Jack.

Children: He was very poor.

Teacher: His mother asked him to take their old cow and trade it for food.

Children: Jack traded the cow for three magic beans.

Teacher: His mother was furious and threw the beans out the window. That night a huge beanstalk grew far up into the clouds.

Children: In the morning

Teacher: Jack climbed the beanstalk and found himself in the castle of a giant! There were beautiful things everywhere, so Jack took a goose that could lay golden eggs and climbed down

Children: to give it to his mother.

Teacher: The giant was furious and came after Jack. As the giant climbed down the stalk to get his goose back,

Children: Jack cut down the beanstalk.

The End

Hattie and the Fox
By Mem Fox

FOCUS THE LEARNING

Good readers visualize as they read. They imagine characters moving around, and they imagine how it would sound if characters talk to each other. We can help ourselves visualize and understand by dramatizing stories. As we read *Hattie and the Fox,* by Mem Fox, your job will be to visualize the story. Make a movie in your head and think about how it could be turned into a play that we could act out.

INTERACTIVE READ-ALOUD
Model and Guide Practice

I am going to hang this chart next to me while I read so we have a place to write our ideas about how to dramatize Hattie and the Fox. We are going to turn it into a play so we need to listen to the story and think about how it might work if we acted it out.

READ THREE PAGES OF TEXT, TO WHERE THE COW SAYS, "WHAT NEXT?" I am going to stop reading and think about this. To dramatize this, we will need something that looks like a bush. I will write that on my chart. We will need Hattie, a goose, a pig, a sheep, a horse, and a cow. I will label those "characters" on my list.

 Think together. Do I have all of the characters we need? Did I leave any animals out?

READ TO THE PLACE WHERE HATTIE SEES A NOSE, TWO EYES, AND TWO EARS BUT THE OTHER ANIMALS CONTINUE NOT TO BE BOTHERED. I am thinking about dramatizing and I think it would help to have signs that tell who is the horse, who is the pig, and so on. I am going to write "signs" on the list. Those are props that would be really helpful.

READ TO THE PLACE WHERE HATTIE SEES THE WHOLE BODY AND FLIES INTO A TREE.

 What are you visualizing? How could we dramatize this part? What should we write on our chart?

READ TO THE END OF THE STORY.

END OF STORY REFLECTION

I am going to start at the beginning and read this one more time. You need to think really hard about making this into a play. Try to picture people acting this out as you listen. If you think of something we need to add to our chart, please let me know and I will stop so we can write it down.

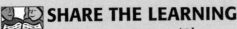

SHARE THE LEARNING
Focus on Drama/Play

Tip for Share the Reading	Tip for Readers Theater Script

Explain that when we dramatize our voices, we need to show the emotions and feelings of our characters. Read the passage to the children sounding really sleepy, as if you just woke up. Ask them to identify the feelings you were showing in the way you said the words. Have the children join in reading in a sleepy, bored voice. Read it again modeling sounding really excited. Guide a conversation about the difference. Share the reading with the children showing a variety of different emotions.

Read *Hattie and the Fox* to the children, and plan how they want to dramatize it. Enjoy reading and dramatizing several times to build fluency and improve dramatic interpretation.

EXTEND THE LEARNING

☆ Have the children dramatize a variety of stories.

☆ Dramatize a nonfiction selection such as the life cycle of a butterfly or the movement of a snake.

☆ Guide children in describing a character then acting out the character's behavior.

☆ Dramatize *The Carrot Seed* by Ruth Krauss or *Don't Let the Pigeon Drive the Bus!* by Mo Willems.

☆ Have the children create illustrations they can use to dramatize a selection.

☆ Dramatize a selection telling the story from the point of view of a character.

ASSESS THE LEARNING

➤ During small group instruction, have students dramatize character voices.

➤ Have students create an illustration and use it to support a reenactment of a story.

INFUSION OF FORMAL LANGUAGE
Test-style language

In a *play*, the story is
A. different.
B. acted out by people.
C. changed.
D. boring.

Which statement is *not* true?
A. When you act out a story, you sit still.
B. When you act out a story, you act like a character.
C. When you act out a story, you say what the character would say.
D. When you act out a story, you sometimes use props.

"Good grief!" said the goose.

 "Well, well!" said the pig.

"Who cares?" said the sheep.

 "So what?" said the horse.

"What next?" said the cow.

Hattie and the Fox

Readers Theater adaptation by Linda Hoyt

I see a nose in the bushes.

Good grief!

Well, well . . .

Who cares?

So what?

What next?

It's a fox!

M O O O O O O O O O O O O !

And the fox ran away!

Tomorrow's Alphabet

By George Shannon

INTERACTIVE READ-ALOUD
Model and Guide Practice

As you read, fold the book back so the children can only see the page with the letter and cannot see the outcome. Read "A is for seed, tomorrow's Apple." What a great pattern! The author chose apple for A, but he didn't say A is for apple. He said, "A is for seed," because some day that seed will grow into a tree and that tree will grow apples! To understand this book, I have to think about how things start and what they turn into.

READ THE B PAGE. B is for eggs . . . what will an egg turn into later? Think together and then I will show the next page.

 Think together. Why would B be for eggs?

CONTINUE TO THE END OF THE SELECTION. Engage the children in partner conversations to think about the relationships that allow them to solve the puzzles.

END OF STORY REFLECTION

That was fun.

 Think together. What was your favorite part of the book? Were there any places you couldn't figure out the answer?

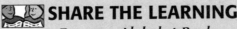

SHARE THE LEARNING
Focus on Alphabet Books

Tip for Share the Reading

Read *Bicycle Alphabet* aloud to the children. Then work with them to discuss and label the parts of the bike in the picture. They might also enjoy making a list of things you can do on a bike. Read the selection again, inviting the children to read chorally with you. Read the selection again, inviting the children to read chorally with you. When ready, have them create illustrations for *Bicycle Alphabet*, rewrite lines reflecting their own thinking, or write additional lines of their own. Reread to celebrate their thinking.

Bicycle Alphabet

A is for bicycle because you put **air** in the tires.

B is for bicycle because it has **brakes**.

C is for bicycle because it can **crash**.

D is for bicycle because you don't ride **double**.

E is for bicycle because **everybody** loves them.

F is for bicycle because they go really **fast**.

G is for bicycle because some bikes have **gears**.

H is for bicycle because bikes have **handlebars**.

Tip for Readers Theater Script

Read *Alphabet Fun* to the children and talk about the alphabet pattern. Read it again, inviting the children to join you chorally. Have students read it with a partner then prepare to perform it for their parents. Have parents sign on the page after their child reads to them.

Alphabet Fun
By Linda Hoyt

B is for caterpillar. Tomorrow's **butterfly**.

C is for kitten. Tomorrow's **cat**.

R is for chick. Tomorrow's **rooster**.

G is for baby. Tomorrow's **grown up**.

EXTEND THE LEARNING

☆ Gather an array of alphabet books. Compare them.

☆ Create an alphabet book focused on names of students. Example: "J is for Justin" and "A is for Alania."

☆ Have each child create an alphabet book.

☆ Make a class alphabet book on a specific topic such as whales.

☆ Make an alphabet book about the classroom, including classroom items and people.

☆ Create an alliteration alphabet book.

☆ During small group instruction, guide children in reading alphabet books.

☆ Confer with readers during independent reading to ensure they know how to navigate an alphabet book.

☆ Read *A, My Name Is Alice* by Jane E. Bayer and enjoy the variation on a typical alphabet book.

☆ Read and perform *Chicka Chicka Boom Boom* by Bill Martin, Jr. and John Archambault.

ASSESS THE LEARNING

> Assess children's ability to recognize and navigate an alphabet book by conferring with individuals during independent reading.

> Assess contributions to class alphabet books for understanding of the structure that binds an alphabet book together.

INFUSION OF FORMAL LANGUAGE
Test-style language

Alphabet books have

  A. at least one page for every letter of the alphabet.

  B. animals.

  C. silly sentences.

  D. questions.

This alphabet book is *mostly* about:

  A. Letters

  B. Reading

  C. Singing

  D. What things will become

Bicycle Alphabet

A is for bicycle because you put **air** in the tires.

B is for bicycle because it has **brakes**.

C is for bicycle because it can **crash**.

D is for bicycle because you don't ride **double**.

E is for bicycle because **everybody** loves them.

F is for bicycle because they go really **fast**.

G is for bicycle because some bikes have **gears**.

H is for bicycle because bikes have **handlebars**.

Alphabet Fun

By Linda Hoyt

B is for caterpillar. Tomorrow's butterfly.

C is for kitten. Tomorrow's **cat**.

R is for chick. Tomorrow's **rooster**.

G is for baby. Tomorrow's **grown up**.

The Very Hungry Caterpillar
By Eric Carle

FOCUS THE LEARNING

Introduction: We all love counting books. Here is one that is already a favorite for many of you, *The Very Hungry Caterpillar* by Eric Carle. Let's warm up and practice counting together. How many shoes are you wearing? How many fingers do you have? How many stories have I read to you today? How many windows in our classroom?

 Turn to your partner. Tell how many people are in your family.

INTERACTIVE READ-ALOUD
Model and Guide Practice

READ PAGES 1 AND 2. Then pause to think aloud. I am going to look back at these two pages and do some counting. On the first page I see there is one egg, one leaf, one moon, and one tree. I see lots and lots of stars. Let's count them together. On the second page I see one caterpillar and one sun. The sun has lots and lots of sunbeams around it. Let's count them.

READ THE PAGES THAT DESCRIBE THE FRUIT HE ATE, TAKING TIME TO COUNT EACH KIND OF FRUIT.

 Which kind of fruit did he eat the most of? Which kind of fruit did he eat the least of?

READ TO THE PAGE THAT TELLS WHAT HE ATE ON SATURDAY. Wow! Look at all of these treats. The first line says he ate it all on Saturday. How would you feel if you ate all of that in one day? Let's count and see how many things he ate.

CONTINUE READING AND COUNTING TO THE END OF THE BOOK.

END OF STORY REFLECTION

Let's think for a minute about all of the things the caterpillar ate. He ate a lot! Think from the beginning of the book all the way to the end and remember as much as you can.

 Count together. How many things can you remember that the caterpillar ate. Let's look through the book and count together to see how much he ate in all.

 **SHARE THE LEARNING**
Focus on Counting Books

Tip for Share the Reading

Explain that you are all going to work together to write your own counting book. You may want to create it on butcher paper so there is just one sentence per page. Engage the children in a conversation about "who" is hungry and then have fun filling in the blanks. After your story is constructed, add illustrations and have fun reading it again and again.

> One day a hungry _____ went for a walk. While he was walking, he got very, very hungry so he ate **1**_____. Then he ate **2**_____.
> He was still hungry so he ate **3**_____.
> The more he walked the hungrier he got so he ate **4**_____ and **5**_____.

Tip for Readers Theater Script

For emergent readers, sing "A Counting Song" together. When you come to a number, say the number clearly and then guide the children in counting from 1 up to the target number. You may want to have objects to count, let them use their fingers, or have children stand to support one-to-one matching. Once they learn the song, provide the script so they can sing and track along. Many children will benefit from crafting illustrations to go with each number. For developing readers, read and sing as the script is written, focusing on smooth tracking under the print and fluent expression. Begin lifting the level of challenge by changing the numbers on the script. You might insert numbers such as 17, 22, 31, . . . and so on to increase difficulty.

"A Counting Song"
As the tune of "The Farmer in the Dell"
By Linda Hoyt

It's time for us to count.
It's time for us to count.
Hi Ho The Derry O
It's time for us to count.

10 . . . 1,2,3,4,5,6,7,8,9,10!

It's time for us to count.
It's time for us to count.
Hi Ho The Derry O
It's time for us to count.

9 . . . 1,2,3,4,5,6,7,8,9

It's time for us to count.
It's time for us to count.
Hi Ho The Derry O
It's time for us to count.

EXTEND THE LEARNING

☆ Guide writers in creating their own counting books, with one page dedicated to each number.

☆ Provide an array of counting books in the classroom to enjoy for Read-Aloud and independent reading.

☆ Consider writing during math time to give children a chance to associate written language and mathematics.

☆ Turn a story into a counting experience by having the children count items in the illustrations and using sticky notes to indicate how many items they are finding.

ASSESS THE LEARNING

> Check for understanding as you observe writers creating their counting books.

> Confer with readers during independent reading as they interact with counting books.

> Provide concrete objects for children to count, and then have them use language to explain what they did. Example: "I counted 17 unifix cubes."

INFUSION OF FORMAL LANGUAGE
Test-style language

This book was *mostly* about:
  A. What the caterpillar ate
  B. How a caterpillar lives
  C. Laying eggs
  D. Butterflies

Which statement is *not* true?
  A. Butterflies are pretty.
  B. Caterpillars need to eat a lot.
  C. Leaves are better for caterpillars than cake.
  D. Caterpillars turn into dogs.

One day a hungry _____ went for a walk. While

he was walking, he got very, very hungry so he ate

1_____. Then he ate **2**_____.

He was still hungry so he ate **3**_____.

The more he walked the hungrier he got so he ate

4_____and **5**_____.

"A Counting Song"

(to the tune of "The Farmer in the Dell")

By Linda Hoyt

It's time for us to count.
It's time for us to count.
Hi Ho The Derry O
It's time for us to count.

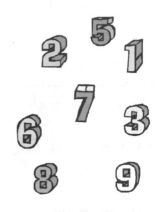

10 . . . 1,2,3,4,5,6,7,8,9,10!

It's time for us to count.
It's time for us to count.
Hi Ho The Derry O
It's time for us to count.

9 . . . 1,2,3,4,5,6,7,8,9

It's time for us to count.
It's time for us to count.
Hi Ho The Derry O
It's time for us to count.

Writing Traits

Engaging, well-written texts provide outstanding models for beginning writers. Standards in this strand explore ideas, organization, voice, and so on, so learners can begin to emulate that writer's work and incorporate those traits into their own writing.

Good Dog, Carl
By Alexandra Day

FOCUS THE LEARNING

Have you ever noticed how much work it is to take care of a baby? When someone takes care of a baby, they have to feed them, change their diapers, and keep them safe because babies don't know what will hurt them.

 Think together. Tell about a time you were around a baby and what you noticed.

INTERACTIVE READ-ALOUD
Model and Guide Practice

In *Good Dog, Carl* by Alexandra Day, the dog is left to babysit! This book is going to be a lot of fun for us because it is wordless. We are going to look at the pictures and come up with our own ideas about words we could use to tell the story. Let's look at the first two pages. Oh, no! The baby is climbing out of the crib and standing on the dog!

 Think together. What do you think the dog will do? Share your ideas.

SHOW THE NEXT TWO-PAGE LAYOUT. The baby is riding on Carl like he is a horse! But Carl put her on the bed so she won't get hurt. He is pretty smart. I can see why the title is *Good Dog, Carl.*

TURN TO THE PLACE WHERE THE BABY FALLS DOWN THE LAUNDRY CHUTE. You will need to explain the laundry chute and why Carl runs down the stairs. *Poor Carl! That baby is making him work really hard.*

 Talk to your thinking partner. What has Carl done so far that you think is really smart? Share your ideas.

CONTINUE TO THE END OF THE STORY. Pause to invite the children to share their ideas about what is happening in the story.

END OF STORY REFLECTION

We had a lot of ideas about what happened in the book. Let's write the story in our own words. That is what writers do. Writers get ideas from books, from pictures, from experiences, and then they write them down. I am going to start writing.... Ready to help me?

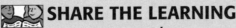 **SHARE THE LEARNING**

Focus on Ideas

Tip for Share the Reading

Writers get ideas for writing from their lives. If you have a dog, a cat, a fish, or just wish you did, those are ideas you can write about. Read *My Dog, Arnie* to the children and discuss what you learn about the author's life just by reading this story. This author clearly enjoys his dog, and it shows in his writing. Read the selection again inviting the children to read in a way that shows how the writer feels about his dog. Have the children make a list of things they know about that they could draw and write about.

My Dog, Arnie

My dog is my friend. He has big floppy ears and a long wet tongue. He has a lot of hair that gets all over me when we play together. Sometimes I brush him so the hair comes off on the brush instead of on my clothes.

I love my dog.

Tip for Readers Theater Script

Remind the children that everyday things sometimes make our best writing. Read "Ice Cream" to the children. Have them describe their favorite ice cream flavors, and then read it again in unison. As they are ready, have them read with partners and independently. Be sure to do some writing about ice cream, chocolate chip cookies, and other favorite foods.

"Ice Cream"
By Linda Hoyt

Chocolate,
Marshmallow,
Strawberry, too.
Ice cream for supper
And breakfast, too.

Mint Chocolate Chip,
Fudge Delight,
Rainbow sherbet
Is out of sight!

EXTEND THE LEARNING

☆ Create a class topic list by hanging a large sheet of paper and a pen on a string. Invite children to write down ideas for writing on the sheet.

☆ Have children keep personal topic lists to help them as writers. It works really well to add to the lists after reading great stories, after classroom experiences, following a field trip, or on Mondays after the students have had a weekend at home.

☆ Model writing after you have read a story and made a connection. Think aloud as you write so the children can understand that the story reminded you of something in your own life that will now become a piece of writing.

☆ Bring in pictures from home and show the children how your personal photos can support you as a writer. Invite the children to bring in photos to help them with ideas, or take digital photos in school and have the children write about them.

☆ Teach children to look around them and learn to describe simple things such as the grass, the bark on a tree, the sound of the traffic going by, and so on.

☆ Read a variety of wordless books, such as *The Snowman* by Raymond Briggs, to generate ideas for writing.

ASSESS THE LEARNING

➤ Confer with writers to assess their ability to generate their own ideas.

➤ Assess writer's ability to write clearly on an assigned topic.

INFUSION OF FORMAL LANGUAGE

Test-style language

Writers get *ideas* from
  A. Books.
  B. Experiences.
  C. Pictures.
  D. All of the above.

The *main idea* of *Good Dog, Carl* is:
  A. Babies make messes.
  B. Babies ride on dogs.
  C. Carl did a good job taking care of the baby.
  D. Babies get hungry.

My Dog, Arnie

My dog is my friend. He has big floppy ears and a long wet tongue. He has a lot of hair that gets all over me when we play together. Sometimes I brush him so the hair comes off on the brush instead of on my clothes.

I love my dog.

"Ice Cream"

By Linda Hoyt

Chocolate,

Marshmallow,

Strawberry, too.

Ice cream for supper

And breakfast, too.

Mint Chocolate Chip,

Fudge Delight,

Rainbow sherbet

Is out of sight!

Goodnight Moon
By Margaret Wise Brown

FOCUS THE LEARNING

Goodnight Moon by Margaret Wise Brown reminds us how nice it is to snuggle into bed and begin to feel sleepy. I love that cozy feeling with the blankets up around me and my head on my pillow.

 Think together. When you lie in your bed and look around, what do you see?

INTERACTIVE READ-ALOUD
Model and Guide Practice

LOOK AT THE COVER. This is a whole book about bedtime and saying goodnight to things in your room. This author got her writing idea from something she does every day, going to bed! As we read the story, be thinking about ideas for writing. If you were going to write about saying goodnight, what ideas would you include in your writing?

READ TO THE PAGE WITH THE COW JUMPING OVER THE MOON. The bunny has said goodnight to several things. Let's remember together.

 Put your heads together. What has the bunny said goodnight to so far? If you were going to write about going to bed, would you include things that are the same or would your ideas be different?

READ TO THE PAGE THAT SHOWS THE ENTIRE ROOM. "Goodnight room" is such a nice way to think about going to sleep, isn't it? Are you thinking about your room? Do you have a special stuffed animal or a favorite chair...maybe a pillow?

 Think together. Is this giving you ideas for writing?

CONTINUE TO THE END OF THE STORY. Stop often to talk about ideas for writing.

END OF STORY REFLECTION

I am going to think for a minute about my bedroom and everything I would want to say goodnight to....There is my lamp, my books, my clock, my pillow. I really like my pillow so I want to be sure to include that. I am going to start by drawing a picture of the things I would say goodnight to so I can remember better when I start my writing. After I draw, I am going to write about everything I want to say goodnight to.

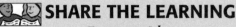

SHARE THE LEARNING
Focus on Ideas

Tip for Share the Reading

Work with the children to think of things you can say good morning to, and complete the poem on the overhead. Read it aloud with expression and then invite the children to join you in a shared reading of their poem. Read it several times to support fluency and expressive interpretation.

> "Good Morning!"
>
> I say good morning to _____
> Good morning to _____
> Good morning to _____
>
> I say good morning to _____
> Good morning to _____
> Good morning to _____
>
> Good Morning!

Tip for Readers Theater Script

For emergent readers, enjoy "Hamburgers" as an echo poem: teacher reads and children echo. As they gain confidence, encourage them to read with partners or independently. For developing readers, after enjoying a fluent expressive reading of the poem, have them write their own versions and perform them.

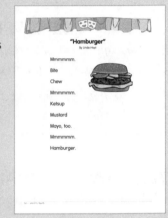

> "Hamburger"
> By Linda Hoyt
>
> Mmmmmm.
> Bite
> Chew
> Mmmmmm.
> Ketsup
> Mustard
> Mayo, too.
> Mmmmmm.
> Hamburger.

EXTEND THE LEARNING

☆ Make a point to pause before Read-Alouds and say: "This is a book about _____." Let's use this as a chance to think about ideas for writing. If something in the book helps you connect to a writing idea, be sure to let me know and I will pause and write your idea on our chart of Ideas to Write About.

☆ Have the children create an illustration about an experience such as going to the dentist. They then tell a partner about the experience while the partner asks questions. Each author then tries to add details and ideas to the picture to show more information. After the illustration is revised, the author meets with a new partner to share and respond to questions about the illustration.

☆ In small group instruction, remind children to be gathering ideas for writing.

☆ Introduce a topic and ask children to draw and write about the topic so they learn to be flexible about writing to a prompt as well as selecting their own topics.

☆ Take a walk with paper and pencils. Think out loud about things you can write about, and show the children how you can make a quick sketch or jot down a few words to remind you of the idea for writing. Have the children work on their own idea lists.

☆ Show children how an idea can be used several times by taking one idea and modeling a personal narrative about that idea then turning the same idea into a poem.

☆ Read *The Mitten* by Jan Brett and show how the pictures in the margins provide more ideas about the story. Encourage children to expand their ideas through art.

☆ Model writing directions for simple classroom tasks, and then have the children create their own sets of directions.

ASSESS THE LEARNING

➤ Monitor children's ability to self-select a topic, generating ideas and text.

➤ Confer with writers during writers workshop to assess their list of ideas.

INFUSION OF FORMAL LANGUAGE
Test-style language

The room in *Goodnight Moon* belongs to:

  A. The bears
  B. The cow
  C. The kitten
  D. The bunny

The *ideas* for the writing are all about:

  A. Pictures on the wall
  B. Kittens with yarn
  C. The moon
  D. Saying goodnight to things you enjoy

"Good Morning!"

I say good morning to _____

Good morning to _____

Good morning to _____

I say good morning to _____

Good morning to _____

Good morning to _____

Good Morning!

"Hamburger"

By Linda Hoyt

Mmmmmm.

Bite

Chew

Mmmmmm.

Ketsup

Mustard

Mayo, too.

Mmmmmm.

Hamburger.

Brown Bear, Brown Bear, What Do You See?
By Bill Martin, Jr.

FOCUS THE LEARNING

Introduction: Have you ever noticed how much better things work for us when we are organized in our classroom? If all of the coats are hung in the closet, the paper is stacked neatly, and pencils are sharp, everything seems to work better for us. It is the same way in a book. Authors need to think about how they are going to organize their writing. The book we are going to read today is organized around having the same type of sentences repeated over and over again. You may have heard the book before, but this time try to listen for the pattern that Bill Martin, Jr., used to organize his book. It is called *Brown Bear, Brown Bear, What Do You See?*

INTERACTIVE READ-ALOUD
Model and Guide Practice

READ TO THE END OF THE PAGE WITH THE RED BIRD.

 Turn to your partner. Did you hear the pattern? What did you notice? Who will be talking next?

CONTINUE TO THE END OF THE STORY. Pause occasionally to give partners time to talk about the language pattern and the animals they are seeing.

END OF STORY REFLECTION

The way Bill Martin, Jr., organized this book, I could tell what each page would be like. I just needed to figure out who would be on the next page. I like that pattern so much I want to practice it again.

Note: If I were in the classroom with you, I would have the children say: "Mrs. Hoyt, Mrs. Hoyt, what do you see?" Then, I would answer: "I see Alex looking at me." The children in unison would then say: "Alex, Alex, what do you see?" and so on.

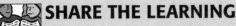 **SHARE THE LEARNING**
Focus on Organization

Tip for Share the Thinking

Model writing using the organizational pattern from the book. Explain that the pattern is one way to organize your writing and thinking.

"_____ _____
What do you see?"
"I see _____ looking at me."

"_____ _____
What do you see?"
"I see _____ looking at me."

"_____ _____
What do you see?"
"I see _____ looking at me."

Tip for Readers Theater Script

For emergent readers, engage the children in looking at the pictures and reciting the pattern for each, ensuring that they remember to look at the next picture to predict which animal is coming next. As they gain confidence, have them read in unison and in partners. Developing readers might enjoy reading and enacting the lines dramatically.

"Frog, Frog, What Do You See?"
Readers Theater adaptation by Linda Hoyt

Frog, frog, What do you see?
I see a rooster looking at me.

Rooster, rooster, What do you see?
I see a cow looking at me.

Cow, cow, What do you see?
I see a spider looking at me.

Spider, spider, What do you see?
I see children looking at me!

EXTEND THE LEARNING

☆ Invite children to create illustrations to go with the modeled writing from the lesson, or take digital pictures of children to post with their pages.

☆ Provide an opportunity for children to do their own writing using the organizational pattern.

☆ Model additional ways to organize writing. After blowing bubbles, show them how you could have one page about the bubble mixture, one page about the bubble wand, and one page about the colors and shapes in their bubbles.

☆ Encourage children to talk about how they will organize their writing before they add text to their illustrations.

☆ Read *I Went Walking* by Sue Williams (Harcourt, 1989), to show what another version of this same organizational pattern sounds like.

ASSESS THE LEARNING

> Have partners use the pattern and listen in to see if they can follow the pattern.

> Confer with writers about organization. Look through their portfolio to see if they are trying more than one organizational style. Even kindergarten children can paginate and create multi-page books with organization.

> Talk about organization of the books you are using in guided reading and see if children can identify the differences.

INFUSION OF FORMAL LANGUAGE
Test-style language

This story was written to
  A. explain about animals.
  B. be a lot of fun to read.
  C. teach us about children.
  D. describe animals.

What was the first animal in the story?
  A. Red Bird
  B. Yellow Duck
  C. Black Sheep
  D. Brown Bear

"_____, _____,

What do you see?"

"I see _____ looking at me."

"_____, _____,

What do you see?"

"I see _____ looking at me."

"_____, _____,

What do you see?"

"I see _____ looking at me."

"Frog, Frog, What Do You See?"

Readers Theater adaptation by Linda Hoyt

Frog, frog, What do you see?

I see a rooster looking at me.

Rooster, rooster, What do you see?

I see a cow looking at me.

Cow, cow, What do you see?

I see a spider looking at me.

Spider, spider, What do you see?

I see children looking at me!

Ten, Nine, Eight

By Molly Bang

INTERACTIVE READ-ALOUD
Model and Guide Practice

SHOW THE TITLE PAGE, DEDICATION PAGE, AND FIRST PAGE OF TEXT (10). I am thinking about the way Molly Bang organized this book. I know she writes about counting things, but I see now that all of the things she is counting fit together around the idea of going to bed.

TURN TO THE NEXT PAGE (9). Cover the text so the children can only see the picture. Most counting books we have read start at 1 and go up. This one starts at the number 10.

 What number do we think is next? Let's count together and see.

READ THE PAGE. "Nine soft friends in a quiet room." This page makes me think of how nice it is to hold a soft, fuzzy stuffed animal. It says they are friends so the girl must like them a lot. It also says the room is quiet. Shhh. Can you picture it? A quiet room with nine soft friends? Ready with your whisper voices? Let's count the animals.

TURN TO THE NEXT PAGE (8). Since we know how Molly Bang organized this book, we know what number is next, don't we?

 How many things do you expect to see on this page?

CONTINUE TO THE END OF THE STORY. Pause occasionally to give partners time to talk about the book.

END OF STORY REFLECTION

If you were going to organize a book around counting, would you start with a big number and count down to 1 or start with 1 and count up?

 Tell each other how you would organize a counting book.

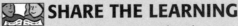 SHARE THE LEARNING
Focus on Organization

Tip for Share the Thinking

Explain that this piece of writing is organized around counting. The children need to help you finish the writing so you can read and enjoy it together. After the piece is completed, read for fluency and expression.

The Hungry Hippo

The hungry hippo ate **1** _____ .

He also ate **2** _____ .

He went for a walk and ate **3** _____ .

The walk made him more hungry so he ate

4 _____ .

He was thinking about dessert so he ate

5 _____ .

Tip for Readers Theater Script

When we organize a piece of writing, we sometimes select transition words to help us. Words like "first," "next," "then," and "finally," help us create a sense of order as we organize our writing. Read *A Bunny for a Pet* to the children emphasizing these transition words, and explain that the writing was organized around these words so the events would be described in the correct order. Have the children join in as they become comfortable, reading the script for fluency and expression. Some students may enjoy adding another line that starts with the word "finally."

A Bunny for a Pet

First, you need to choose a bunny. You will want to choose one that is friendly and does not bite.

Next, you need a cage for your bunny. You will also need a dish for water.

Then, you can take your bunny home and give it a name!

EXTEND THE LEARNING

☆ Have children create an illustration that tells a story of something you have done together in class. It could tell the story of a science experiment, planting seeds, or going to recess. Have them organize their illustration so that it shows the beginning, the middle, and the end of the experience.

☆ Model a piece of writing that replicates the style of *Ten, Nine, Eight* but in different environments. You might craft something like: "Ten little chicks snuggling next to mom, 9 fluffy ducklings swimming in the pond, 8 puffy penguins sitting on dad's feet . . ."

☆ Create a class counting book using items around the room: "26 desks waiting for a reader, 25 counting blocks standing in a row, 24 pencils standing in a can . . ."

☆ Scaffold individuals in creating personal counting books.

☆ Show students a variety of organizational patterns for books. Remind them of organizing around beginning, middle, end or alphabet books like *Q is for Duck*.

☆ Have students review their writing folders to see how they have been organizing their writing.

ASSESS THE LEARNING

➤ Meet with small groups for interactive writing. Assess their ability to identify and apply organization to the piece.

➤ Assess their writing folders to determine how many organizational patterns are present.

INFUSION OF FORMAL LANGUAGE
Test-style language

In this counting book, the author *organized* the writing around:

  A. Letters

  B. Animals

  C. Numbers

  D. People

Another name for this story could have been:

  A. Toys

  B. Dad

  C. Bedtime

  D. Molly

The Hungry Hippo

The hungry hippo ate **1** _____.

He also ate **2** _____.

He went for a walk and ate **3** _____.

The walk made him more hungry so he ate

4 _____.

He was thinking about dessert so he ate

5 _____.

A Bunny for a Pet

By Linda Hoyt

First, you need to choose a bunny. You will want to choose one that is friendly and does not bite.

Next, you need a cage for your bunny. You will also need a dish for water.

Then, you can take your bunny home and give it a name!

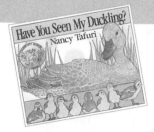

Have You Seen My Duckling?
By Nancy Tafuri

FOCUS THE LEARNING

Introduction: Writers express voice in their writing when we understand the feelings and attitudes of characters or sense the author's passion for a topic. In *Have You Seen My Duckling?* the mother is searching for her lost duckling. Since there aren't very many words, we are going to add words that will help us understand what is happening and how the characters are feeling. I am going to place a large sticky note (3 x 5) on each page so we can write your ideas right onto the book.

INTERACTIVE READ-ALOUD
Model and Guide Practice

READ PAGE 1. Then pause to think aloud. I am thinking of what I could say that would communicate how I feel about this. As a writer I understand the ducklings and what they are thinking, I need to use my writers voice to help a reader understand what I am thinking. I am going to place one sticky note on the left page near the single duckling, and I am going to write, "Mister Butterfly! Wait. I want to look at you." If the duckling could talk, I bet that is what he would say. I am going to use an exclamation mark to show he is really excited. I am going to put another sticky note next to the nest. On this one I am going to write, "Hey everybody, look! There goes Max. We have to get him back!" As a writer I want my reader to know that there are a lot of feelings here.

READ PAGES 2–3. I am going to put three sticky notes on these pages. The first one goes by the nest. I will write: "Mom! Mom! Hurry. Max is gone. He chased the butterfly and disappeared!" Now I am going to put one by Mother Duck. I will write, "Oh, dear. I went to try to find food and Max is in trouble again. Why can't he stay where I put him?" My last sticky note is going up by Max and the butterfly. I will write, "Come on Mr. Butterfly, slow down. You are flying so fast I can't catch up."

Turn to your thinking partner. How am I doing at giving my writing voice? Are my words helping you to understand what the characters are thinking and feeling? Can you tell how I feel about what is happening?

SHOW PAGES 4–5.

You know what to do. Think together. Where should we put the sticky notes and what should they say? Remember we want lots of voice in our writing. After students contribute ideas, select the one that has the strongest voice and write into the book.

CONTINUE READING. Add text as you go through the book, stopping to have students turn and talk with a partner.

END OF STORY REFLECTION
Reread the book from cover to cover using the text the children have created as you read aloud. Talk with them about voice and how the characters' feelings and thoughts come alive.

Turn and talk to your partner. On which pages do you think we did the best job of developing voice for our characters?

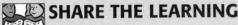 **SHARE THE LEARNING**

Focus on Voice

Tip for Share the Reading

Place the text on the overhead projector and read it aloud with expression. Guide a conversation focused on the voice in this piece about caves. Explain to the students that there are no characters but we still get a very strong sense of connection to the topic because the writing has such strong voice and the writer's feelings about the setting are very evident.

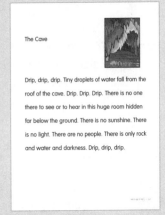

The Cave

Drip, drip, drip. Tiny droplets of water fall from the roof of the cave. Drip. Drip. Drip. There is no one there to see or to hear in this huge room hidden far below the ground. There is no sunshine. There is no light. There are no people. There is only rock and water and darkness. Drip, drip, drip.

Tip for Readers Theater Script

Guide a conversation about learning to ride a bike. What is it like? How does it feel? Were you ever afraid? Could we write about bike riding in a way that our voice, our feelings, our emotions would be clear in our writing? Read "The Bike Ride" to the children showing emotion as you read. Pride, fear, and elation should all come through in the poem. Invite the children to read along with you showing the changing emotions in their voices. As learners gain confidence, have them read the poem with partners and individually.

"The Bike Ride"
By Linda Hoyt

Hands on the handle bars
Feet on the pedals
   I can do it.

Pushing off
Rolling along
   I can do it.

Dad's holding on
Keeping me up
   I can do it.

Oh, no, he let go!
I'm on my own
   I can do it!

EXTEND THE LEARNING

☆ Read a selection to the students about a favorite animal such as a frog or a caterpillar. Then have the students "become" the animal and write in the first person. Example: "I am a frog. I have smooth slippery skin and love to capture flies with my long sticky tongue. I start life as an egg at the bottom of the pond but quickly turn into a tadpole and begin to develop lungs and the ability to hop on land."

☆ Provide an array of wordless books and sticky notes. Then have the students work in partners to think of words that could be added either orally or in writing to add voice to the story.

☆ Illustrations have a big impact on voice. Guide students in reviewing an array of picture books and talking about the pictures. Which illustrations draw you in and give you a sense of the personality of the characters? Have children look at their illustrations. What could they add to show the personality of the people they are portraying?

ASSESS THE LEARNING

➤ Engage students with a wordless book and assess their ability to add text orally or in writing that deepens the voice.

➤ Analyze the "I am" writing to see if the writing gives voice to the animal.

➤ Gather small groups for interactive writing with a focus on voice in writing. Assess individual's ability to generate statements that reflect voice in writing.

INFUSION OF FORMAL LANGUAGE

Test-style language

There is enough information to suggest that
   A. Mother Duck worked very hard to find her duckling.
   B. the other animals were worried.
   C. the missing duck was lost.
   D. the brothers and sisters were mad at the missing duckling.

All of these are true *except*:
   A. There was a butterfly.
   B. The turtle came back with the missing duckling.
   C. The frog helped out.
   D. Mother Duck was not there in the beginning of the story.

The Cave

Drip, drip, drip. Tiny droplets of water fall from the roof of the cave. Drip. Drip. Drip. There is no one there to see or to hear in this huge room hidden far below the ground. There is no sunshine. There is no light. There are no people. There is only rock and water and darkness. Drip, drip, drip.

"The Bike Ride"

By Linda Hoyt

Hands on the handle bars

Feet on the pedals

   I can do it.

Pushing off

Rolling along

   I can do it.

Dad's holding on

Keeping me up

   I can do it.

Oh, no, he let go!

I'm on my own

   I can do it!

Farmer Duck
By Martin Waddell

INTERACTIVE READ-ALOUD
Model and Guide Practice

READ THE FIRST TWO-PAGE LAYOUT. I am looking at the picture. I can tell from looking at the picture that the man is in bed eating chocolates and reading the newspaper, and the duck is bringing him food! I remember from the cover that the duck was digging in the dirt. This duck does a lot! Here is a place where the voice of the author is beginning to show. The author must have a good sense of humor. I am going to read page 1 again. Listen to the words and think about the author who wrote them. The pictures tell us about the author's voice as well.

What in the picture reminds us that the author has a sense of humor? (Point out the underwear on the footboard.)

TURN TO THE NEXT TWO-PAGE LAYOUT. Notice the farmer in the window and the duck in the mud with the cow.

Talk to your thinking partner. Look at the picture. What can you learn from the picture? Read the text after they have talked about the picture. What are we noticing about the voice of the author? I think it is interesting that the author just has the duck say "quack," when animals in books usually speak words. That is part of this author's sense of humor and voice coming through.

TURN TO THE LAYOUT THAT SHOWS THE DUCK SAWING, DIGGING, WASHING DISHES, AND IRONING.

Thinking partners, what can you learn from these pages? Is the author's voice coming through? How do you think the author feels about the duck? The farmer? How can you tell?

READ TO THE PLACE WHERE THE ANIMALS BUMP THE FARMER OUT OF THE BED. Let's think about the author, the person who wrote this story. What are we learning about the author? What is the author doing that helps us hear his voice?

STOP OFTEN TO LOOK AT THE PICTURES. They do a lot to expose the author's voice and how he feels about the characters. (Notice the hen cuddling up to the duck, the cow with the crossed arms in the meeting, the faces of the animals as they chase the farmer out of the house.)

CONTINUE TO THE END OF THE STORY. Pause on each two-page layout to give partners time to talk about the voice of the author.

END OF STORY REFLECTION

We learned a lot about the voice of this author. Let's think about what we learned...We learned that the author has a good sense of humor and chose words and events that made us laugh. We learned that the author didn't like the farmer very much. He made the farmer all hairy and messy and lazy. We learned that pictures and words both help us understand the voice of the author.

Think about the author's voice and the way he felt about the duck. How did the author feel about the duck, and how do you know?

SHARE THE LEARNING
Focus on Voice

Tip for Share the Reading

Read the selection to the students with expression. Then ask them to think about the author of the piece. What does the author want us to understand? In this piece, the author writes as though she is the wind. Saying, "I am the wind," makes the author and the wind closer together in our thinking. Let's try it. "I am a bird. I stretch my wings and lift off of the branch. I _____."

I am the wind.
I howl in winter and blow softly through the leaves in summer.
I move seeds from place to place and lift the wings of beautiful birds.
I am the wind.
Whoosh.

Tip for Readers Theater Script

Read "Hooray for Surprises" to the children and ask them to visualize what is happening. Read it again as an echo reading: teacher reads a line, children echo. Next, divide the children into teams to read their assigned parts. Rehearse until the script can be read with fluency and expression. Talk about the voice of the author. How does the author's voice show in this piece? What did the author do to share the excitement of the children?

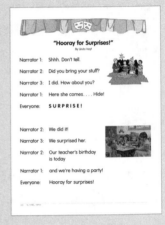

"Hooray for Surprises!"
By Linda Hoyt

Narrator 1: Shhh. Don't tell.
Narrator 2: Did you bring your stuff?
Narrator 3: I did. How about you?
Narrator 1: Here she comes. . . . Hide!
Everyone: **SURPRISE!**

Narrator 2: We did it!
Narrator 3: We surprised her.
Narrator 2: Our teacher's birthday is today
Narrator 1: and we're having a party!
Everyone: Hooray for surprises!

EXTEND THE LEARNING

☆ Have the children create pieces of writing using the first person, "I am." Talk about their voice in the writing.

☆ During small group instruction, have students talk about the voice of the writer. What is the author doing to show feelings, emotions, humor?

☆ Model a piece of writing with a strong emphasis on voice. Use "sound words" and exclamation marks, and try to create a piece with a lot of voice and emotion so the children can see how you think about voice in a conscious way. Example: "Pip. Peep! A tiny bill begins to show through the crack in the egg. Pip. Peep!

☆ During Read-Alouds, draw children's attention to the voice of the author and what you can learn about an author through the stories an author creates.

☆ Confer with writers to talk about ways to bring out their voices in their writing.

ASSESS THE LEARNING

> During small group instruction, engage children in conversations about voice.

> Confer with individuals to see if they can pick up information about author voice from illustrations.

INFUSION OF FORMAL LANGUAGE
Test-style language

Illustrations are important. They help us to
  A. think about what is happening.
  B. understand how an author feels about characters.
  C. understand the story.
  D. All of the above.

Another name for this story might be:
  A. *The Animals Take Over*
  B. *The Lazy Farmer Wins*
  C. *The Duck Works Hard*
  D. *Animals Have a Meeting*

I am the wind.

I howl in winter and blow softly through

the leaves in summer.

I move seeds from place to place and lift

the wings of beautiful birds.

I am the wind.

Whoosh.

"Hooray for Surprises!"

By Linda Hoyt

Narrator 1: Shhh. Don't tell.

Narrator 2: Did you bring your stuff?

Narrator 3: I did. How about you?

Narrator 1: Here she comes. . . . Hide!

Everyone: **S U R P R I S E !**

Narrator 2: We did it!

Narrator 3: We surprised her.

Narrator 2: Our teacher's birthday is today

Narrator 1: and we're having a party!

Everyone: Hooray for surprises!

Rosie's Walk

By Pat Hutchins

FOCUS THE LEARNING

Introduction: Today I am going to ask you to think together about the words we choose in talking and writing and how important it is to choose words that tell exactly what we mean. For example, I could say "_____ (name a child), please stand up." Now watch what happens when I say "_____, please stand up quickly!" I chose words that gave more information, and it had a different result. Here is another example. I could ask someone to *walk* to the door, or I could ask someone to *tiptoe* to the door.

 Share your thinking. What is the difference between walk and tiptoe?

We are going to read *Rosie's Walk* by Pat Hutchins. Pay attention to the words she chooses and how much they tell us about what is happening.

INTERACTIVE READ-ALOUD
Model and Guide Practice

READ PAGES 1 AND 2 (ACROSS THE YARD). I am thinking about the words used in this book and what they tell me. I think the words "across the yard" tell me a lot. The author could have said Rosie "went for a walk," but I would have been wondering *where* Rosie walked. By using the words "across the yard," I know Rosie didn't walk around in a circle; she went in a line across the yard. Who can show us how you would walk *across* our classroom?

LOOK AT THE PAGES WHERE THE FOX STEPS ON THE RAKE. LOOK WHAT HAPPENED WHILE SHE WAS WALKING ACROSS THE YARD!

 Share your thinking on what might be happening. What could we say about what is happening to the fox? What words should we choose?

TURN TO THE PAGE ABOUT THE POND. Now it says Rosie went "around the pond." How is "around" different from "across."

 Turn to your thinking partner. Are these words the same, or are they different? What do they help us understand?

CONTINUE TO THE END OF THE STORY. Pause to point out word choices and to give partners time to talk.

END OF STORY REFLECTION

Let's think together about some of the helpful words that Pat Hutchins used in this book. I remember she used *around* and *across.*

Your turn. Which helpful words are you remembering?

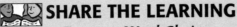 ## SHARE THE LEARNING
Focus on Word Choice

Tip for Share the Thinking

Work with the students to make careful word choices that tell as much as possible. After you create the story, students might enjoy acting it out, reading it chorally or taking a copy home to show their parents.

> Callie the cow went for a walk. She went
> _____ the slippery rock and _____
> the branch of the tree. She _____ up
> the hill and _____ the barn. She was
> really hungry so she_____
> _____.

Tip for Readers Theater Script

For emergent readers, enjoy "Harvey's Run" as an echo poem ignoring the sound words and focusing on echoing the lines of the poem. Talk about the word choices in the poem and how they help us understand what is happening. As students gain confidence, assign a few students to make the sounds to go with each line. With continued reading, have children read the poem together, reading the text and the sound words. For developing readers, enjoy the poem as a whole class or partner experience emphasizing word choice and fluency.

"Harvey's Run"
By Linda Hoyt

Harvey the horse went for a run	(clip, clop)
Through the grass	(swish, swish)
Under the tree	(crunch, crunch)
Over the fence	(yee ha)
Into the barn	(clip, clop)
Just in time for dinner	

EXTEND THE LEARNING

☆ Read a wide range of books with wonderful word choices, drawing the children's attention to the words and how good word choices help a reader.

☆ Guide writers in thinking more seriously about word choices. Create charts with alternatives to weak words like: *went, came, said.* Help children build a repertoire of options.

☆ Introduce the concept of *opposite* to expand word choices. What is the opposite of up? Young? Easy? And so on.

ASSESS THE LEARNING

➤ During small group instruction, guide readers to notice well-chosen words or to discuss changing words in the text to make them more precise.

➤ Confer with readers during independent reading to see if they can identify well-chosen words or make suggestions about better word selections.

➤ Assess their writing to determine quality of word choices, and then confer with those who need additional scaffolding to grow in word choice.

INFUSION OF FORMAL LANGUAGE
Test-style language

Which of the following tells us *where* Rosie walked?

  A. Fox
  B. Dinner
  C. Through the fence
  D. Hen

Which of the following is the *best* word choice to tell about being quiet?

  A. Walk
  B. Tiptoe
  C. Run
  D. Went

Callie the cow went for a walk. She went

_____ the slippery rock and _____

the branch of the tree. She _____ up

the hill and _____ the barn. She was

really hungry so she_____

_____.

"Harvey's Run"

By Linda Hoyt

Harvey the horse went for a run	(clip, clop)
Through the grass	(swish, swish)
Under the tree	(crunch, crunch)
Over the fence	(yee ha)
Into the barn	(clip, clop)
Just in time for dinner	

Diary of a Worm
By Doreen Cronin

FOCUS THE LEARNING

(Note: It would be really helpful to provide an experience with real earthworms from a garden or a sporting goods store before and after reading this selection.)

What do you know about earthworms? Have you ever seen one up close?

 Think together. What do you know about worms?

In *Dairy of a Worm*, Doreen Cronin uses a lot of real information about worms and organizes the information like a diary. It shows what happens on different days in the life of a pretend worm. You will have fun learning about real worms and laughing when she adds things real worms just can't do. While we read, watch for the word choices the author makes . . .

INTERACTIVE READ-ALOUD
Model and Guide Practice

One of the important things earthworms do is tunnel through the ground. They move through the soil and leave a tunnel behind. This allows the soil to get air which is good. Read through the place where the spider is holding the worm by a thread. The author used some great words. When Dad was eating the newspaper, it says, "Chomp." Did you know that worms like to eat paper?

 Think together. What does chomp mean? Can you show what someone would do if they were chomping?

READ TO THE PLACE WHERE IT RAINED AND THE KIDS ARE PLAYING HOPSCOTCH. There is a lot of humor here. On the page with the shovel, do you see the bait can? Fishermen use worms for bait! On the next page it rained. That means that the worms' tunnels fill with water and they will drown, so they have to come up to get air. That is why we see worms on the sidewalk after a rain. They just want to breathe. It says hopscotch is a DANGEROUS game.

 Why is it dangerous to worms? Is dangerous a good word choice here?

READ THROUGH THE PAGES ON APRIL 20. There are some great words here. I noticed "snuck up" and "screamed."

 Talk to your thinking partner. Think together about these words. What do they mean, and are they good choices for these pages?

CONTINUE TO THE END OF THE SELECTION. Pause occasionally to point out strong word choices and humor as well as real information about worms. Be sure to notice words like nightmare, giant, cool, talented, Secret Service agent, careful, mistake, grubby, tracking.

END OF STORY REFLECTION

There were lots of great words in that book. Let's think together and write down some of the terrific words the author chose to use. After we make a list, we can use these wonderful words to tell what we remember from the story.

Think together. What terrific words do you remember? Be thinking about how you can use our words to tell about the story.

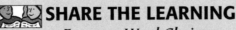 **SHARE THE LEARNING**
Focus on Word Choice

Tip for Share the Reading

Read the first paragraph to the children and talk about earthworms, comparing this passage to what was learned in the book. Focus on word choices within the passage. Notice the Where and What in the headings as well as word choices such as *swallow, usually, weak, drives, surface.* Talk about these words and how making careful word choices helps a reader to understand. Discuss and then add good choices for the missing words in the second paragraph. Read the passage to model fluency. Then have the children join in chorally to celebrate their learning.

Where does a worm live?

A worm usually lives in warm, dark soil. It becomes very weak in daylight and in cold air. A rainstorm is the best time to find them on the surface as the rain drives the air out of their burrows and they come to the surface to breathe.

What does a worm eat?

_____ eat leaves and other vegetables they can find in the _____. Sometimes, when the ground is very hard, they swallow dirt and _____ it out behind them so they can make their tunnels.

Tip for Readers Theater Script

Guide a conversation about things polar bears can do in "I am a Polar Bear." Then have the children dramatize movements such as lumber, slide, etc. Show them how you can read the script and insert either words from the top of the page or words that they think describe how a polar bear could move. Have children rehearse reading their scripts fluently, and then present their scripts as they dramatize polar bear movements. Reread for fluency and expression, and continue conversations about word choice.

"I am a Polar Bear"
By Linda Hoyt

Stretch   Crawl   Leap   Tiptoe   Lumber   Swim   Slide

I am a. _____
I can _____

I am a. _____
I can _____

I am a. _____
I can _____

EXTEND THE LEARNING

☆ Read many stories and poems and talk about word choices.

☆ Keep lists of wonderous words you find in a visible place and encourage the children to use them in oral communication as well as in writing.

☆ Read nonfiction selections and consider word choices.

☆ Create cloze activities and help the children make great word choices.

☆ Use Alphaboxes (Hoyt, 1999) to gather words on a topic, and then use those words in writing.

ASSESS THE LEARNING

> Have children discuss word choices in Read-Aloud selections, and identify interesting words.

> Confer with writers about word choices to assess ability to make thoughtful choices.

INFUSION OF FORMAL LANGUAGE
Test-style language

Diary of a Worm is *mostly* about:

  A. Worms in school

  B. Worms on the sidewalk

  C. Worms in tunnels

  D. Things worms can do

In the story we learned that worms *cannot*:

  A. Walk upside down

  B. Dig tunnels

  C. Eat newspaper

  D. Go to school

Where does a worm live?

A worm usually lives in warm, dark soil. It becomes very weak in daylight and in cold air. A rainstorm is

the best time to find them on the surface as the rain drives the air out of their burrows and they come to the surface to breathe.

What does a worm eat?

_____ eat leaves and other vegetables they can find in the _____. Sometimes, when the ground is very hard, they swallow dirt and _____ it out behind them so they can make their tunnels.

"I am a Polar Bear"

By Linda Hoyt

Stretch   Crawl   Leap   Tiptoe   Lumber   Swim   Slide

I am a.

I can _____.

I am a.

I can _____.

I am a.

I can _____.

Where the Wild Things Are

By Maurice Sendak

FOCUS THE LEARNING

Introduction: I'm going to tell you a story. "We went to the park. It was a sunny day. We flew kites. We went on the swing. We had a picnic." What do you notice about the sentences? They are all very short, aren't they? And four start with "We." These short and choppy sentences are boring to listen to! I'll try again—"It was a sunny day, so we went to the park. We flew kites, went on the swing, and enjoyed a tasty picnic." There, that's better! In my second story, the sentences had fluency. Sentence fluency happens when language flows and has a natural rhythm to it—it sounds like people talk. The sentences are different lengths and start in different ways. Authors try to create sentence fluency in their writing. Let's read *Where the Wild Things Are* and think about sentence fluency.

INTERACTIVE READ-ALOUD
Model and Guide Practice

READ TO THE PAGE THAT ENDS "... WITHOUT EATING ANYTHING." Did you notice that I only read one sentence, but that it took several pages to read it? (Read again if necessary.) What I noticed while I was reading is that the sentences were easy to read out loud. They flowed smoothly as I talked. That is a good test for sentence fluency.

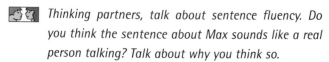 *Thinking partners, talk about sentence fluency. Do you think the sentence about Max sounds like a real person talking? Talk about why you think so.*

Let's keep reading to see when the next sentence ends!

READ UNTIL THE PAGE THAT ENDS "... WHERE THE WILD THINGS ARE." Wow—the author wrote a long sentence that goes across a lot of pages! But when I read it, it really flows. It sounds like someone talking.

Talk with your thinking partner about sentence fluency. How does this story sound when you listen to it? What makes it sound like the author is "talking" to you?

CONTINUE READING, PAUSING TO DISCUSS SENTENCE FLUENCY.
As children listen, ask them what makes the story so interesting to hear. You might point out that some pages have many words while some have few, and that the sentences do not all start the same way. Stop at the page where the Wild Things roar and gnash and roll their eyes when Max tells him he is leaving.

Have you ever told a story saying "and then," "and then," and "and then" without stopping? We tell stories this way when we are excited. When the author writes this way, the story is exciting.

END OF STORY REFLECTION
Maurice Sendak uses sentences in such an interesting way! Some sentences are long, and some are short. When I read aloud, it sounds like me telling a friend about something exciting. It makes sense to tell such an exciting story this way!

Which part of this story did you like the most? If you could meet the author, what would you want to ask him about the way he wrote the story?

SHARE THE LEARNING
Focus on Sentence Fluency

Tip for Share the Reading

Read the sentences dramatically and ask the children to visualize what is happening. Explain that they need to think together about continuing the story. What would they say next? How would they say it? Have children generate several ideas before adding to the text. When you select a sentence to add, be sure to point out that you are choosing a sentence for its fluency. It needs to be a different length than the sentence before it and have a different beginning. After sentences have been added, read the piece chorally to celebrate the fluency in their writing.

> "I'm Max, king of the Wild Things. Sit down, you big things and be good!"
>
> "Shh," said a Wild Thing. "The king wants it quiet!" _____
> _____
> _____
> _____
> _____
> _____

Tip for Readers Theater Script

Guide a conversation about different things that children can be in their imaginations. Read *In My Room* to the children while they visualize what is happening. Read it again and have them dramatize. On a third reading, have them join you in chorally reading the script. As they are ready, assign parts and celebrate the script for fluency and expression.

	In My Room
	by Lynette Brent
All:	In my room
Reader 1:	I can be a monster.
All:	In my room
Reader 2:	I can be a pirate.
All:	In my room
Reader 3:	I can be an astronaut.
All:	In my room
Reader 4:	I can be a cowboy.
All:	In my room
Reader 5:	I can be a monkey.
All:	In my room
Reader 6:	I can be a rock star.
All:	In my room
Reader 7:	I can be a superhero.
All:	In my room
	I can pretend to be anything I want.

EXTEND THE LEARNING

☆ Pull books from Booklinks in this resource that have examples of sentence fluency. Encourage children to find fluent writing in nonfiction texts as well as fiction.

☆ Write a short choppy sentence on chart paper, or a series of short choppy sentences. Work with children to make these sentences more fluent. Discuss strategies with children, such as varying sentence lengths and starting sentences in different ways.

☆ Work with children to create a "checklist" for sentence fluency. Guide them in thinking some sentences sound the same way? Are the sentences different lengths? Does the writing sound the way a person would normally talk?

ASSESS THE LEARNING

> Listen in as children talk about sentence fluency with their thinking partners. Are children able to identify what makes great fluent writing?

> Return to a piece of writing a child has done and discuss the piece with the writer. Ask him or her to find a good example of sentence fluency and a place where the writing could be changed to be even more fluent.

INFUSION OF FORMAL LANGUAGE
Test-style language

Max tamed the Wild Things by
  A. giving them a hot supper.
  B. doing a magic trick and telling them, "Be still."
  C. rolling his eyes and gnashing his teeth.
  D. letting the Wild Things have a rumpus.

Max gave up being king of the Wild Things because
  A. he was afraid of the Wild Things.
  B. the Wild Things were sleeping.
  C. he smelled food and was very hungry.
  D. his mother told him to come home.

"I'm Max, king of the Wild Things. Sit down, you big things and be good!"

"Shh," said a Wild Thing. "The king wants it quiet!" _____

_____

_____

_____

_____

_____

In My Room

By Lynnette Brent

All:	In my room
Reader 1:	I can be a monster.
All:	In my room
Reader 2:	I can be a pirate.
All:	In my room
Reader 3:	I can be an astronaut.
All:	In my room
Reader 4:	I can be a cowboy.
All:	In my room
Reader 5:	I can be a monkey.
All:	In my room
Reader 6:	I can be a rock star.
All:	In my room
Reader 7:	I can be a superhero.
All:	In my room
	I can pretend to be anything I want.

The Snowy Day
By Ezra Jack Keats

FOCUS THE LEARNING

Introduction: "Sit on by the floor me a book please to read!" Could you understand what I just said? Probably not! The words were all mixed up. Let me try again. "Please sit by me on the floor to read a book!" Okay, that's much better. The words flowed together in a way that made sense. My second sentence had something called *sentence fluency*. When we speak, our language flows in a natural way. When writers use sentence fluency, their sentences flow. But it's more than just having words in the right order—it's the way that the words sound. Some sentences are long. Some are short. But they connect together, and they sound great when we read them! Let's read *The Snowy Day* to see how the author put his sentences together. Let's look for sentence fluency.

INTERACTIVE READ-ALOUD
Model and Guide Practice

READ PAGE 7. Look at Peter's face and the way he sits in the bed! I can tell he can't wait to get out in that snow.

 Thinking partners, listen carefully to the words again as I read the page. Talk about sentence fluency. What makes the words on the page nice to listen to? What makes this page sound like a real person talking?

STOP AT PAGE 11. I love the way the author put the words: "crunch, crunch, crunch." Think about stepping into snow. If the snow is just a little crusty on top, your feet would sink in and make that noise: "crunch, crunch, crunch."

 Look at how the author added sound words into the writing. Doesn't that sound great? It really adds to the sentence fluency, because that sentence sounds a bit different, and it's really fun to read out loud.

CONTINUE READING THE STORY. Pause to talk about sentence fluency. Encourage students to turn to thinking partners and say words and sentences again, savoring how they sound in their mouths and to their ears! You might stop, for example, on page 16 to emphasize reading the sentence with "plop"! On page 19, the words "not yet" make Peter sound like a real little boy who wants to play with the big kids. Children will find other places where sentence fluency brings the words to life and makes the story interesting to read.

END OF STORY REFLECTION

READ THE BOOK ONCE THROUGH AGAIN FOR CHILDREN.

 Thinking partners, talk about the sentence fluency in this book. How do the sentences make it sound like a real person talking? What feeling did you have about Peter and about the snow when you heard the author's words? Remember, a good test for sentence fluency is to read something out loud and see how it sounds. The Snowy Day was great to read aloud. The sentences really flowed together. Go back to your seat and take out a piece of writing. Read it aloud to yourself and think about sentence fluency. Do your sentences work together? Are they different lengths, or do they all sound the same?

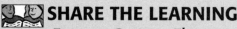

SHARE THE LEARNING
Focus on Sentence Fluency

Tip for Share the Reading	Tip for Readers Theater Script

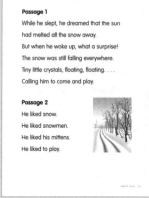

Read passage 1 to the children. Help them to see that some sentences are longer than others yet they flow together and when read aloud they sound really smooth. Help them to also notice that each sentence starts in a different way.

Passage 1

While he slept, he dreamed that the sun had melted all the snow away. But when he woke up, what a surprise! The snow was still falling everywhere. Tiny little crystals, floating, floating. . . . Calling him to come and play.

Passage 2

He liked snow.
He liked snowmen.
He liked his mittens.
He liked to play.

Read the second passage aloud. Ask the children to talk about sentence fluency. Does this passage sound as good? How could you rewrite this to give it sentence fluency?

Read "Snow" straight through, and ask the children to visualize as you read. Point out the repeating refrain and talk about sentence fluency. Does this poem have sentence fluency? Is it smooth when read aloud? Have the children read the repeating refrain on the script while you read the teacher section.

"Snow"
By Lynnette Brent and Linda Hoyt

Children:	The snow fell softly to the ground.
Teacher:	I saw its whiteness all around. I listened for a snowy sound. But I heard a quiet stillness.
Children:	The snow fell softly to the ground.
Teacher:	I rolled a snowball all around. I made snow bricks with a pan I found. And built a snowman nice and round.
Children:	The snow fell softly to the ground.
Teacher:	I thought about snowflakes all around.
Children:	The snow fell softly to the ground.

EXTEND THE LEARNING

☆ Read aloud another book that demonstrates sentence fluency. You might choose, for example, *How the Grinch Stole Christmas* or *Olivia*.

☆ Return to a piece of writing that you created with children. Read the sentences and ask children to suggest ways in which to make those sentences more fluent.

☆ Have children choose wordless picture books from your library and create "text" for these books.

☆ Do sentence scrambles. Write a sentence from a familiar story on sentence strips and then cut it up. Scramble the words and have the children unscramble them so the sentence sounds fluent and makes sense.

☆ Analyze books used in small group instruction for sentence fluency. Have the children make suggestions about ways the sentences could be improved.

ASSESS THE LEARNING

➤ As children discuss sentence fluency, listen in to be sure that they understand what makes writing fluent.

➤ Confer with children about sentence fluency in their own writing and give feedback to help the writer grow in using sentence fluency.

INFUSION OF FORMAL LANGUAGE
Test-style language

The *main purpose* of this story is to
  A. explain why snow falls in winter.
  B. give rules for safely playing outside.
  C. tell about one boy's adventures in snow.
  D. describe the way snow melts in a warm room.

All of these are true except:
  A. Peter hits a tree with a stick.
  B. Peter has a dream about snow.
  C. Older boys have a snowball fight.
  D. Peter's mother plays with him in the snow.

Passage 1

While he slept, he dreamed that the sun

had melted all the snow away.

But when he woke up, what a surprise!

The snow was still falling everywhere.

Tiny little crystals, floating, floating. . . .

Calling him to come and play.

Passage 2

He liked snow.

He liked snowmen.

He liked his mittens.

He liked to play.

"Snow"

By Lynnette Brent and Linda Hoyt

Children: The snow fell softly to the ground.

Teacher: I saw its whiteness all around.
            I listened for a snowy sound.
            But I heard a quiet stillness.

Children: The snow fell softly to the ground.

Teacher: I rolled a snowball all around.
            I made snow bricks with a pan I found.
            And built a snowman nice and round.

Children: The snow fell softly to the ground.

Teacher: I thought about snowflakes all around.

Children: The snow fell softly to the ground.

No, David!

By David Shannon

FOCUS THE LEARNING

No, David! by David Shannon is filled with one of my favorite writing tools. It is called an exclamation mark. It looks like this: "!" When we see an exclamation mark in a book, that means that the author wants us to get really excited and to show a lot of emotion.

INTERACTIVE READ-ALOUD
Model and Guide Practice

SHOW THE COVER, READ THE TITLE, THEN PAUSE TO THINK ALOUD. Here is an exclamation mark already. It is important to notice exclamation marks and see that they are different from a period: "." Because there is an exclamation mark, I know I need to read the title with Gusto! **"No, David!"** You give it a try.

TURN TO THE TITLE PAGE. As I look at the title page, I can see that it is a woman's body. Look at the way she is standing. How do you think she is feeling?

 How would she say "No, David"? Why do you think so?

READ TO THE PAGE WHERE DAVID IS REACHING FOR THE COOKIE JAR. It looks like he is about to fall off the chair. I am also thinking that if he gets the cookie jar, it will fall down and break. I am going to say "No, David" in several ways. Listen and tell me which one fits best. Read the line like you are sleepy, bored, not paying attention, and very angry.

 Turn to your thinking partner. Which one fits best? Which one should get the exclamation mark?

READ TO THE PAGE WHERE HE IS IN THE BATHTUB.

 Think with your partner. Would it work to put a period after "No, David" on this page? Why not?

CONTINUE READING. Pause frequently to look at periods and exclamation marks and reading the text to show the differences in oral interpretation.

END OF STORY REFLECTION

There were a lot of exclamation marks in this book. Let's go back through the pages and count them.

 Turn and talk to your partner. Did the author need that many exclamation marks? Would it have been OK to use some periods here and there?

SHARE THE LEARNING
Focus on Conventions

Tip for Share the Reading

Read the lines to the children one at a time. With each one, practice reading it with a period at the end and then practice it with an exclamation mark. Guide a conversation about how to decide on ending punctuation and shifting our voices to match.

That hurt

I am feeling sleepy

It is time to read

Watch Out

Stop There's a car coming

It's a beautiful day

Tip for Readers Theater Script

Have a conversation about the Fourth of July: the temperature outside, fireworks and the sounds they can make, etc. Read "The Fourth of July" to the children in a flat, mono-tone voice. Then guide them in a conversation about adding exclamation marks. Where would they want to add them to add interest and excitement to the poem? After they add the punctuation, have students read "The Fourth of July" in unison, then in partners to lift the reading to a fluent and expressive level.

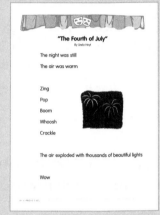

"The Fourth of July"
By Linda Hoyt

The night was still
The air was warm

Zing
Pop
Boom
Whoosh
Crackle

The air exploded with thousands of beautiful lights

Wow

EXTEND THE LEARNING

☆ During small group instruction, guide children in a conversation about exclamation marks. Have them try reading sentences in a book as though it has an exclamation mark instead of a period and see how it changes the meaning.

☆ Place sentences in a pocket chart. Do not add punctuation. Have the children make decisions about appropriate punctuation to add.

☆ Model writing while the children watch and think out loud about selecting exclamation marks vs. periods.

☆ Search for exclamation marks in Read-Aloud and small group books.

☆ Challenge the children to find one place in a piece of writing where they could add an exclamation mark. Have them read their selections to each other.

ASSESS THE LEARNING

➤ Confer with individuals to see if they can shift their oral reading in response to an exclamation mark.

➤ Confer with writers to search for or add exclamation marks in their writing folders.

That hurt

I am feeling sleepy

It is time to read

Watch Out

Stop There's a car coming

It's a beautiful day

"The Fourth of July"

By Linda Hoyt

The night was still

The air was warm

Zing

Pop

Boom

Whoosh

Crackle

The air exploded with thousands of beautiful lights

Wow

Don't Let the Pigeon Drive the Bus!
By Mo Willems

FOCUS THE LEARNING

Read this selection once for enjoyment then again for this lesson. I am going to make our three favorite punctuation marks on the board so we can look at them and think together. We all know a period, an exclamation mark, and a question mark. We use these for different purposes when we write. In *Don't Let the Pigeon Drive the Bus!* Mo Willems uses all three to help us understand what the pigeon is trying to do.

 Think together. When do you use a question mark? An explanation mark? A period?

INTERACTIVE READ-ALOUD
Model and Guide Practice

READ THE TITLE PAGE. Then show the illustration of the driver leaving…and the pigeon peering in on the opposite page. Look! I have already found a question mark, a period, and an exclamation mark. Let's look at the question mark first. He said, "Listen, I've got to leave for a little while, so can you watch things for me until I get back?" That is a question. Questions need answers. That seems like a good place to use a question mark.

TURN TO THE NEXT PAGE, WHERE THE DRIVER IS WALKING AWAY. There aren't any words here, but I have a question for the driver. I am going to use a sticky note to write my question and add it to the book. I am going to say, "Hey, Mr. Driver. How long are you going to be gone?" I need to use a question mark because it needs an answer. I don't want to spend a long time watching his bus for him.

 Think together. Do you have any questions for the driver or the pigeon?

READ TO THE PAGE WHERE THE PIGEON SAYS, "HEY, CAN I DRIVE THE BUS?" Did you notice the question mark?

Why did the author use a question mark here? Do you have some questions you want to ask the pigeon?

CONTINUE TO THE END OF THE STORY. Pause often to talk about questions they can add to the book and the end punctuation the author used.

END OF STORY REFLECTION

If you could talk to the author, Mo Willems, what would you want to ask him? What are your questions? Now that the story is over, what do we want to ask the pigeon?

 Think together. What are your questions?

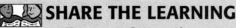 **SHARE THE LEARNING**
Focus on Conventions

Tip for Share the Thinking

Read the statements to the children one at a time, and with each one, decide if it is a question or not. Add the appropriate ending punctuation after the children decide. After the punctuation is added, read the lines with expression.

May I please drive the bus

My cousin drives buses all of the time

May I steer

Would you let me drive if I give you $5

I am a good driver

Tip for Readers Theater Script

Sing "Don't Let the Pigeon Drive the Bus!" for the children so they catch onto the tune and the words. Invite them to sing along until it becomes familiar. Then, pass out the script and have them track along as they sing. As they gain confidence, have them sing with partners and take the song home to read and perform for their parents.

"Don't Let the Pigeon Drive the Bus!"
(to the tune of "Mary Had a Little Lamb")
Readers Theater script by Linda Hoyt

A pigeon wants to drive a bus,
drive a bus,
drive a bus.
A pigeon wants to drive a bus.
He really wants his way!

He begged and begged and begged some more
Begged some more,
begged some more.
He begged and begged and begged some more.
He's one determined bird!

He threw a tantrum, then felt sad,
Then felt sad
Then felt sad.
He threw a tantrum, then felt sad
Until he saw the truck.

EXTEND THE LEARNING

☆ Read the book again and focus on exclamation marks and periods.

☆ Select a nonfiction Read-Aloud with a lot of questions in it. Example: Why Do Whales Have Belly Buttons? Show the children how questions can actually make good titles.

☆ Place a text in a pocket chart and have the children add punctuation.

☆ Encourage readers to change ending punctuation to make it more interesting.

☆ Read *Frog and Toad* books or *The Grouchy Ladybug* to consider quotation marks.

☆ Model extended sentences such as, "I can splash *and* swim in the pool."

☆ Model writing continuously to show how to begin a sentence with a capital letter, and how to end it with a period, exclamation mark, or question mark.

ASSESS THE LEARNING

➤ Conference with writers during writers workshop to assess understanding of conventions.

➤ Analyze writing samples to determine which conventions are appearing in unedited work.

➤ Confer with readers and have them show you how they use end punctuation to shift their oral reading.

INFUSION OF FORMAL LANGUAGE
Test-style language

Question marks are used:

  A. To show you are done

  B. For people's names

  C. At the end of a question

  D. When you are really excited

In this book you could *infer* that

  A. driving the bus was really important to the pigeon.

  B. pigeons don't know how to drive buses.

  C. the bus driver was worried that the pigeon would try to drive.

  D. All of the above.

May I please drive the bus

My cousin drives buses all of the time

May I steer

Would you let me drive if I give you $5

I am a good driver

"Don't Let the Pigeon Drive the Bus!"

(to the tune of "Mary Had a Little Lamb")

Reader's Theater script by Linda Hoyt

A pigeon wants to drive a bus,

drive a bus,

drive a bus.

A pigeon wants to drive a bus.

He really wants his way!

He begged and begged and begged some more

Begged some more,

begged some more.

He begged and begged and begged some more.

He's one determined bird!

He threw a tantrum, then felt sad,

Then felt sad

Then felt sad.

He threw a tantrum, then felt sad

Until he saw the truck.